Edith Karlsson

EDITH KARLSON

HORA LUPI

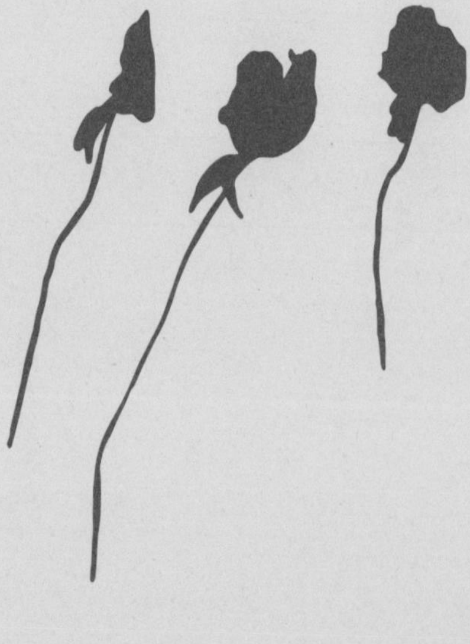

TABLE OF CONTENTS

Maria Arusoo

THE MAKING OF *HORA LUPI*

On behalf of the Estonian Centre for Contemporary Art, I am extremely pleased to present Edith Karlson's exhibition *Hora lupi*, created for the 14th Estonian pavilion at the 60th International Art Exhibition — La Biennale di Venezia and the book published alongside the exhibition.

The beginnings of this project go back to November 2022, when an international jury consisting of Antonia Alampi, Annie Fletcher, Geir Haraldseth, Jaanus Samma, Maria-Kristiina Soomre, and myself visited a legendary sculpture studio complex constructed in the 1970s, located on the outskirts of Tallinn in the pine woods. The complex, that has been, and still is, home to dozens of artist studios, has also housed Edith Karlson's since 2008. Wherever we looked in her studio, experiments with form and material caught our eye. Among them were lone characters from her previous exhibitions and burgeoning ideas for the future, many of which have since become sculptures and installations. Ceramic snakes slithering up bodiless transparent polymer resin suits; singular forms of hands or birds; animal skeletons gathered from forests and roadsides; models of animal heads; and various abstract objects only just beginning to take form. This, and so much more, we found in the phantasmagorical and vivid world of Edith Karlson.

At the time, Edith was carrying a not yet fully articulated feeling about the direction she wanted to explore, let us call it the burgeoning moment of a trajectory. A crossing point of emotional duality, where, on the one hand, everything is still possible, and yet there is hope, on the other, that something has irreversibly shifted and there is no going back. On the studio floor next to the wall, Edith's long-time friend, the chihuahua Kusti, was dozing, serenely observing the discussion. This was our first look into the strange world of Edith Karlson's sculptures, its multifarious characters all now brought fully into the light at the Estonian pavilion at the Venice Biennale.

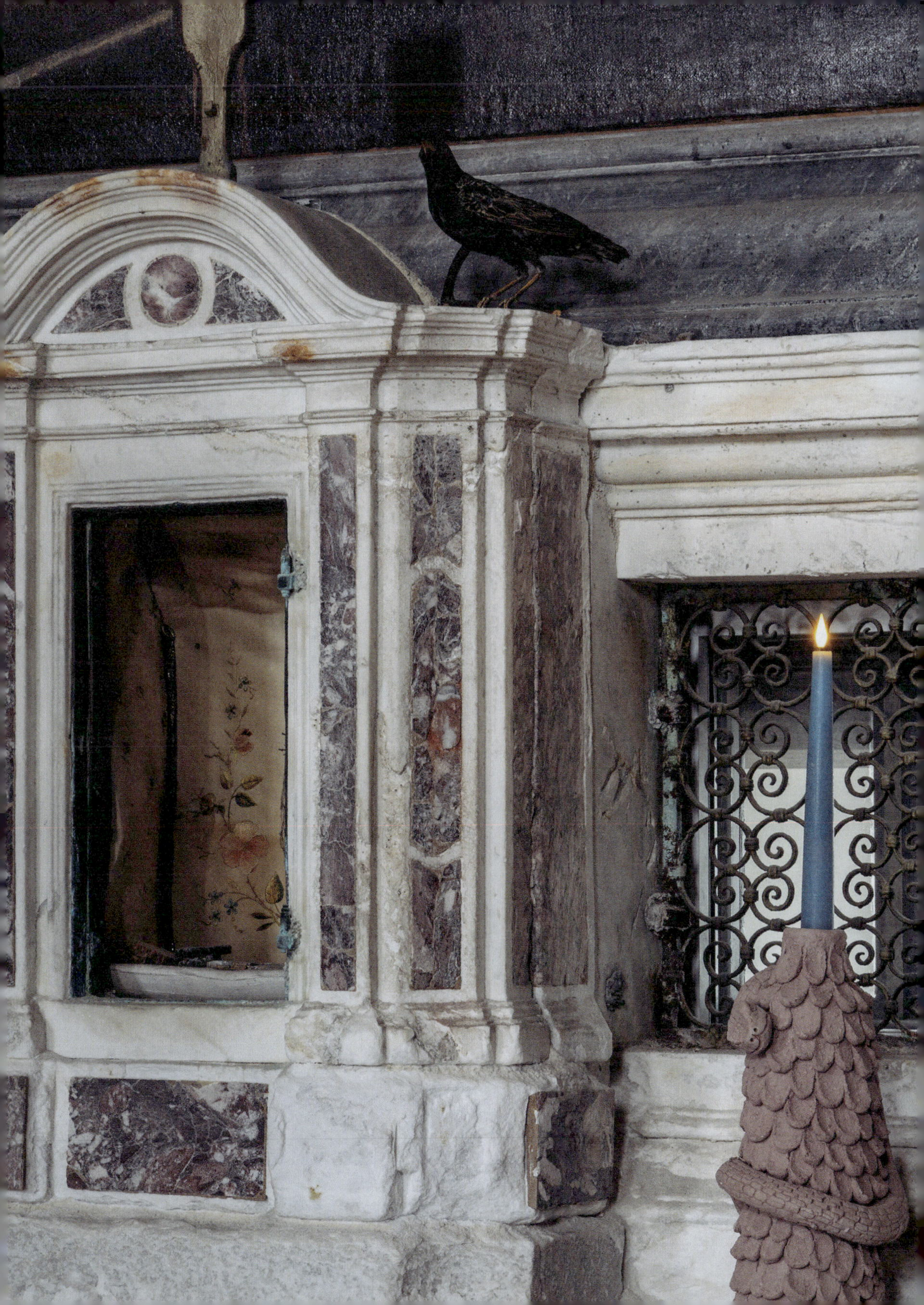

Edith Karlson is empathic and sensitive to material, her work best interpreted through the notion of ambivalence. Her individual works as well as her sculpture groups and exhibitions are extremely dense in their dramaturgy, often inspired by personal experience and tactile interpretations of her surroundings. Despite this, Karlson's artistic position leaves the viewer enough space to approach the works independently and without pressure. Karlson values each viewer's individual journey, where their personal experience is allowed to relate to and collide with hers. Karlson's layered worlds do not hide behind conceptual masks and never sidestep opportunities to trigger our emotions. However, through their metamorphoses something surprising always surfaces. Edith Karlson's humans are almost never merely humans and her animals are something more than animals, too. They are not necessarily chimeras, mermaids, or monsters either — nothing that we can exactly pin to form or mythology. Her plethora of characters are hybrids, they blend into one another and thus find new form. Her starting points can be extremely personal. *Hora lupi* contains casts of the hands of both the artist's grandmothers, which hold lace handkerchiefs, crying an

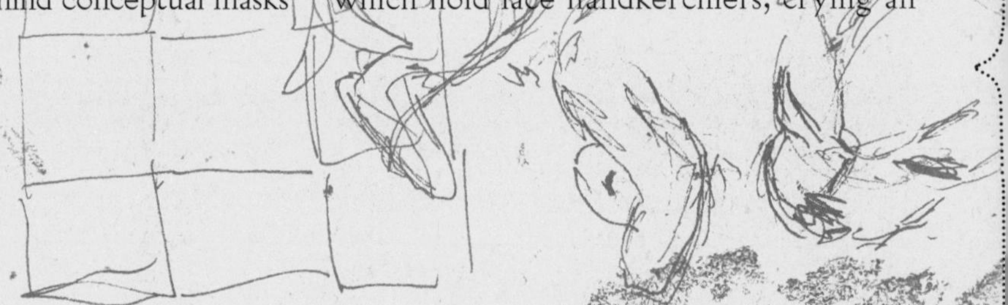

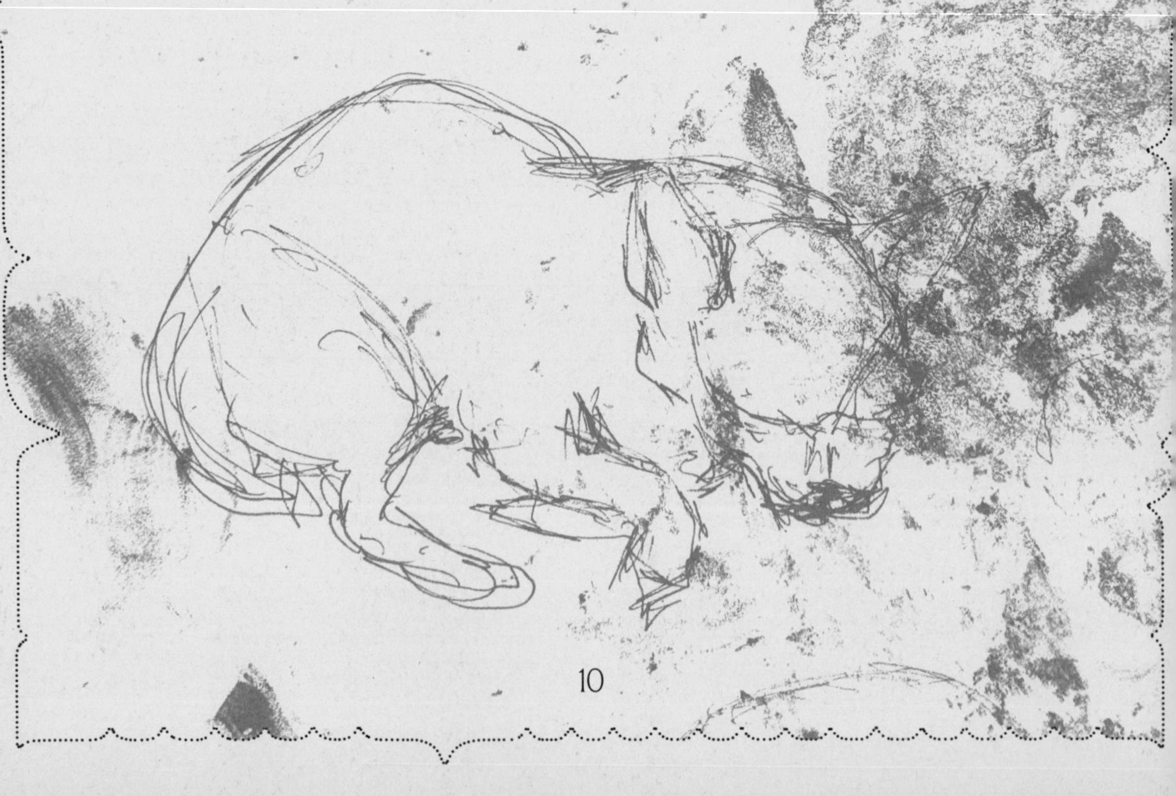

endless stream of grief. Then there are the casts of the bodies of the artist's friends and assistants, which have evolved into sirens with fish heads or crying women, as well as toy soldiers found in old drawers that have now increased in size hundredfold, fighting each other in the middle of the exhibition space, in addition to surreal artworks created by the artist's son Nikolai.

Edith's *Umwelt* always follows her, and these deeply personal touches and immense phys ical work which she puts into her projects translates in this instance, I dare to believe, into an all-encompassing exhibition that pro foundly touches the viewer.

Karlson places great value on the space and the environment in which she sets up her exhibitions — it is her primary impetus. In 2023, we began our search for the space for the 2024 Estonian pavilion. Together with Edith Karlson and Eero Epner, the exhibition's dramaturgical consultant, we made several research trips to Venice and visited former storage spaces, a wine cellar, a recently closed historic apothecary, a glass mogul's palazzo, workshops, countless other spaces modified into galleries, and, for a moment, we even considered a space once used by elderly venetian men to play board games that had been closed for thirty years. Even so, the feeling of not having yet arrived at the right space kept us moving forward until, on a searing August day, we did, finally, arrive. The sense of having arrived was so strong from the very first visit that the process gained momentum with such speed that there was no way back. The exhibition was not so much inspired by the church but rather by the hole in the floor in one of the rooms — it fills with lagoon water during high tide and runs dry during low tide. The collapsed floor became the impetus for *Hora lupi*.

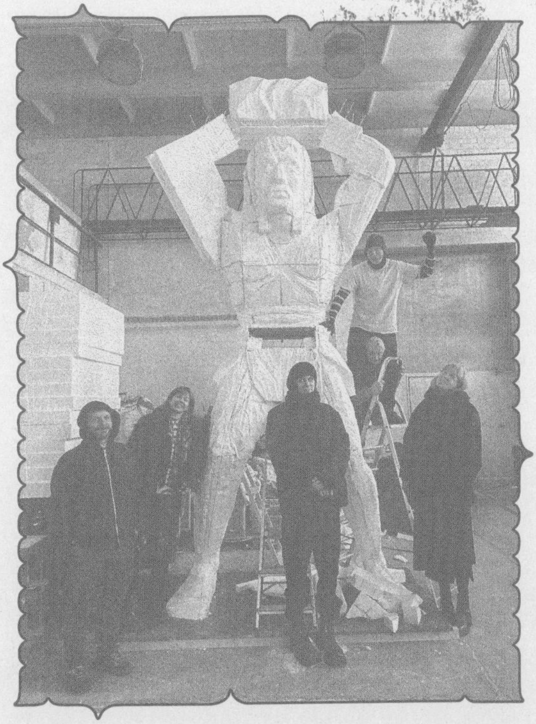

While working on the project, the artist had described a feeling of falling, the moment where you've already fallen off the edge with no possibility of return, however what lies ahead is still unclear. Euphoria and fear simultaneously boil within you, as do hope and a sense of surrendering to inevitability — everything is still possible, but the path back to safety is cut off. Processes have been set in motion and you just have to go with the flow, humbly and without anguish.

Having made her way to the Chiesa di Santa Maria delle Penitenti next to the Cannaregio canal, the artist had arrived. This building, a melancholy and decaying memory of lost glory, a temple being devoured by time with its dust-covered artefacts, fractured marble, and salt-coated walls was precisely the place Edith Karlson had been imagining, perhaps without even being conscious of it.

During the incubation period of the Venice project, Edith had been thinking about a sculpture — a siren, a strange hybrid with the torso of a woman, the head of a fish, and the tail of a mermaid. A curious sea creature to accompany her from the seaside city of Tallinn to the lagoons of Venice. Now the siren had found her place — she could recline next to the gaping hole in the church floor. From here onwards, Karlson did not begin creating a new world, instead, it seemed as if all the characters of *Hora lupi* were merely returning to the place that they had always belonged. This is how all the sculptural trios of *Hora lupi* were born, from the crying women to the savages.

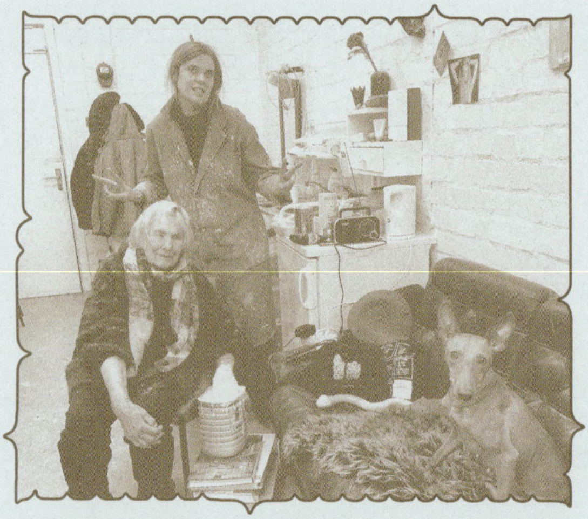

In the semi-closed chambers, snake skins seem to have been forgotten, ceramic snakes peer out from behind the altars, and simple clay eggs are placed next to the tabernacle. In the high vases next to the main entrance, flowers moulded from human asses decorate the space. From high up in the vault, dozens of storks look down at visitors, one of them safeguarding a deep red glass heart the artist created together with Berengo glass makers in the furnace on Murano island. Finally, in a narrow room filled with memories and grief, in front of an unusually narrow bed, lies a sculpture of a chihuahua, the artist's dog Kusti who recently passed away and whose memory is now forever modelled in clay.

Entering the church, it feels like we are secretly witnessing a *mise en scène* of some sort rather than looking at an exhibition. Echoing around the vault, we hear a haunting version of Henry Purcell's 1691 operatic tune *The Cold Song*, performed by the artist herself and arranged by Raul Saaremets. Initially, Karlson was inspired by the 1981 version sung by Klaus Nomi, a track she was listening to during the period of preparation for the project.

Let me, let me
Let me, let me
Freeze again...

drawing you in and freezing time.

Let me, let me
Freeze again to death!

In the psychogeographical map of Venice, *Hora lupi* is located on the outskirts. Chiesa di Santa Maria is an eighteenth century church in Cannaregio with a view of a former slaughterhouse, looking towards the Ponte della Libertà, the bridge connecting the islands to the mainland. In this book, Piero Vespigniani, the architect of the Estonian pavilion writes about the history of the church, its architecture, and various functions. Cecilia Alemani looks at Edith Karlson's entangled life and work in a conversation with Edith after visiting her Tallinn studio while the artist was preparing for Venice. A more poetic insight into the world of Edith Karlson is provided by the poetry of Quinn Latimer; Eero Epner takes a closer look at both *Hora lupi* and Edith Karlson's work more broadly; Dieter Roelstraete writes about contemporary art

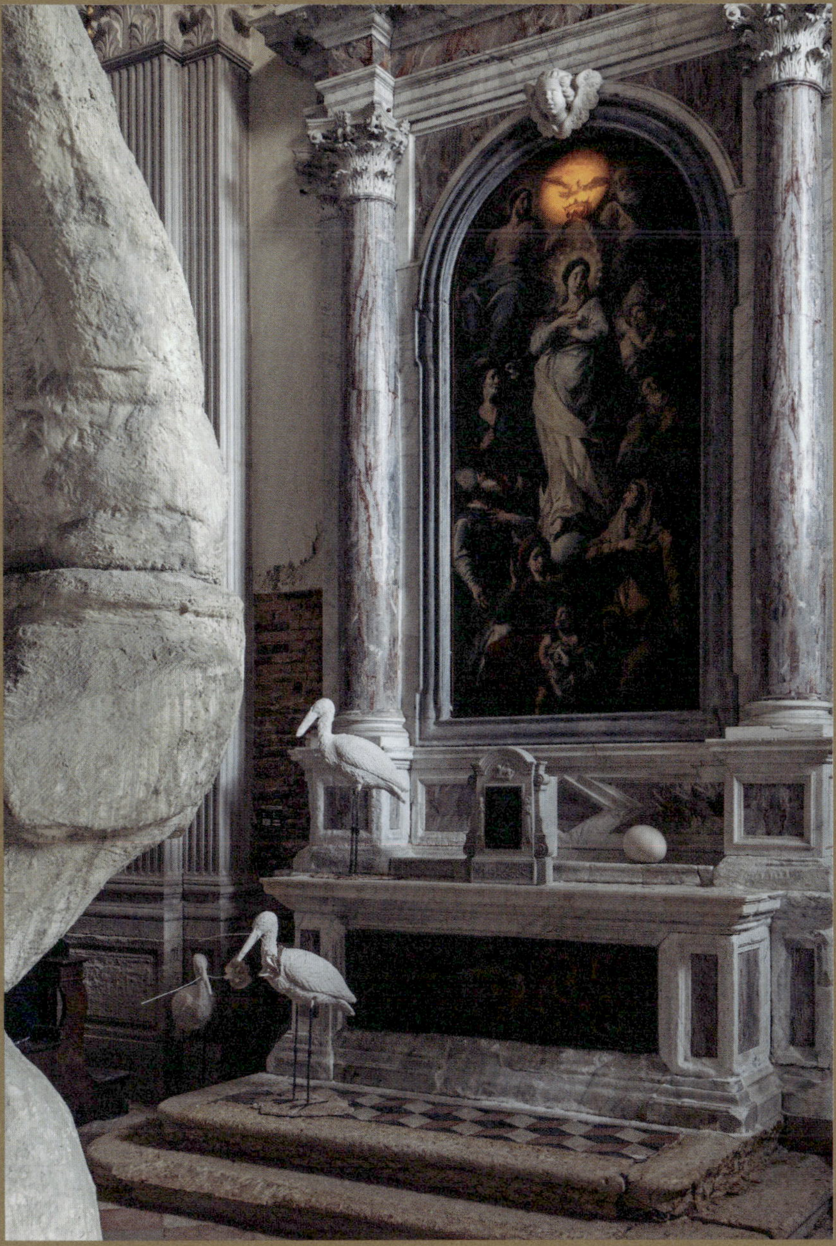

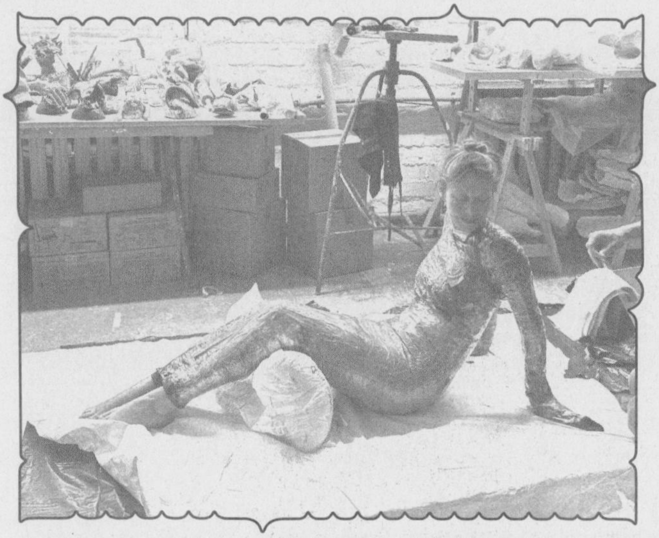

in church settings and the current moment "affectionately" labelled the "assholocene"; and, as per the artist's request, horror stories written by Estonian children have also found their way into the book, as Karlson is often inspired by children's vivid imagination and as yet unsolidified flow of ideas.

We are truly grateful to everyone who contributed to the making of this book — from editors to the graphic designers Jojo & me, who also created the visual identi ty for the Estonian pavilion.

This extensive project was made possible thanks to the dedicated and continuous work of numerous people. I would like to thank the team of the Estonian Centre for Contemporary Art, the co-editor of this book Keiu Krikmann, the head of production for the exhibition Sten Ojavee, the project coordinators Marika Agu and Mikk Lahesalu, and the communications manager Kaarin Kivirähk, who also invited Stina Pley and Alexia Menikou to be part of the team. The pavilion would not have been completed without the technical mastery of Tõnu Narro, Mihkel Lember (Technical Director) and Johannes Säre (Dream Team) or without lighting design by Oliver Kulpsoo, and sound design by Raul Saaremets. The artist was supported every step of the way by her studio assistants Loora Kaubi and Eva Mahhov and her expanded team— Art Allmägi, Sander Haugas, Erik Liiv, Maria Luiga, Nikolai Saaremets, Hanna Samoson, and our Italian coordinator Valeria Romagnini.

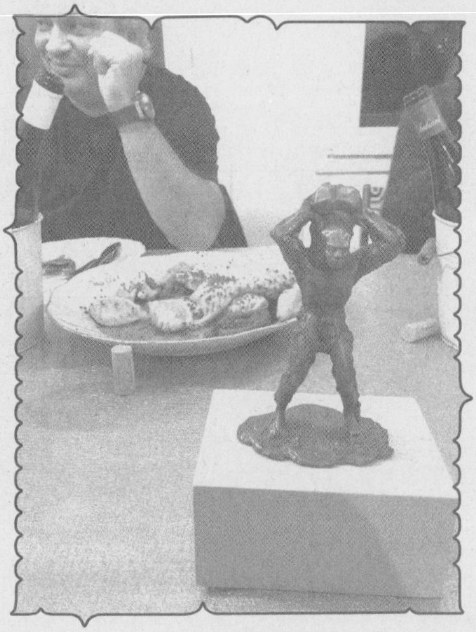

We would also like to thank the supporters of the Estonian pavilion for their unyielding trust and contribution which made it all possible. The project involved numerous other people — the full list of names is available in the colophon.

Each contribution was invaluable, and it was only due to the wonderful, supportive, and harmoni ous teamwork — with Edith Karlson always at the very centre of it — that this project has been such a success.

Thinking of *Hora lupi* and trying to summarise the process, I have been thinking about comparing it to a flowing river. From the moment we came to the beautiful but melancholy and decaying Chiesa Santa Maria delle Penitenti standing in the shadows of its former glory, the river found its bed and its current has been strong and unstoppable. At times, the role of the team around Edith Karlson was to clean the river from drift wood and sediment, so that water could flow in full force and so, the incessant flow still carries us all to this day.

I hope the readers of this book have a chance to get to know the wonderful work of Edith Karlson in more depth, to enjoy her absurdist and humorous approach, to laugh and cry together with the artist in our notably darkening world, at times still pierced by sharp rainbow-coloured rays of hope.

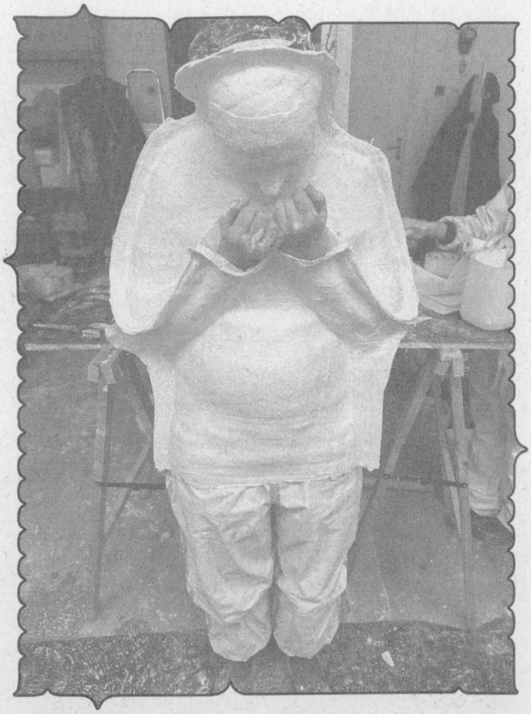

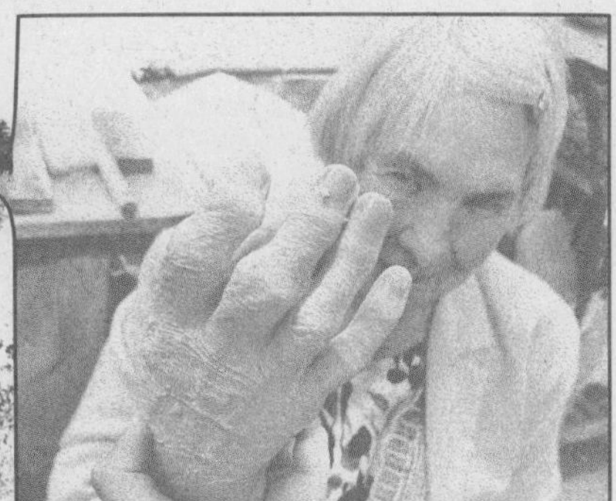

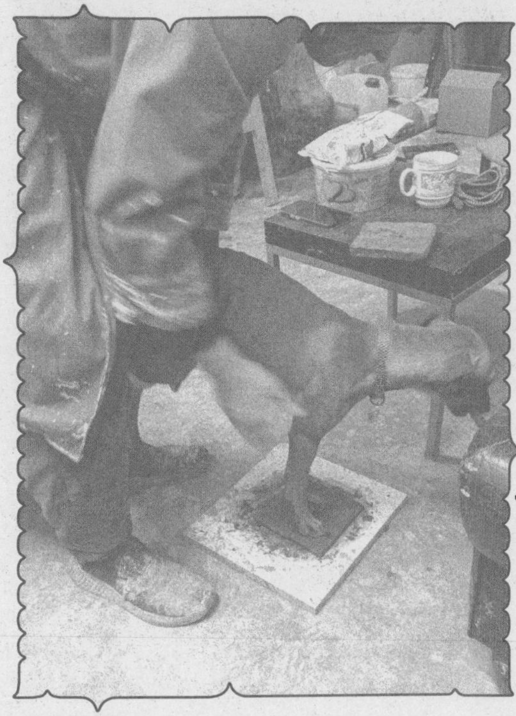

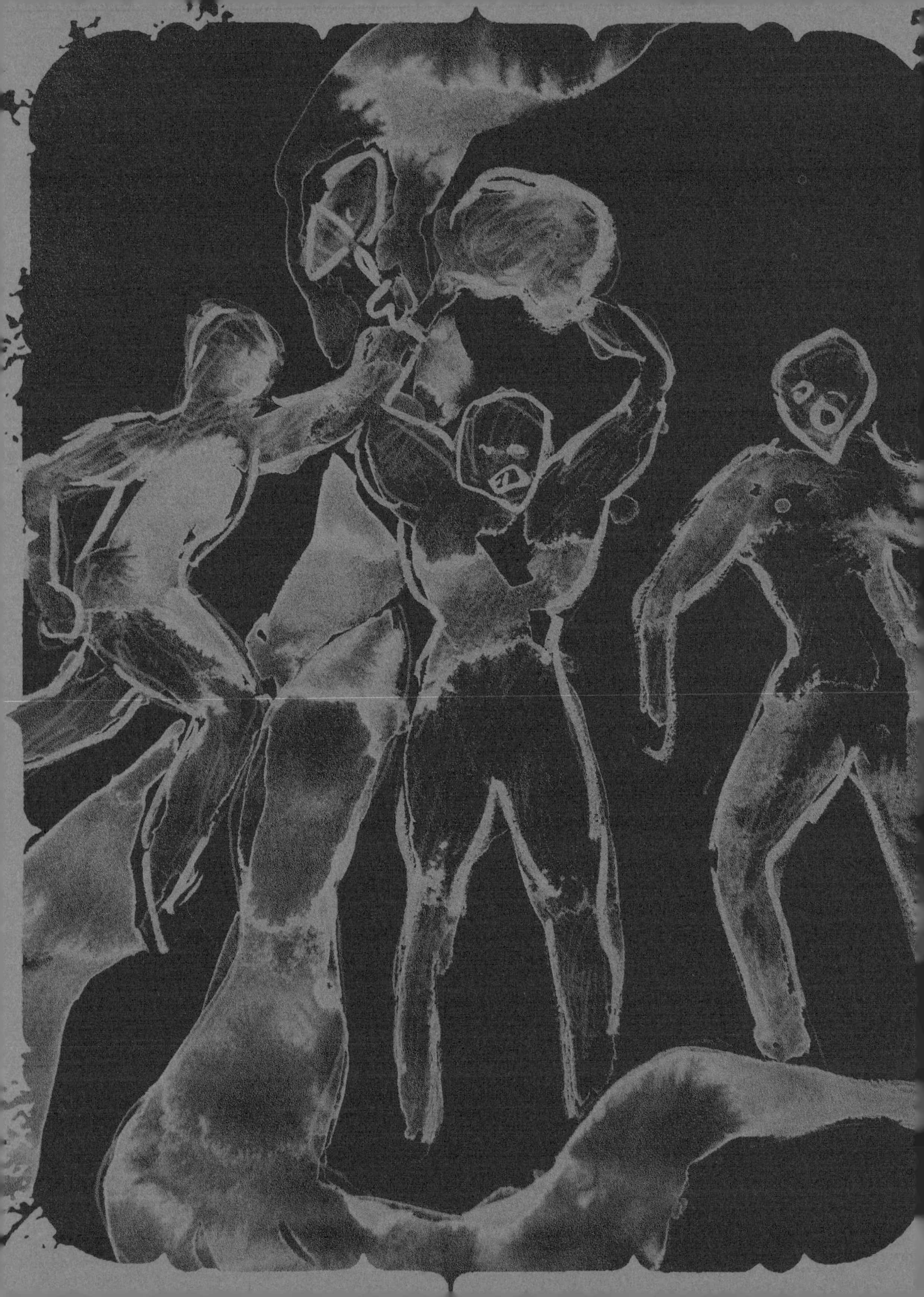

Quinn Latimer

WOLVES FOR HOURS (AN ANIMAL IN THE SHEETS)

For Edith Karlson

I

Winter. Hypnosis of snow, its pale technology.
White snakes! Dark waters.

Melancholy. The hour is late and bleak and stunning.
Night circles me like a dog.

Macabre visions of rites, a kind of — what — society. No.
Bestiary.

Each animal holds another animal in its mouth —
by the scruff of the neck or by the beak.

Each animal holds a string of beads in its mouth.

The beaded string loops up and down, as another
animal mouth lifts it, and another, and another.

Necklace that loops around the room, against the
white throat of the wall, clasped in a series of animal mouths.

No words, only beads. No animals, only me.

Some dance track looping the distance —
profane feminine voices, a foreign tongue, a familiar beat.

I am looking at old images in a pdf of an artist's book.
Images that change form, gender.

I am looking at new images, gleaned from the long night,
of the artist's future exhibition.

It is just discernable over the water, on the island.
Some pink licking at the blue-black horizon,
the color of an animal's rough tongue.

The exhibition is in a church alongside a canal on a lagoon.

Interiors, exteriors. Brick walls, marble columns,
red-veined like meat, pale like fat.

Charity of courtyards, angels of waterways and laundries.
Fallen alters, fallen women.

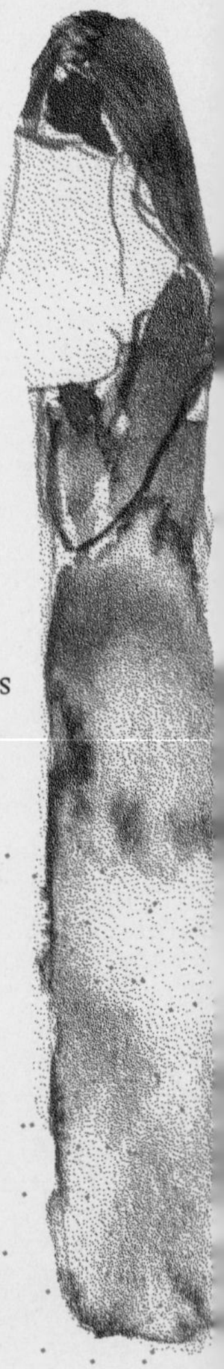

Sinking and mineral, our baroque sewage, our animal sediment,
our ladies of lucid and ludic impoverishment and servitude.
Not quite penitent. History!

The church is an animal, cleaning itself. With its rough tongue,
like a little clay fish, licking down its damp, dirty fur.
Then its iridescent scales.

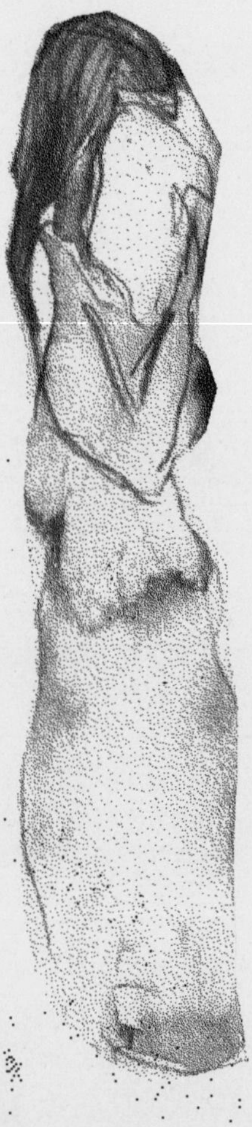

The animal is cleaning itself and then everyone else.

Her interior externalized as a kind of relief,
with long indices of expert metamorphosis.

Cherubs become fathers become monsters become grandmothers
become snakes become saints become storks become slaves
become sculptures become sex workers become city-states
become babies become allegories become angels become kittens
become interiors become exteriors become bodies become
cleaners become orders become hours become wolves become
systems become language become meat become memories
become ruins become dogs become clay become concrete
become climate become algorithms become humans.

Come, come. Put your mask on.

Become dust, stardust.
Memory of what you once were.

That is, werewolves, witches, heretics, cats, cults, fishes, floors.

History of forms, their emotional index and violent mutability.
History of bodies: same.

To be an animal, to be female, to be poor, is to make everyone
else clean against your transforming filth.
Debt she's born with, and by she, I mean me, and everyone else.

Her filth is gendered, her poverty gendered, her period style
gendered, her spiritual conditions carceral and gendered, her
irony gendered, her jokes dirty and despairing and gendered.

Her swanlike neck hovering over the floor like a snake,
a series of snakes, slithering across the brittle grounds.
Green then black then white.

Her hands red and raw and older than her face. Terracotta.

Her narrative naked and genre: a female body writ across the
dripping forest or the dusty grounds of the church, dead and
sculptural, that begins every story.

And by genre, I mean stable forms, unstable bodies.
Ideologies and variations of.

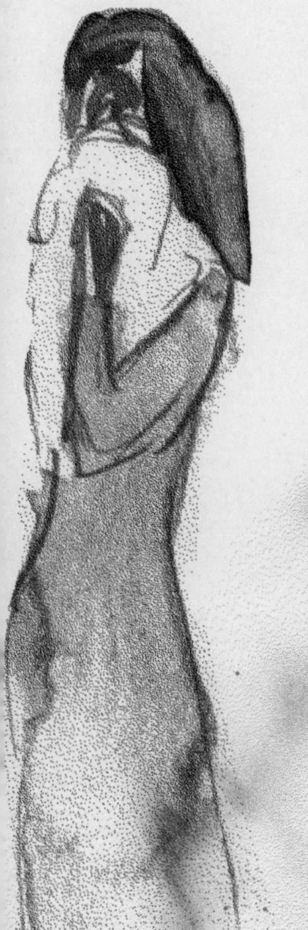

And by gendered and sculptural, I mean animal.
Made animal or returned to it.

What is the difference?
She is an animal in the sheets. Cleaning them.

To have this body — such irony! this rough vessel! this fishy head!
this rote title! — is to become allegory. Or an exhibition.

Solidarity in numbers, in hybridity and alienation,
pleasure and oppression.

Our glittery bestiary, at once rough and ritual.
The easy moral, the devoted company.

The long, strange dramaturgy of social world, lonely life.

Its lackluster rites.

City-state of the soul! I joke.
My melancholic refrains.

So the citations arrive
(as on thin vaporetto in the foggy, wastrel night):

Gender is the length we go to in order to be loved,
a writer once wrote in his novel devoted to some early
auto-verses and profane and medieval crushes.

Incarceration is the length we go to in order to be free, I write
now in a poem inside contemporary climes of infinite brutality.

Pandemics strobe such sentiments,
sentences nocturnal and without off-ramps.

So many crimes, canals, books, artists, political and personal
failures, discarded technologies and poor images,
idiot ideologues and valances of organized violence.

So many masks, birds, bones, pleas, deities, pieties.

First a church, then a prison, then an exhibition.
Each a kind of model of the world.

Devotion and power, supremacy and mourning,
production and reproduction, their continuum.

The camp of gender, for example:
built at dawn, dismantled each night.

Church as workhouse, economy of bodies, belief in money,
a pretty penny, given the patina of humility, charity.

Let's just say: It was not a pretty poem, a smooth sculpture, an
acceptable object, a popular algorithm, a just system,
a real religion, an easy child. But it worked.

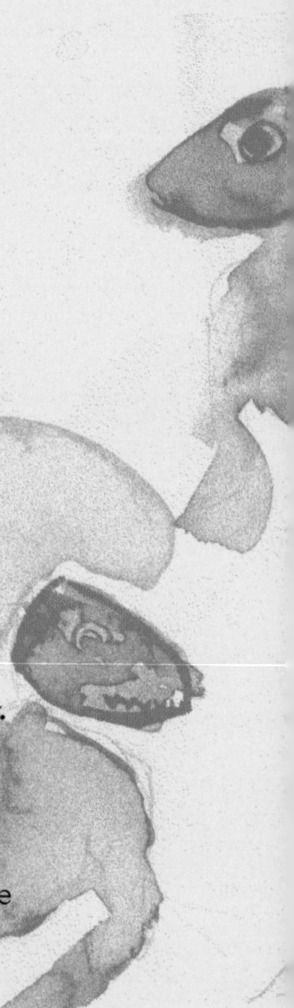

She *worked*, I once wrote about another artist. That is to say,
about this artist and every artist that came after.

Her gender simply the length by which I went to work for her.

To love someone means to work for them.

To love an idea means to work for it.

To love like an animal means to become all labor. Labor you take
to be your leisure, sacred or profane, who is to say.

The trance of the social.

Body after body, same, same, then different.

Choice the mineral fiction of youth, error and economy
of your age. Cruel desires, cheap sunglasses, a red lip.

Submit to your errors, your filth, your shame.
Clean yourself up.

And by yourself, we mean the world.

M.

Spring. Dust, red. Floods in the plazas!

Ritual of reindeer, of poppies, of carnival,
of some Sahara come north.

Animals with flowers in
their mouths.

Every animal is an artist, the
male artist once said to
his commercialized cult.

Every animal is a female artist, the woman
artist replied in her retrospective fever.

Sardonic and with despair, she said this, but also with real pleasure.

Their assembled northern cults — nationalist,
internationalist, economic, gendered, exhibitionary —
took this information and spread it throughout the lands and
seas as glitteringly abject offerings.

They laid them at the feet of their concrete
and clay deities gleaned from the east, their
fading moneyed miracles plucked from
the west, their pale and
excruciating institutions
mimicries of the fat
columns of the south.

Some dance track
looping the distance —
voices feminine and
foreign as always.

West that became
North. East that became South. Girl that became wolf.
Woman that became fish. Foreigner that became feminine.
Butch that became femme. Object that became language.
Fiction that became the real.

Familiar equations, storied transformations.

Some sirenic meadow that was once part woman,
part bird or fish, but all witch.

No body but a voice, filling the field,
drifting across the water.

To build a body — kind of woman, kind of animal,
kind of alarm — around that voice to
make sense of its strangeness, its animality.

The head of a fish, the breasts of a young woman,
the tail of a siren, the ears of a wolf, wings of an angel,
feet of a bird, rough hands of a matriarch.

An algorithm — that is, a technology —
for difference, its emergence and emergency.

The violence it should always be greeted with (this is ideology).

Alarm that signals the hour of the wolf at sea.
Hour of the alarm for the daughter at land.
Alarm that rings their manifestations: hybrid, myriad, maenad.

Maenads wearing snakes, leopard print;
spinning tales; raving mad.

Sirens that alert you to some violent becoming —
forests, tundra, courtyard, canal, laurel, cow, stasis.

Water become rupture become island become church become
prison become ruin become exhibition. Girl become tree
become wolf become terracotta become allegory become
season become algorithm.

Large language systems, with the largess of empire and
emptiness of Northern California,
our lucite technologies, clacking like clear heels.

*Every language is just a dialect with an army and
a navy*, someone once said. *Every woman is a fiction,
fluorescent and irritating,* someone else replied.

You must find your form, the poet then said to the critic.
You must find your forms, the maenad advised her followers.
You must flee your form, the figure said, finally, to itself, mouth
and hands red and raw.

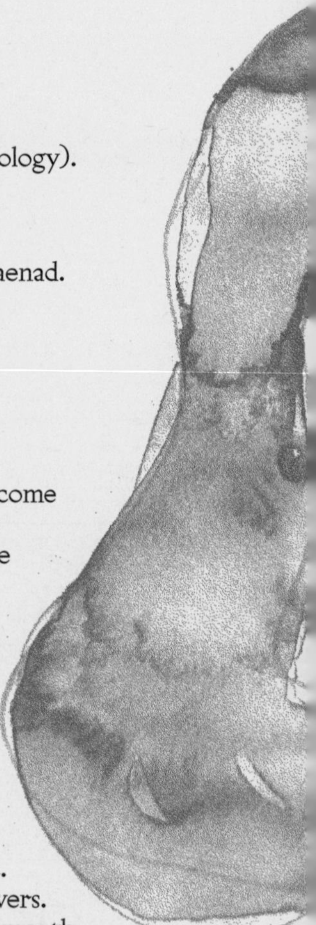

And yet the regulations of our church of
the penitent once went:

Entrants to be between twelve and thirty years,
living in Venice at least a year, healthy in mind and body,
not pregnant, and having withdrawn from prostitution for
at least three months.

So many numbers: twelve, thirty, one year, three months. Nine
months. Again and again, without end.

Again and again, even though we know love's landscape /
and the little churchyard with its lamenting names /
and the terrible reticent gorge in which the others /
end, as the poet wrote.

The little churchyard with its lamenting names:
mind and body, wolf and woman, fish and bird,
snake and swan, land and water, city and state.

Now loop them all together. Beads on a single string.

Mouths open and aching and animal.
Hungry for company, the warmth of another body.

Our hunger turned into our labor. Our bodies built
to make sense of the strangeness of our voices.
Our mouths singing and starving and laughing.

Our minds working and working, high-pitched. Our institutions
and islands sinking and dragging. Our waters dirty and rising.

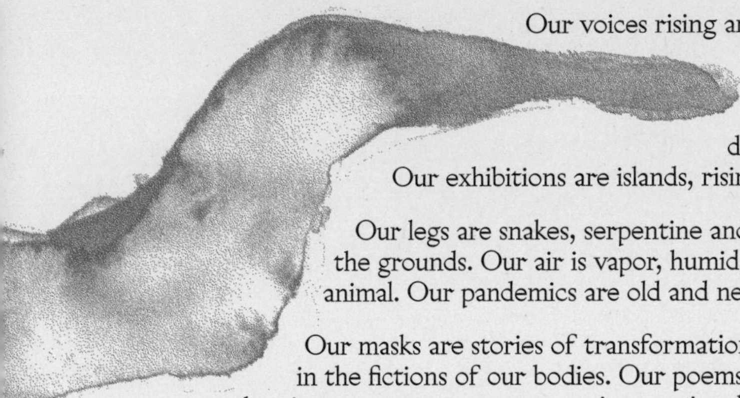

Our voices rising and falling.
Our women are
working and
mourning,
devoted as animals.
Our exhibitions are islands, rising and falling.

Our legs are snakes, serpentine and looping across
the grounds. Our air is vapor, humid, dirty, almost
animal. Our pandemics are old and new and constant.

Our masks are stories of transformation and incarceration
in the fictions of our bodies. Our poems are long and
looping as extraneous essays on international exhibitions.

Our artists are animals scratching inside the long and
looping night. Our night rooms are melancholic,
our jokes macabre. Our animals are in series,
stunning and sunning themselves on the docks.
Our pleasures are historical and ideological and cruel.

Our self-soothing is a pop song, sung in a foreign language,
ever new. Our song is a poem for future animals, future
exhibitions. Our future is a song, apocalyptic and looped.

Our wolf is a girl, laughing and starving and writing.
Our hour is her name, howling and moralizing.
Our bodies are animals, crossing the glowing matrices.
Our field is a feeling, fluorescent and forever.

Our trance is social, an exhibition of animals.
Our sheets are filthy, scrawled with lyric and language.
Our walls are up but coming down, brick by brick.
Our strangers are women, brickhouses,
and allegorical — watch them glow and toil.

Our wolves are stories,
howling at the purple perimeter.
Our borders are fictions,
featuring darkening waters, inky skies.

Shhh. Night!

Hour of the girl-animal.

Hour of the wall scrawled with equations,
devotions, laments, exorcisms.

Hour of the uncharitable memoir,
its narcotic sentences.

Hour of grandmother's acid confessional.

Hour of her daughter building, fucking,
thinking, dreaming, singing, sighing.

Hour of the birthing of a bestiary in clay and concrete,
islands and institutions, charity and violence.

Hour of the red mouth, blue heart,
green and irradiating dream.
Like a cat it slinks across the courtyard.

Hour of death cults. Bombs that read *victim / victor,*
in floral fonts. Victories called *total* and *final* without irony.
Streaming violence until the humid morning.

Hour of waiting for it to be over. Hour of arrival.
Of animals, wet and dry on the docks.

Our sun is an anxious dog, circling us like language.

Our moon is a neurotic wolf,
showing us her bright teeth in black rooms.

Mask of days, nights of pale sheets.
Presence of aching, nascent technologies.

Our hour is an animal, sniffing the clock on the wall.

Hands ancient and moving.

Come, come. Good boy.

Tell us the time.

Note: Italicized lines are by Robert Glück, Anne Carson, Joseph Beuys, Rosemarie Trockel, Max Weinreich, Richard Howard, Rainer Maria Rilke, imaginary maenads, and, at various times, myself.

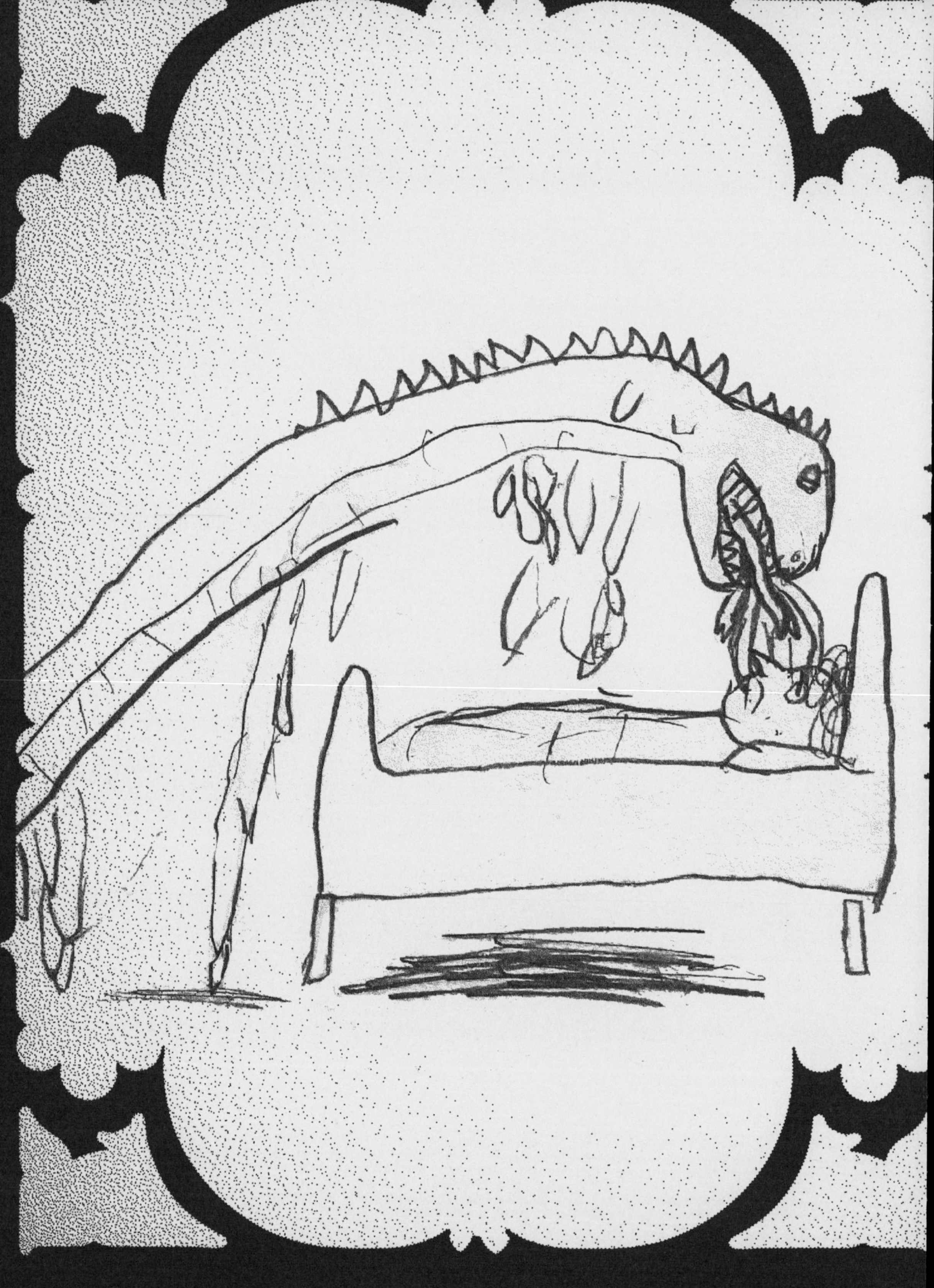

Risto Pärna
10 years old

BIG SLIMY SNAKE

There was a child who every one always bullied. Every day, the child felt bad. There was nowhere the child would feel good. Even at home, the child was beaten. One day the child became something strange. They turned into a big slimy snake. One night, the snake decided to go and visit one of the bullies. The slimy snake slid into the house through a window. The boy was asleep. The slimy snake started eating the boy's mouth. From the mouth of the slimy snake, white maggots crawled into the mouth of the bully.

In the morning when the boy woke up, he was green in the face. The boy had maggots in his mouth. The maggots had eaten the boy's intestines. The maggots spilled out of the boy's mouth. The boy fell down. And that is how the story ended. The big slimy snake will come to your house at night and will do the same to you.

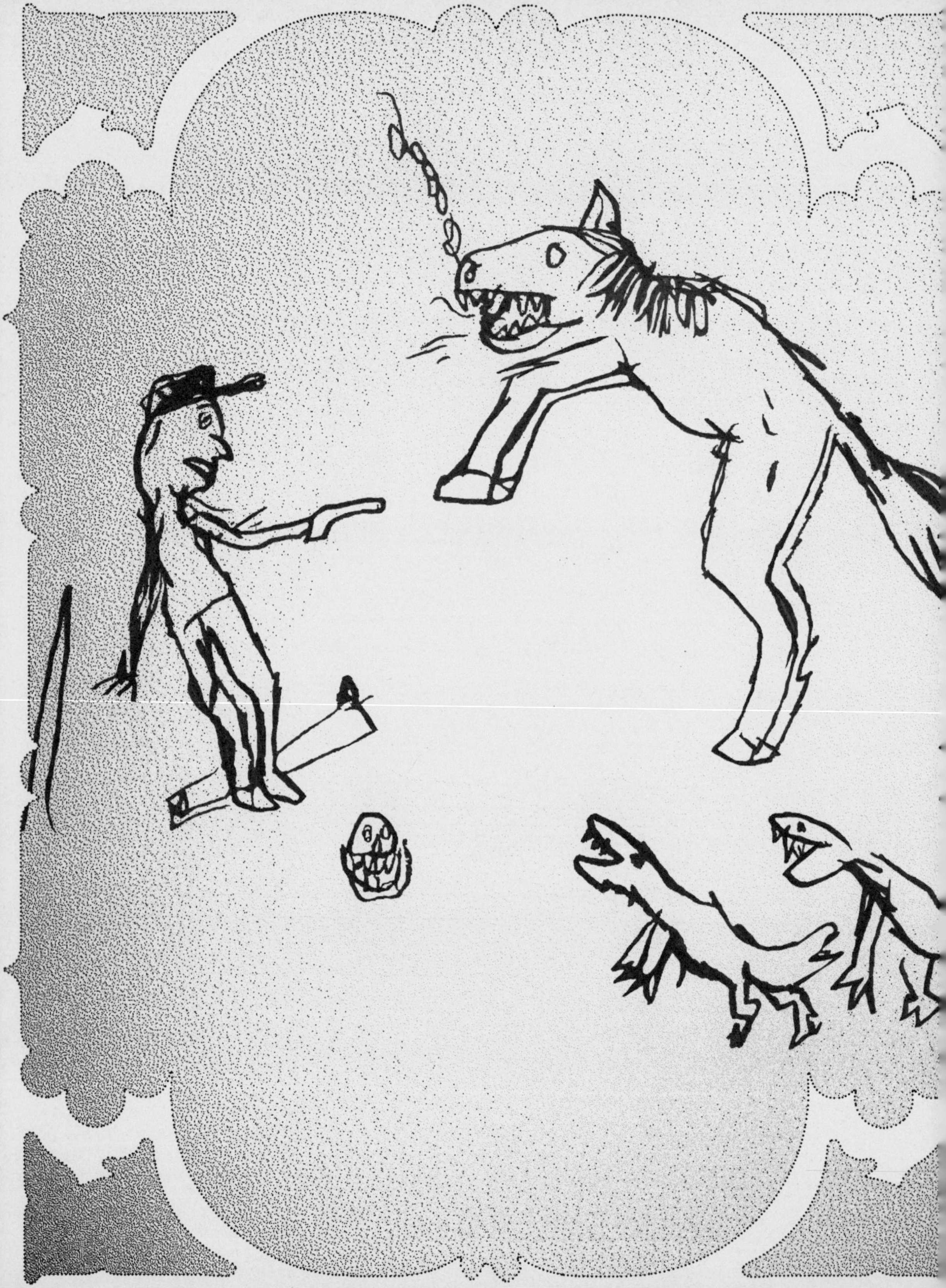

Bärbel Balodis
9 years old

DARK HORSE

Once upon a time, a dark horse lived in the woods. The horse had red eyes, a long dark mane, and she was very large. She had ran off from a farm because everyone was mean to her. Now, the horse lived in a little cave in the forest. At night, she haunted the farm. When she came to the farm, her eyes glowed and her nostrils released red smoke.

People were very afraid of her. Brave men went to the woods to find her but none of them ever returned.

One day, the horse returned to the stable. People were scared that she would take someone into the woods with her. The horse ran towards them but then suddenly changed direction and galloped into the pen and took a foal with her. Now everybody noticed that the foal's eyes were red like her mother's. Suddenly, the horse stopped in front of the house and noticed puppies trapped in a plastic bag. The puppies were yelping and asking for help. The horse gave them a sniff and helped them get out of the plastic bag. The puppies barked and were happy. The horse, the foal, and the puppies all went into the woods and lived there happily ever after. Never again did they return to the horrible farm. As revenge, the people of the farm still hear the frightening horse neighing and dogs howling at night.

Mona Lee Tšetõrkina
11 years old

BLACK CATS ARE NOT SCARY

There once was a family who had mice in their house. The mice ate all their food and they were concerned. The mother had a friend whose cat was going to have kittens.

One day the mother's friend's cat gave birth to five kittens. The first was white, the second tabby, the third brown, the fourth black, and the fifth beige. The mother's friend had already given away the brown and the tabby and kept the beige for himself. The mother's friend invited the family for a visit and asked if they wanted the black cat. "A black cat brings bad luck," said the mother. But the mother had no other choice because meanwhile the white cat had disappeared.

So now the family had a black cat who was friendly and did not break any vases. The cat stayed vigilant all night and the mice didn't even get a chance to sniff the food because the brave cat caught them all. But the mother was still not sure about the cat. Deep down, she wished the cat would run away.

Two weeks later, the family decided to go for a walk in the woods. All of a sudden, the mother found the white cat that belonged to her friend, the one that had disappeared. She picked the little one up and took it home. "A white cat brings luck," said the mother cheerfully. She drove the black cat out of the house. The black cat went back to the mother's friend and NEVER wanted to see the mother again.

At night, instead of catching mice, the white cat broke vases, tore curtains, and broke other fragile things. The mother got fed up and she took the white cat back to the woods. In the evening, the white cat was back in front of the house. The family let the cat back in because nobody wanted to take the cat away again in the dark.

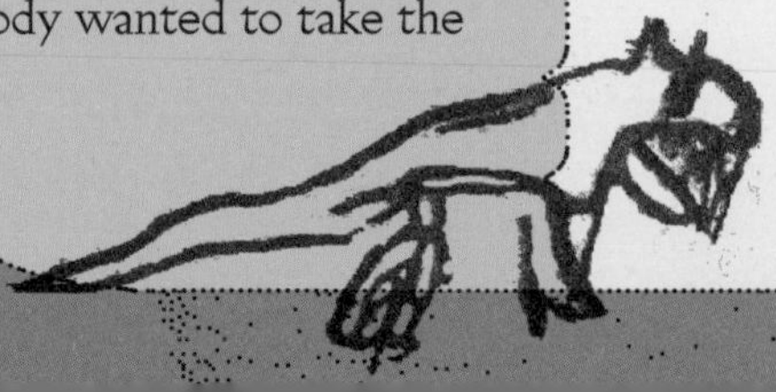

The mother could not sleep that night. The next morning, she took the cat into another city. The same night, the cat was back in the house again. The mother got mad, threw the white cat out, and double-locked the door. That night, she discovered the white cat was in her bed.

The following morning, the mother took the white cat on a boat with her. When the boat reached an island, the mother took the cat into the woods then ran back to boat, which took her home. The mother locked the door at night with four locks this time and calmly went to bed.

At night, the mother discovered that the same white cat was in her bed again, only now the cat's pale blue eyes had become black and the paws and chest were covered in blood. The cat growled, arched its back and bared its teeth, which were dripping with blood. A loud scream was heard from the room and the only one who was seen leaving the room was the blood-stained white cat.

Would you want a white cat?

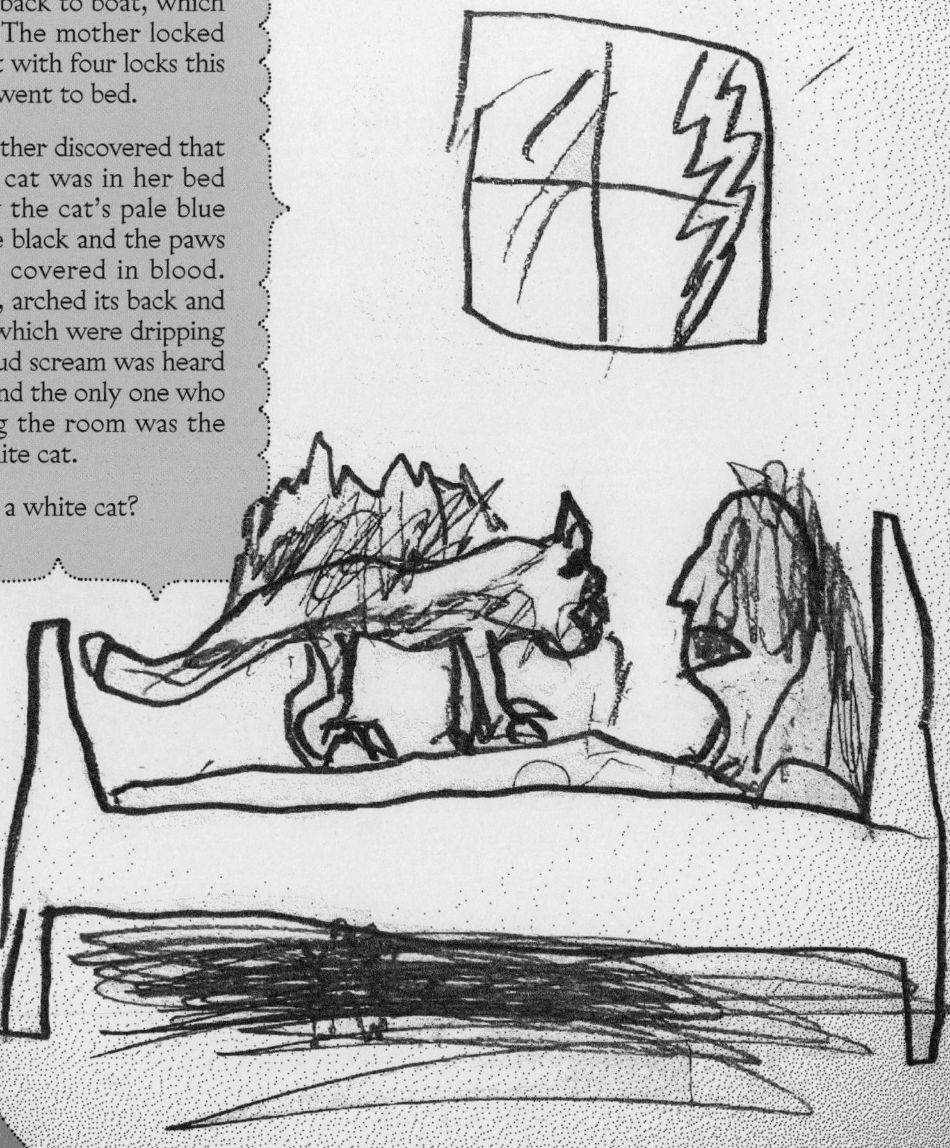

Melany Raud

11 years old

ALL OUR FEARS

At night, I am afraid to leave my room.

I am afraid to fall asleep at night.

I am afraid someone will chase me in the dark.

I am afraid that if my hamster bites me, I, too, will turn into a hamster.

I am afraid of white rats. My mother is afraid too.

My mother is also afraid that someone will come into our house at night and steal the children.

My brother is afraid of frogs because they are slimy. He is afraid of wolves because they have sharp teeth and claws. He is afraid of foxes because he thinks they look scary.

I would like to go to sleep now but I can't because I am afraid.

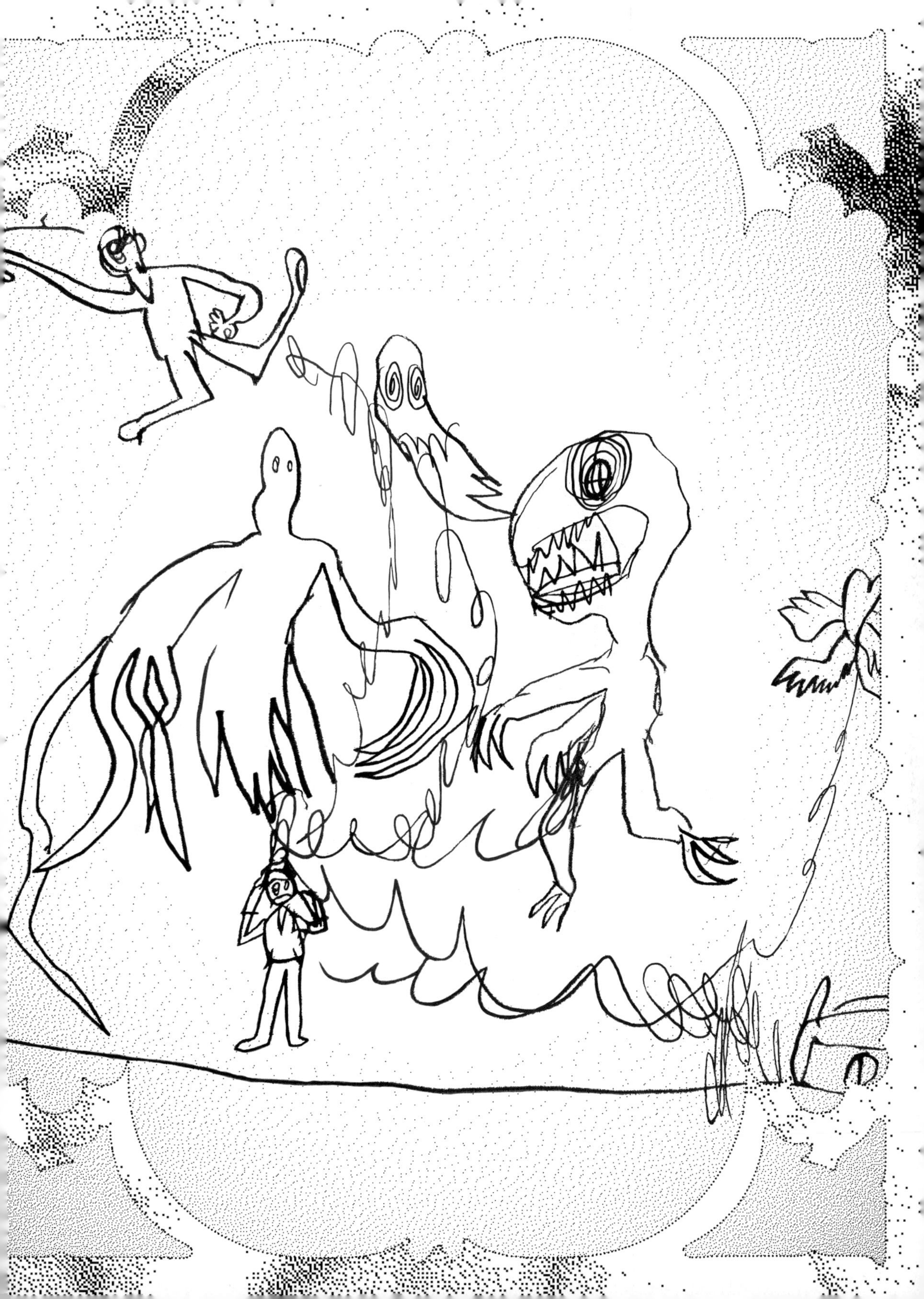

Emilia Palmipuu

THE HOLE

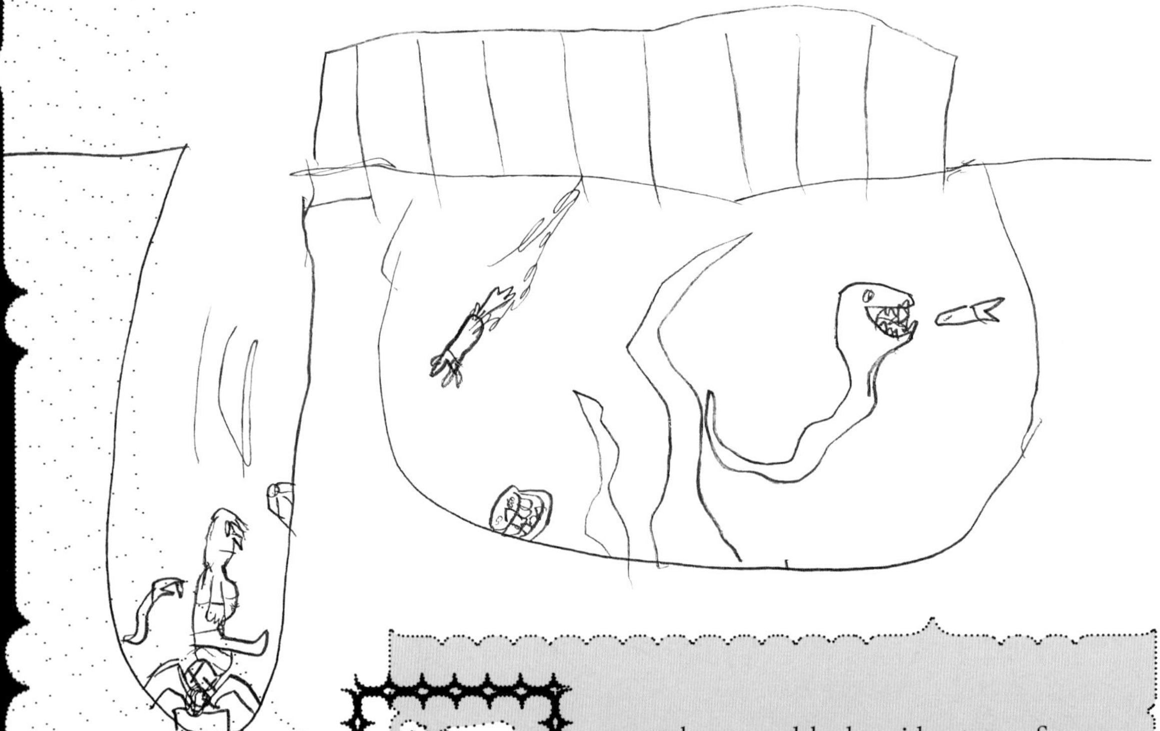

I was at home and had an idea to go for a walk in the woods. I got dressed and went to the woods. Suddenly it was dark. I didn't see so well anymore and took a wrong turn. I walked and walked until I reached a bridge. I crossed the bridge but there was a hole on the other side, so I fell into an abyss. In the dark, I felt snakes and hairy spiders crawling all over me. And then, one of them bit me. I turned into a giant spider.

I sat and waited for the next child I could bite. But along came a big fat man instead who crushed me to death as he fell. The spiders and snakes held a beautiful funeral for me.

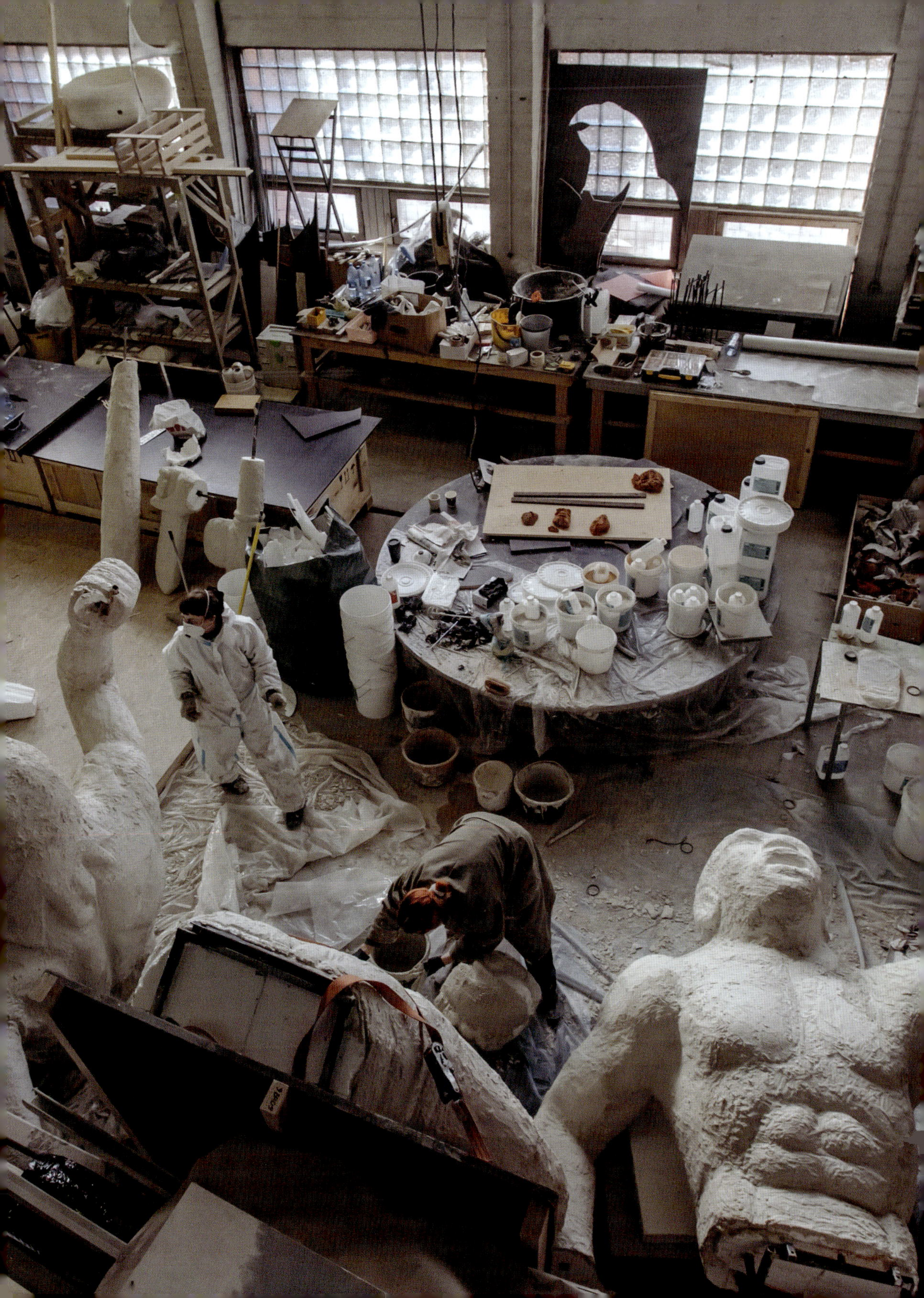

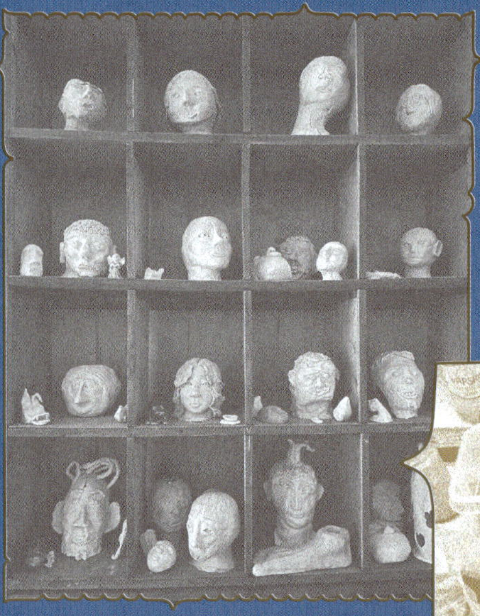
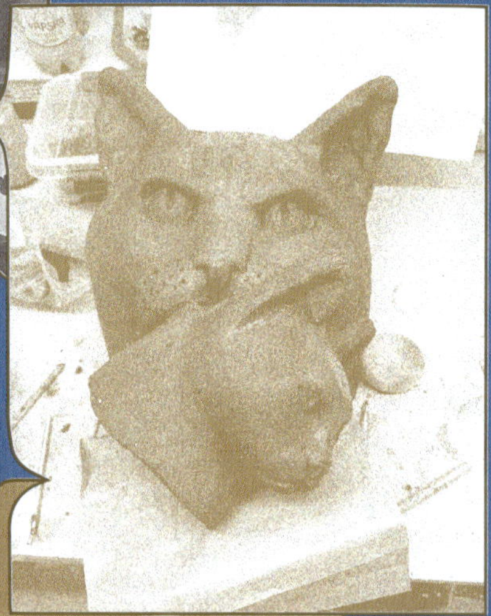
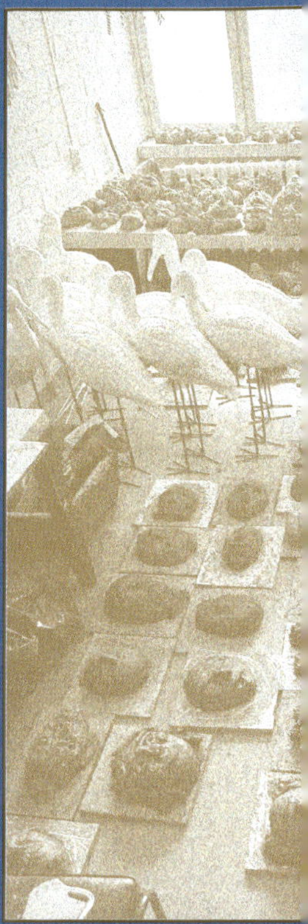
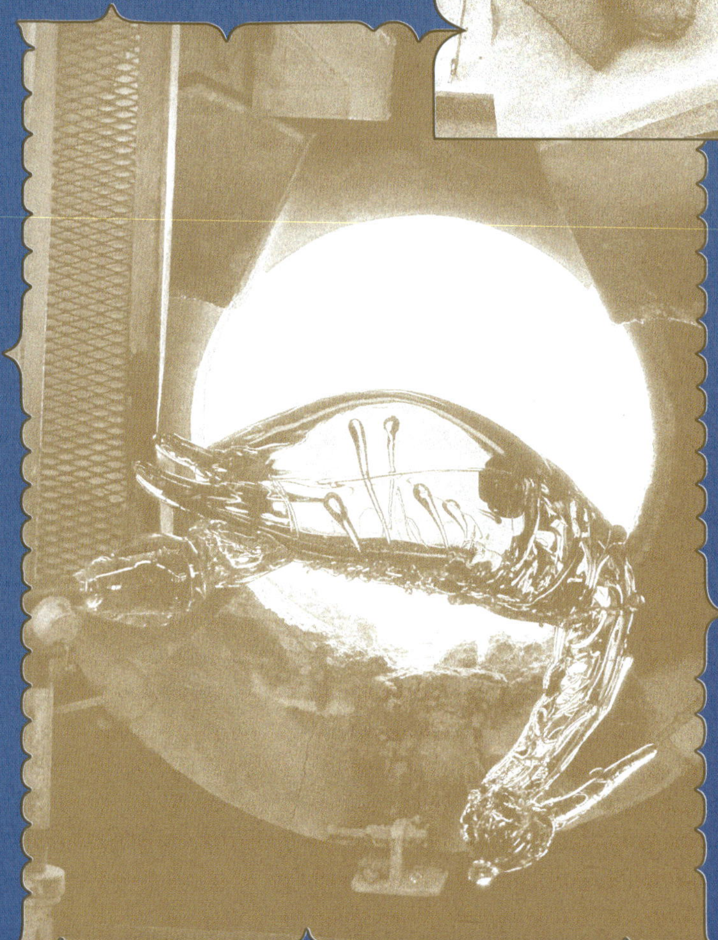
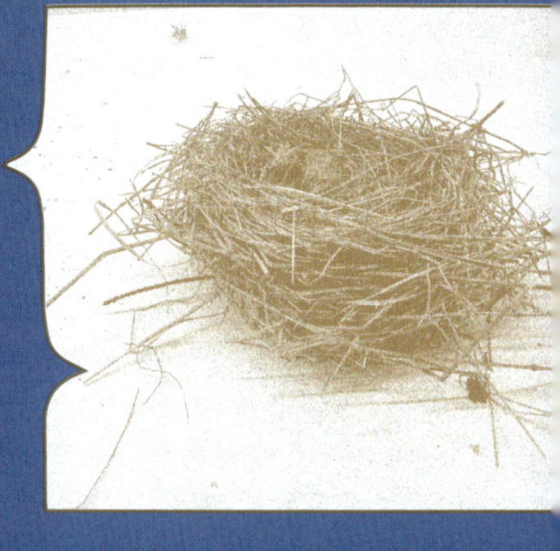

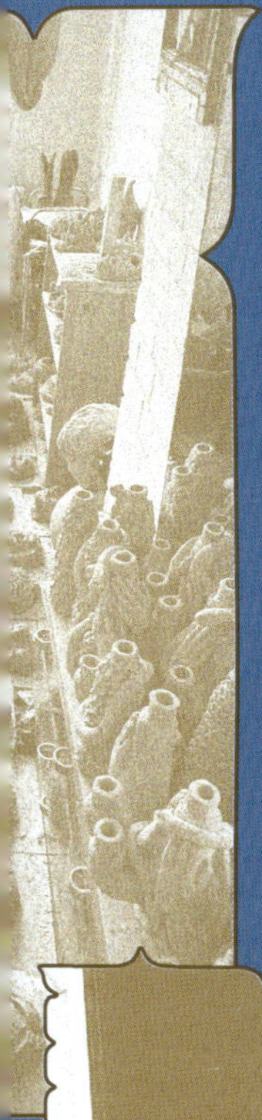
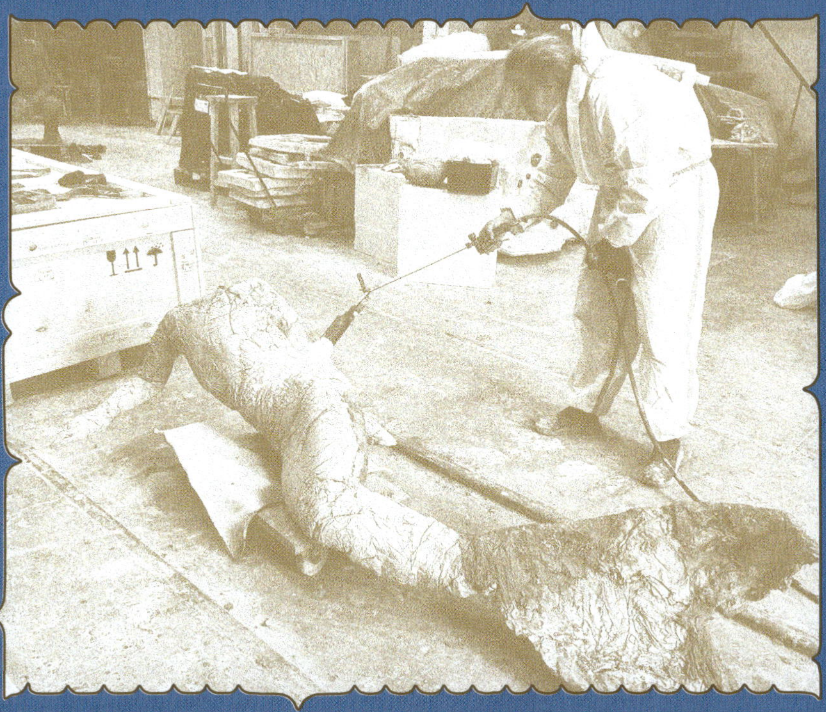
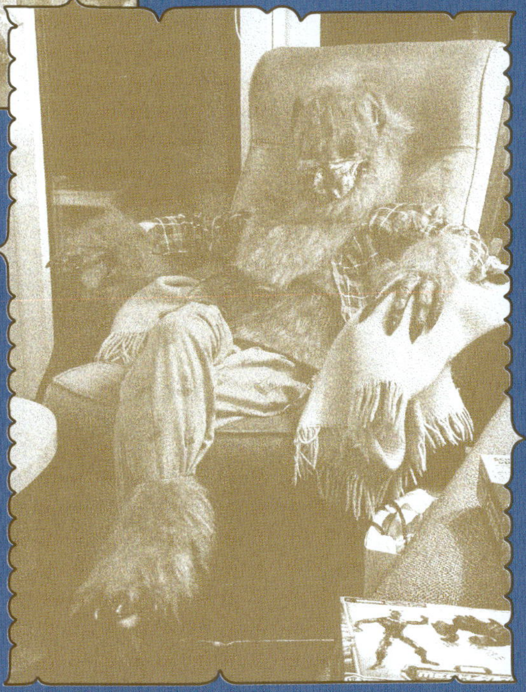
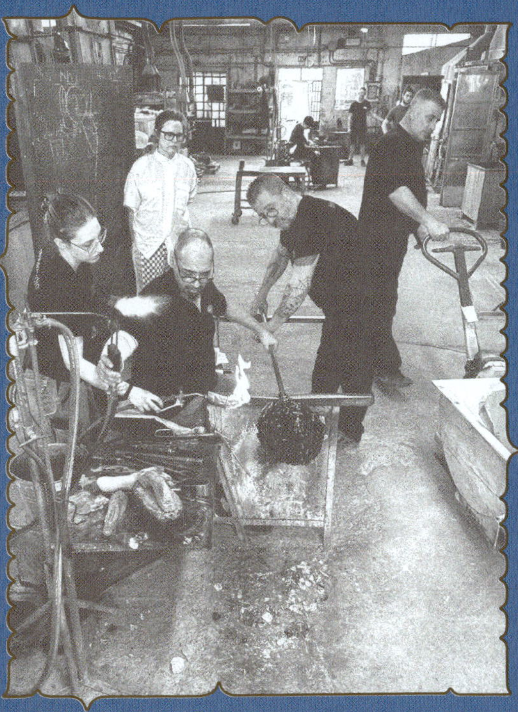

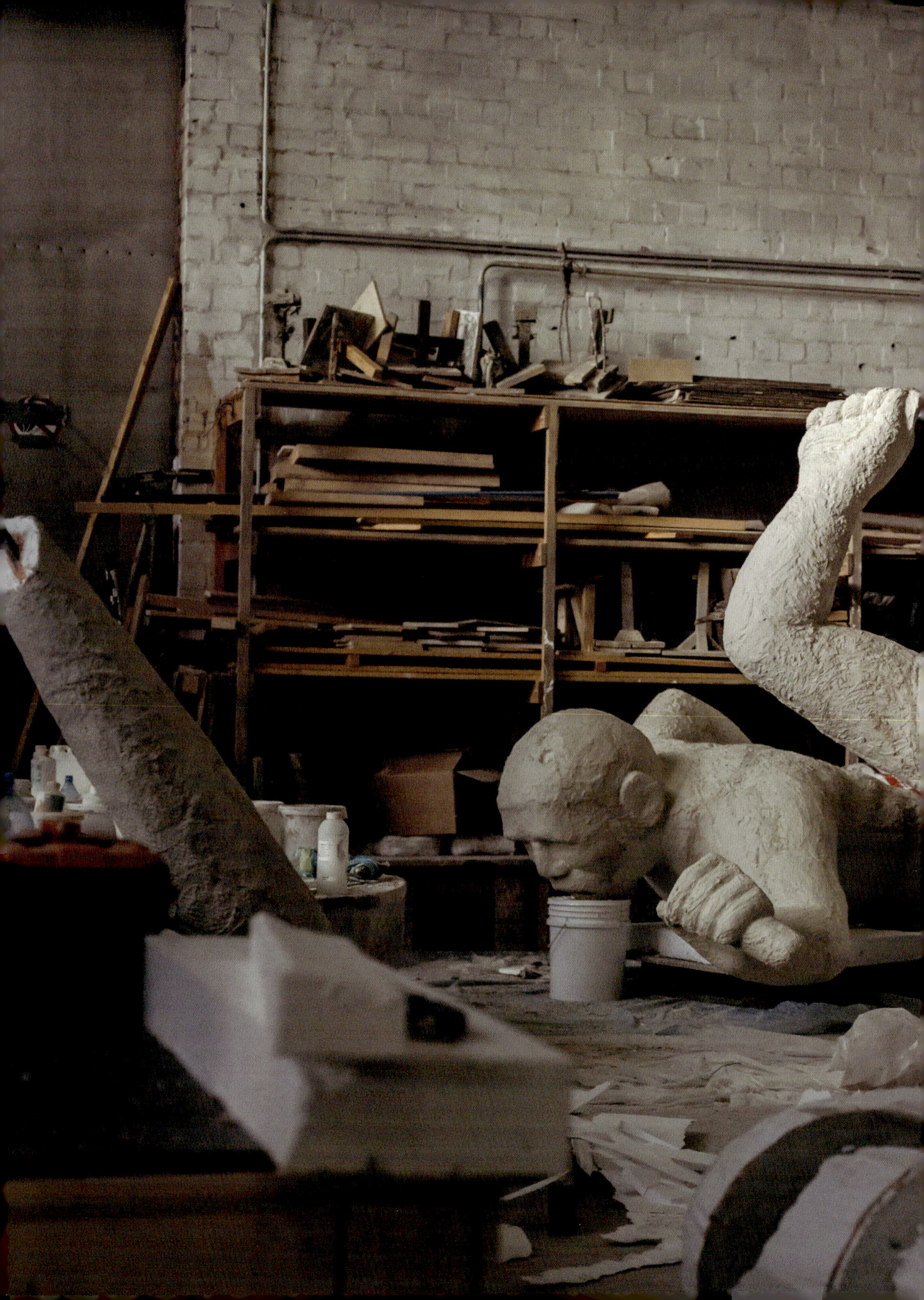

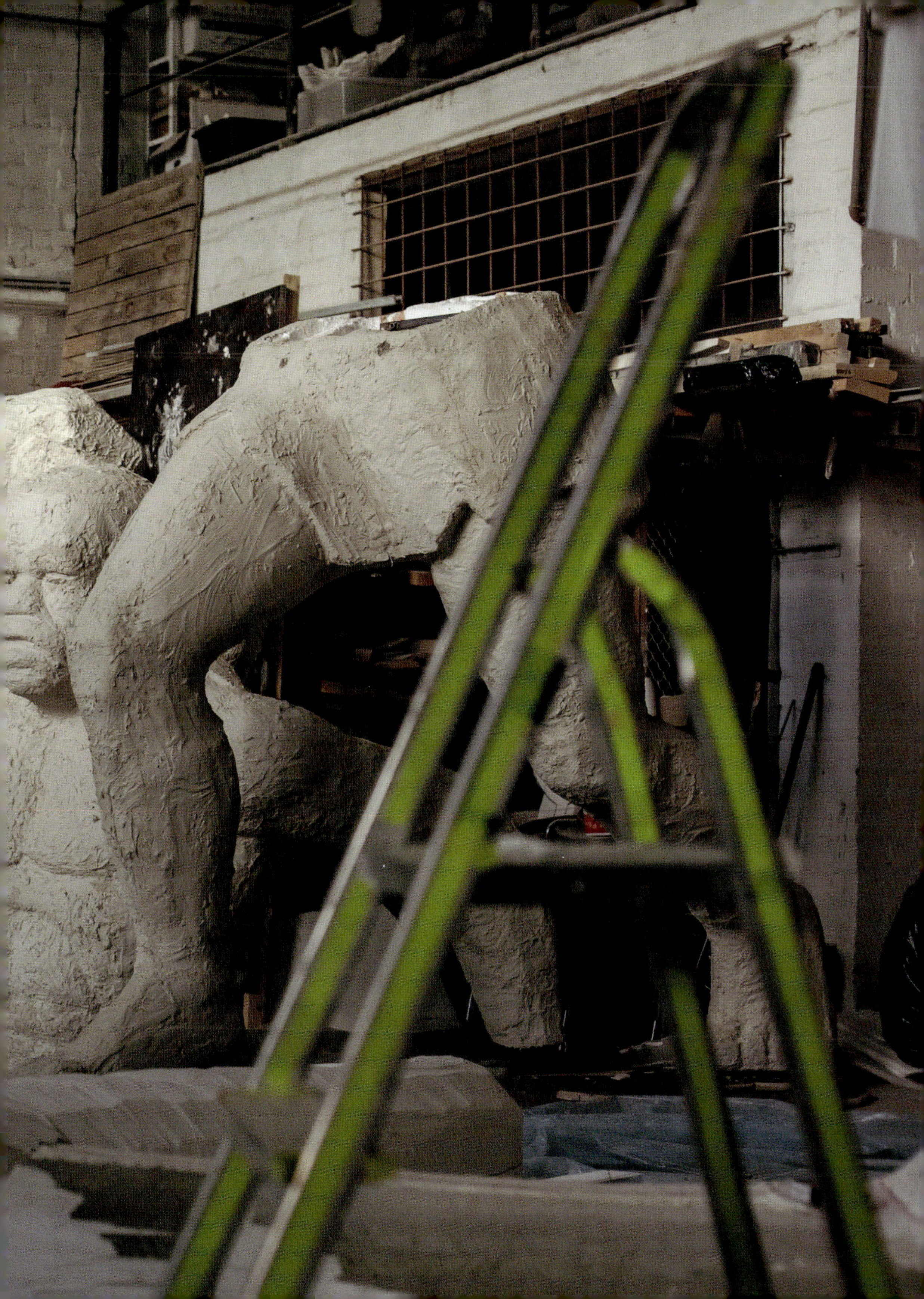

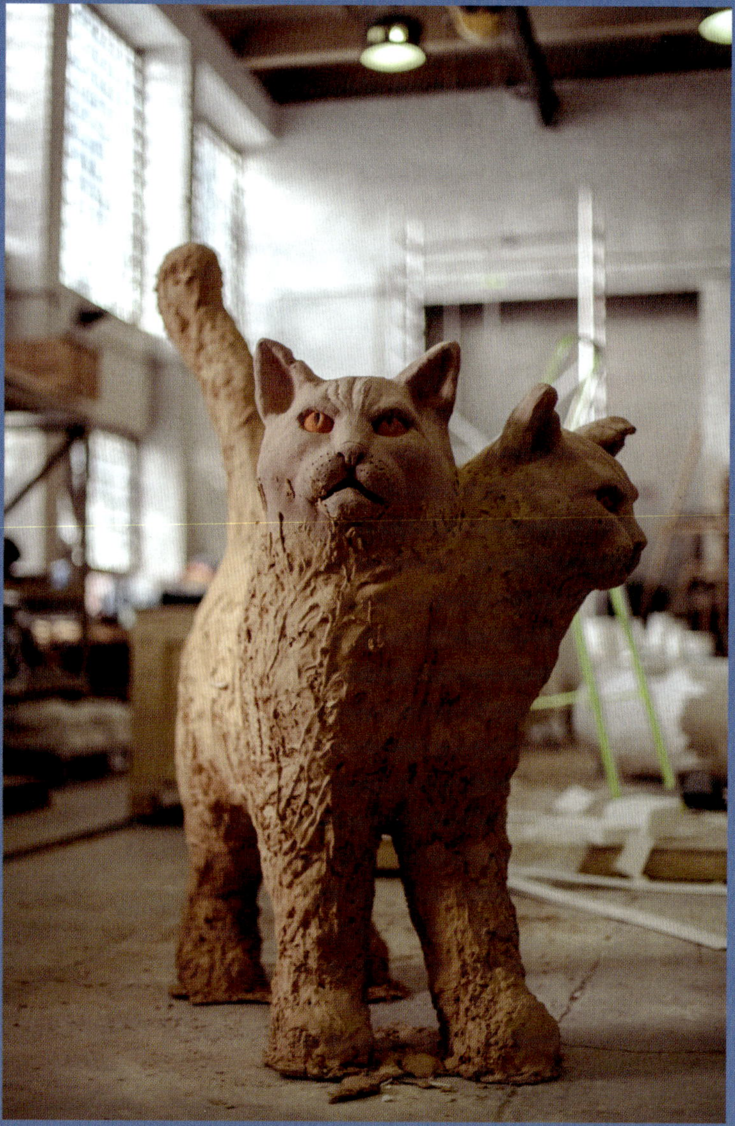

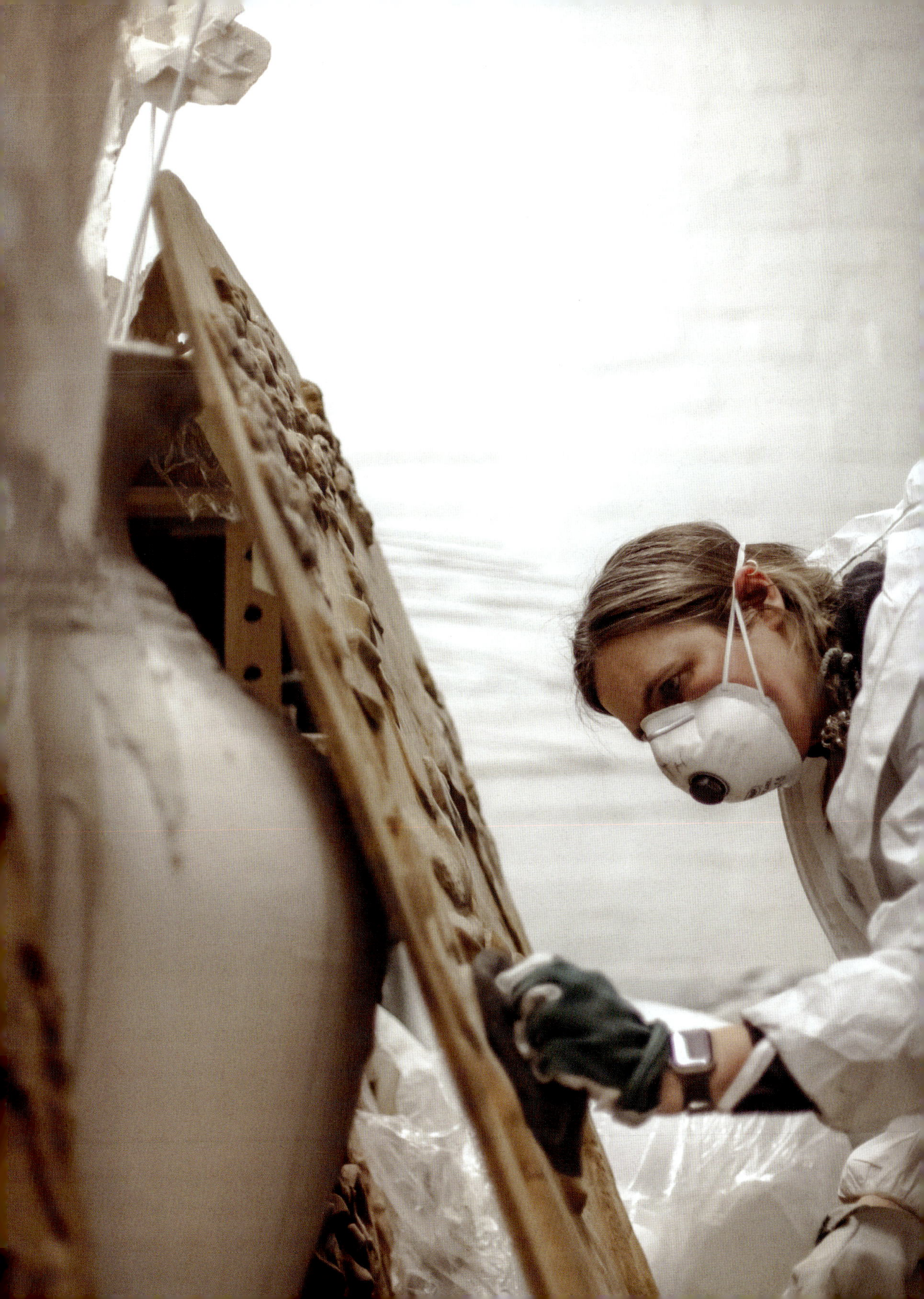

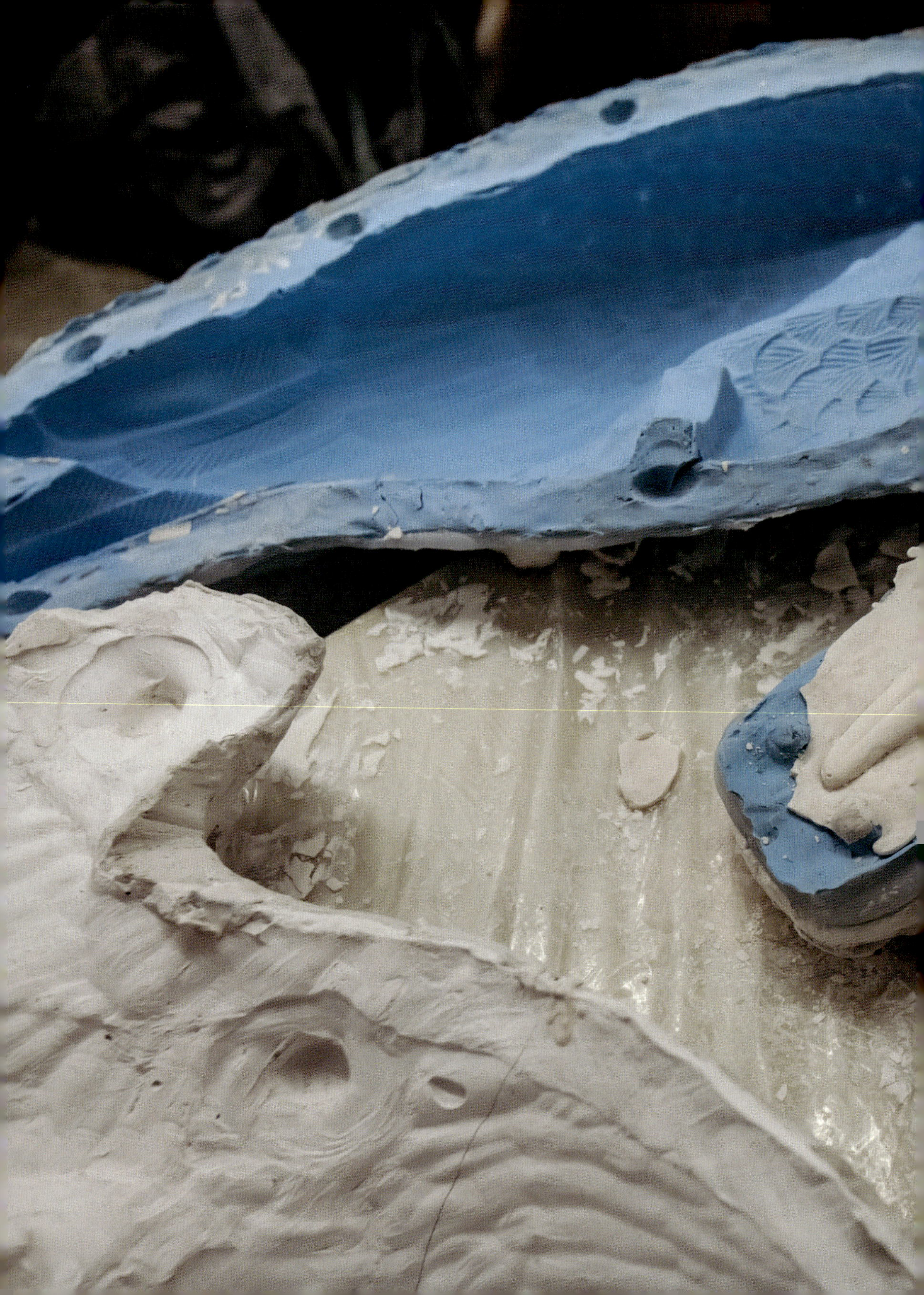

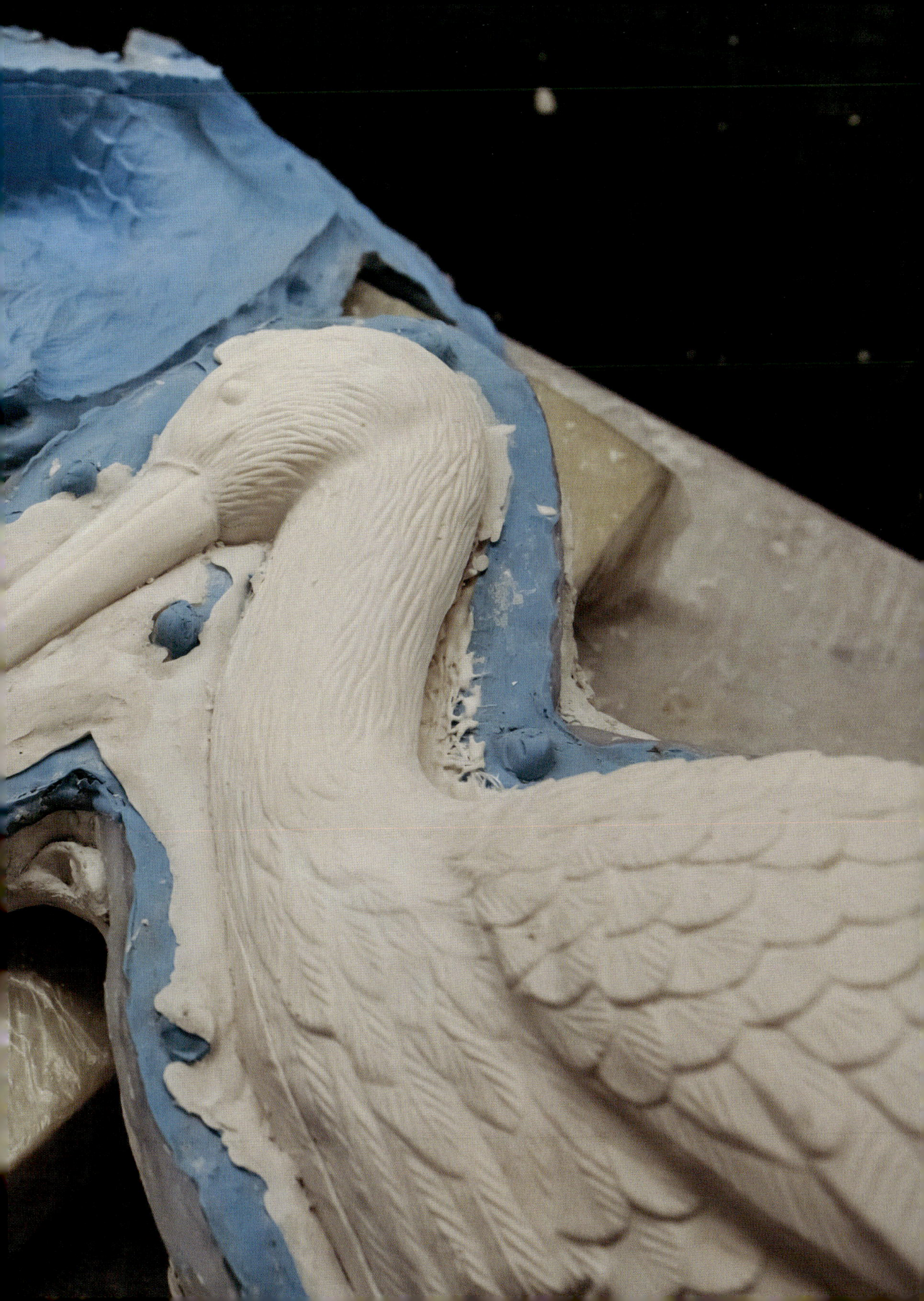

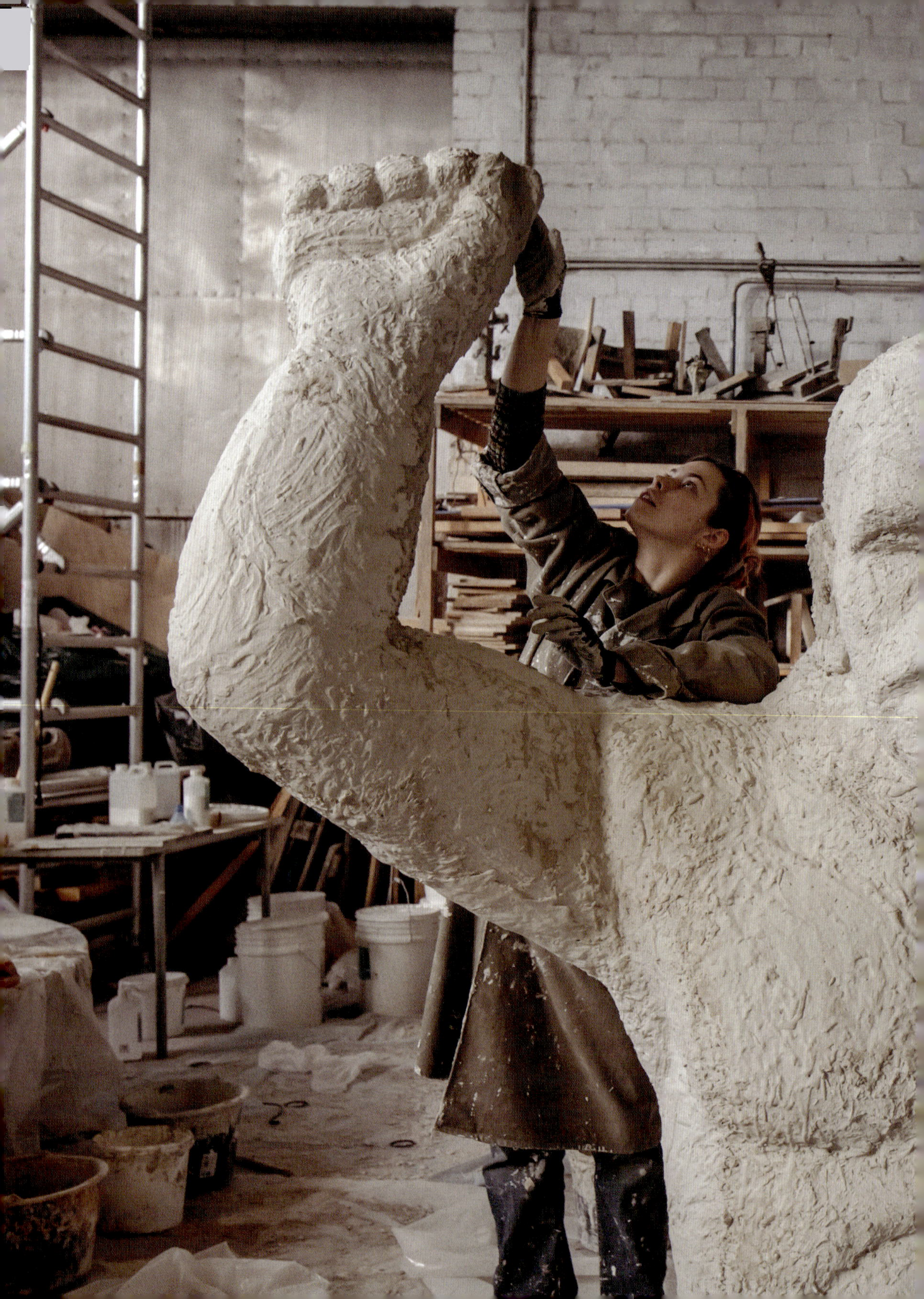

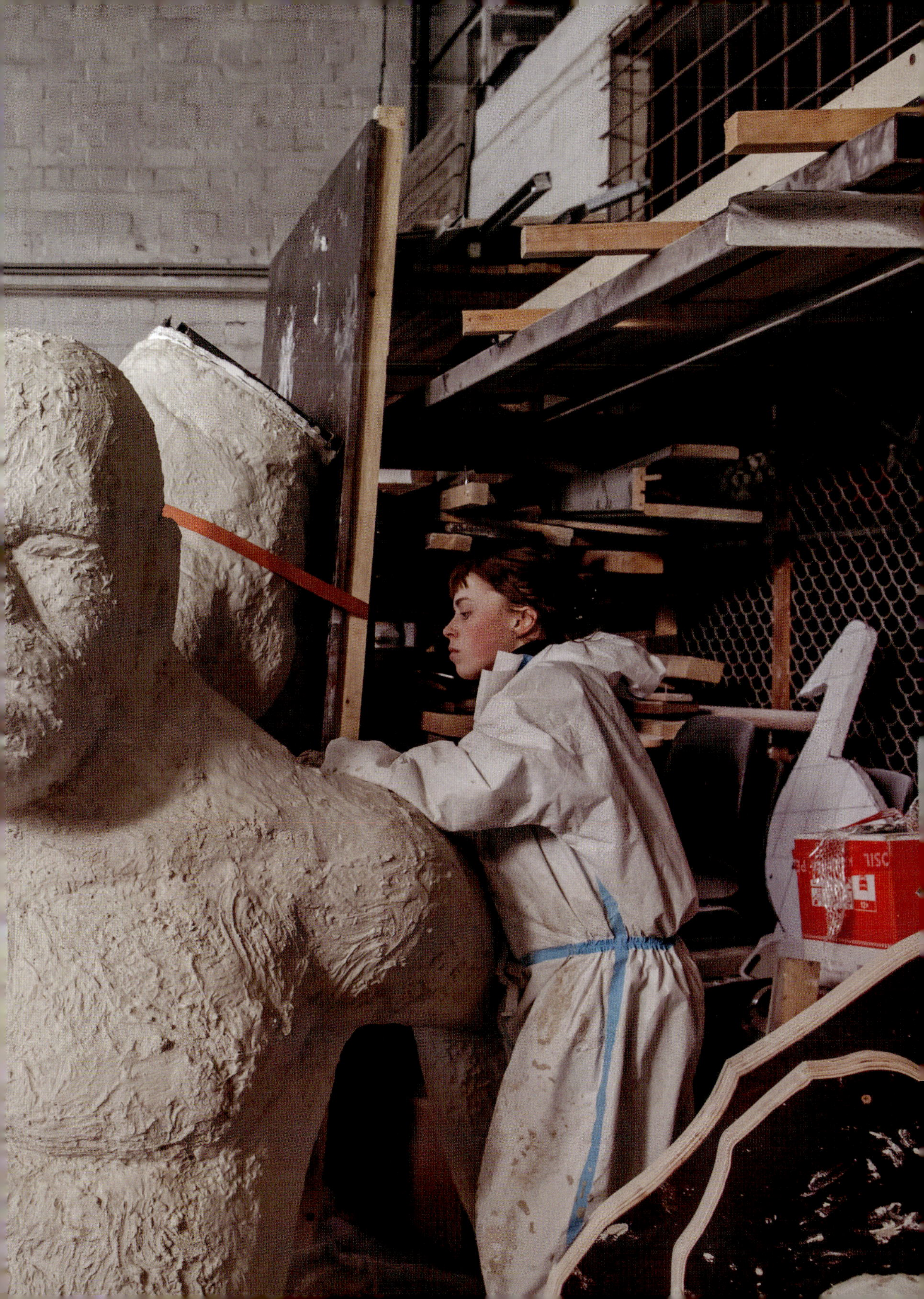

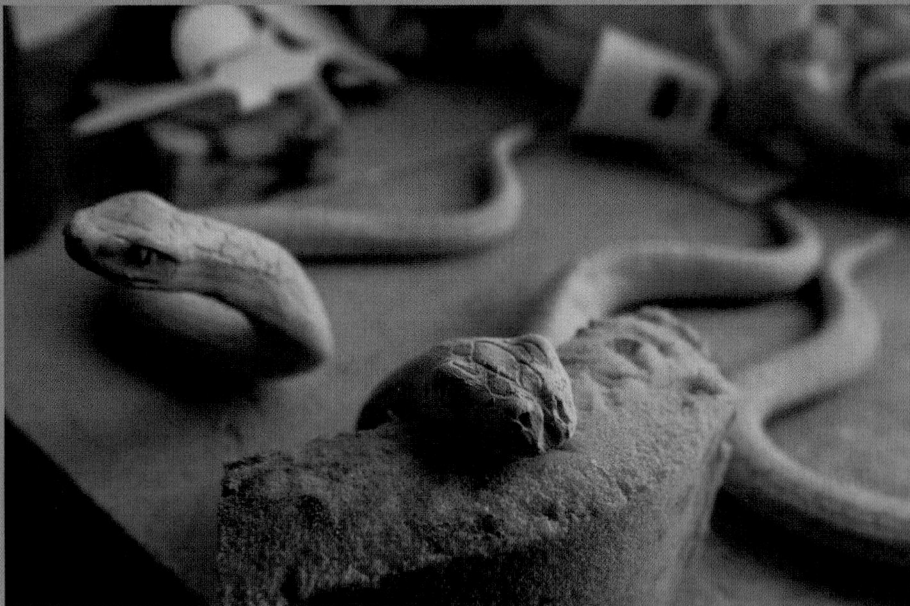

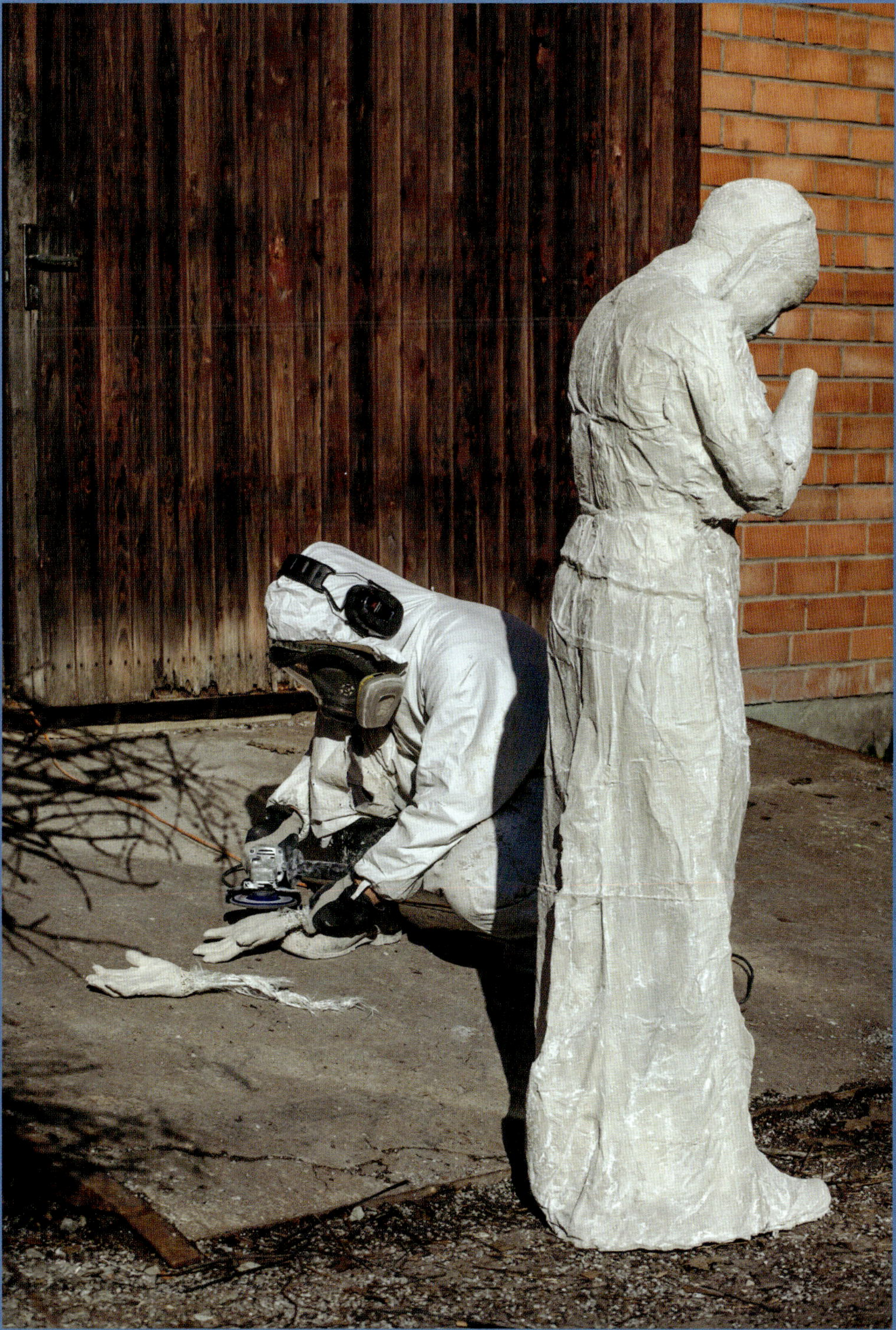

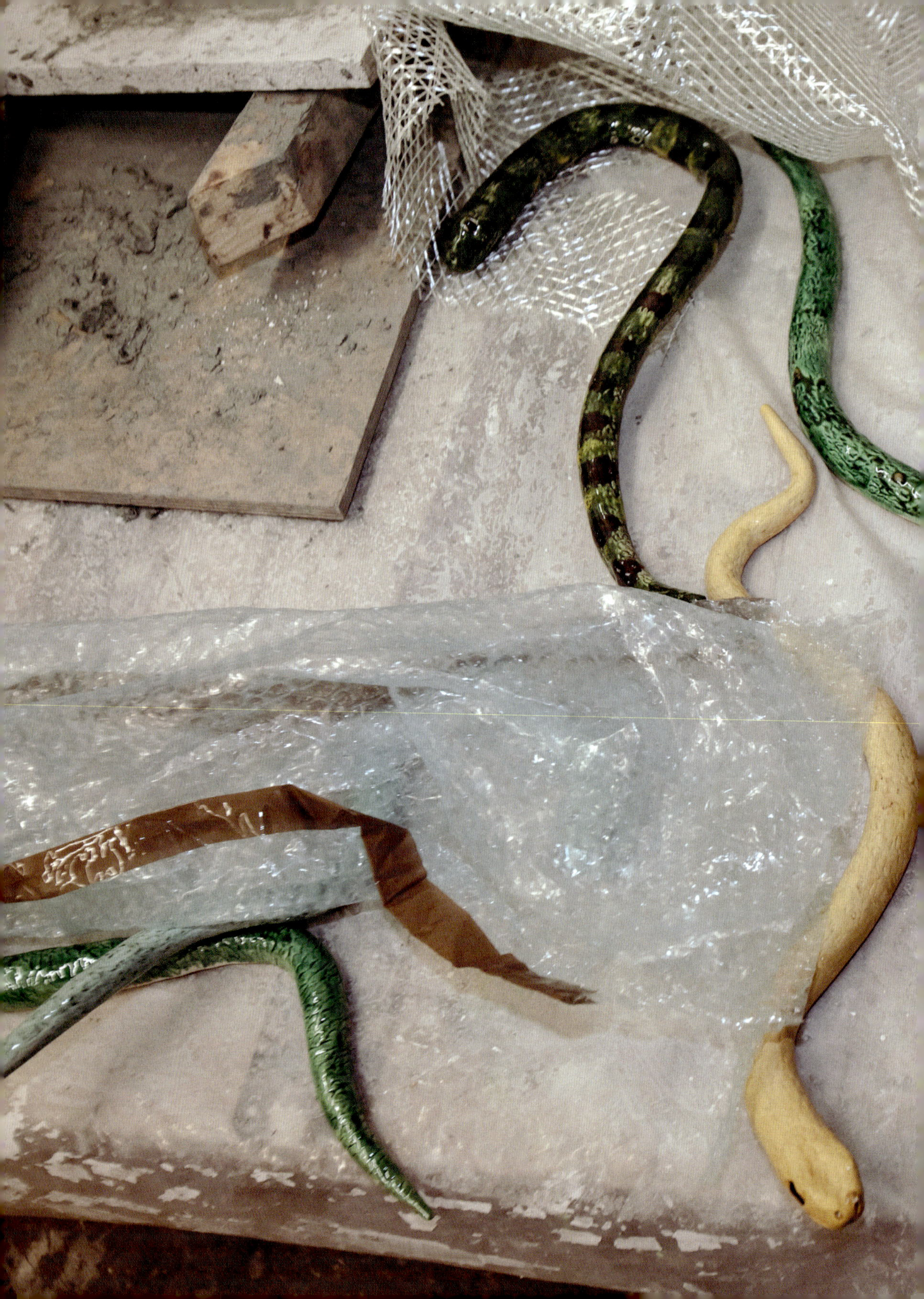

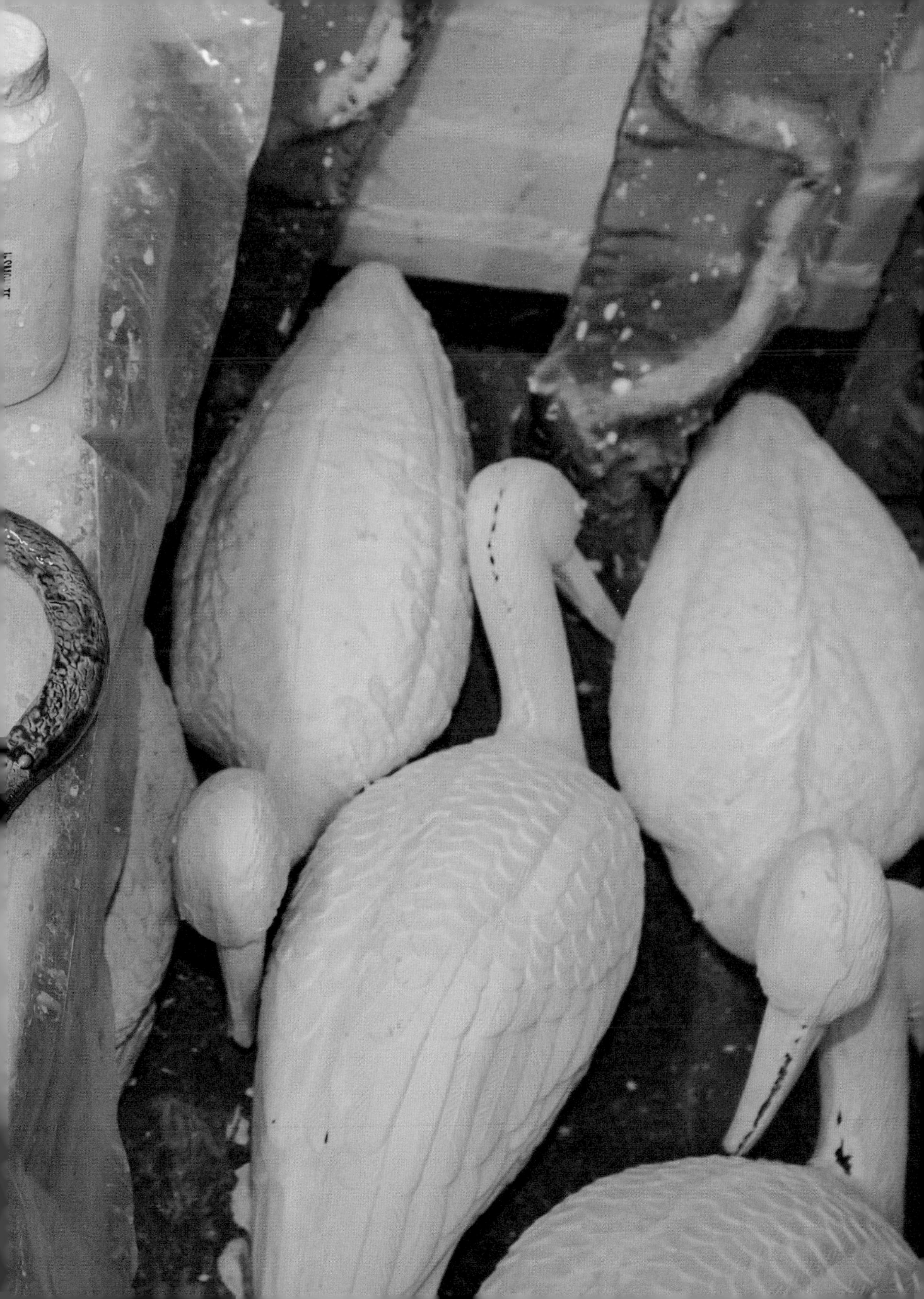

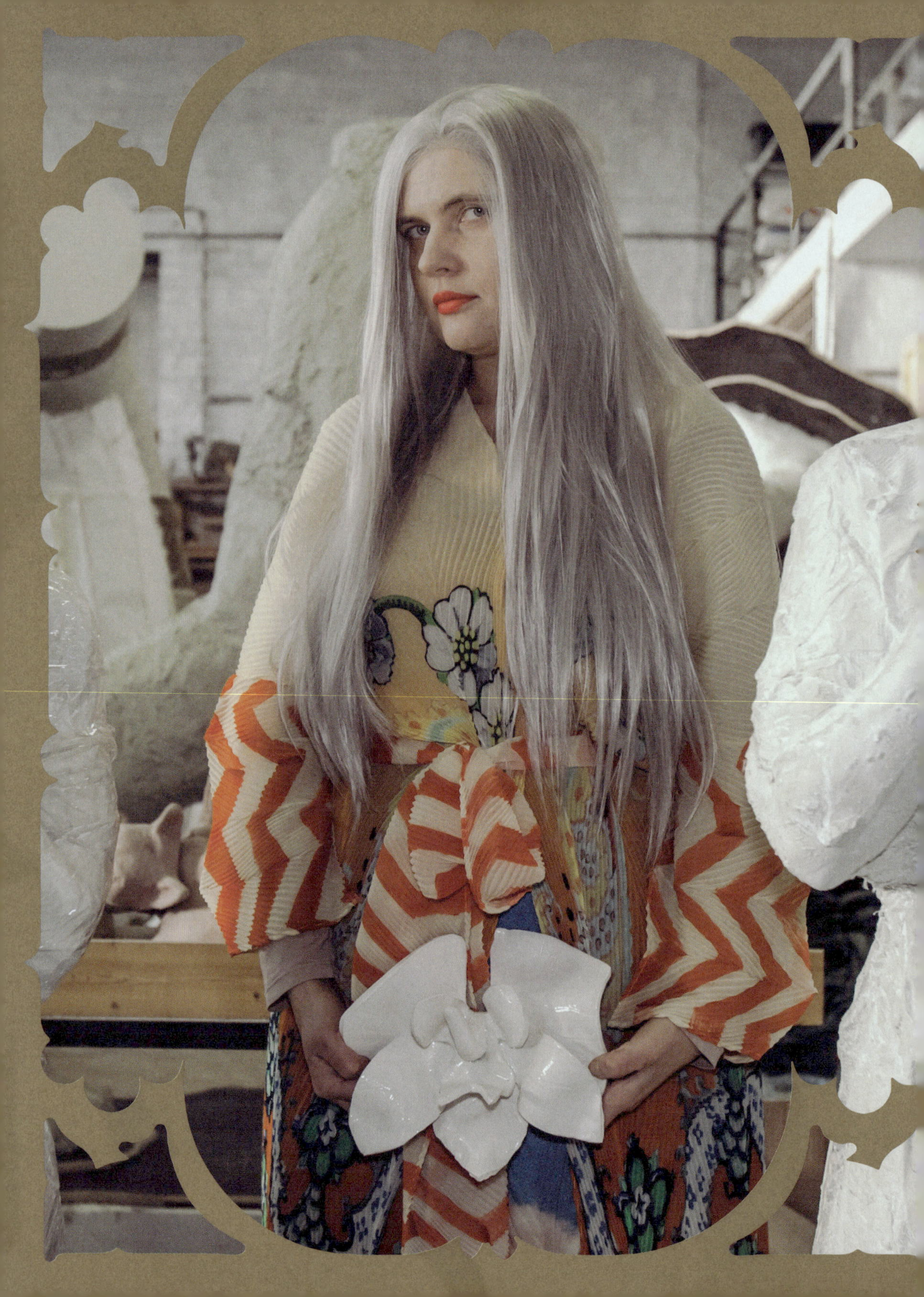

Interview with Edith Karlson by Cecilia Alemani

A NEVER-ENDING CHAIN OF SHIT BINDS US FOR ALL ETERNITY

When I visited your studio in Tallinn last September, I was greeted in the courtyard outside of the building by a group of grey, towering figures, made of what seemed to be cement, their faces completely hidden by layers of veils or coverings. In hindsight, it seems a telling encounter with your work: I immediately thought of the classical reference to Rodin's *The Burghers of Calais* while at the same time they evoked something unfinished, unmonumental, and quite creepy. Who are these figures?

I began the series *Drama is in Your Head* in 2011 and worked with it until 2018. With the exception of a few projects, until 2018, that was the title for all of my works. The work you saw was *Drama is in Your Head II*. It was first presented in 2013. I had just turned thirty. I filled the gallery with ghostly concrete figures about the size of a six-to-eight-year-old child, gathered around a concrete table with a vase of dried flowers on it, which I had gotten for my birthday. This work addressed my trauma of the social pressure and expectations about what a thirty-year-old woman should have achieved in her life. At the time, I had nothing but a tiny dog and a computer. I felt I had failed as a person. Not to mention I remembered all too vividly how old thirty-year-old people seemed to me when I was seventeen — so incredibly old! That was a truly difficult time. Now, looking back, it's funny, of course, and you could say that life is difficult indeed when you're working on yourself.

You seem very confident when it comes to materials: bronze, concrete, clay, but also plastic and organic elements. Formally, your sculptures are incredibly tactile, sensual, even when abject, or not finished. Do you like to make everything yourself? Do you ever delegate or outsource parts of your production?

My attitude towards material is that I like to take it easy. I don't consider one material higher than another. I have a rather classical education in sculpture, which in the Estonian context means that sculptors mainly work with clay. All sorts of exciting materials like silicones, resins, and epoxies became widespread in Estonia, which was part of the Soviet Union, way later than many other places in the world and so I'm curious to experiment with different materials. I'm not one to measure and weigh everything out super precisely, which means that often things go wrong. But it also often happens that in the end, the wrong thing turns out to be precisely what I needed. And in general, yes, I've mostly done everything on my own. I'm bad at delegating and outsourcing but recently, the volume of production has grown and it is no longer humanly possible for me to do everything alone. I've found super lovely and effective people, who sometimes help me out and I'm learning to be better at delegating. But still, I have to admit — I can't not go over the final details myself, with my own hands.

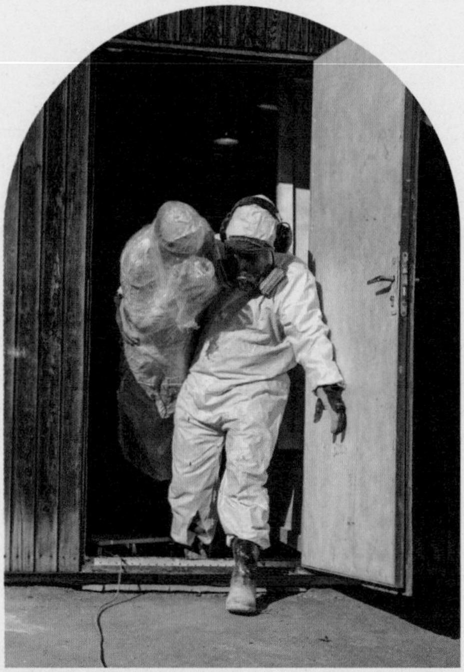

Your subjects seem also to hover between human and non-human, evoking hybrid beings like mermaids and cyborgs, suspended between natural and artificial. How do you arrive to these forms?

Juxtapositions, contrasts, but also the absurd, have always been a fascinating and endless playground for me. It is difficult to explain how I arrive to different images and forms; it is always a journey. I think all my pieces are connected to one another; each new thing grows out of an older one. I express myself rather poorly in words, so I try to do it better through my art. A good old cliché.

Do you find inspiration in literature?

It has happened, of course. But not so much in specific words, I connect more to certain atmospheres. Among my favourites are Olga Tokarczuk's *Drive Your Plow Over the Bones of the Dead,* Ingmar Bergman's *Laterna Magica,* Siri Hustvedt's *The Blazing World* and there are many others as well. The last book I read was Kate Chopin's *Désirée's Baby and Other Stories.* Chopin is considered a precursor of feminist and modernist literature. She lived between 1850 and 1904, which is a far away enough time that the language and style of the book made me feel like I was reading sci-fi. Romantic and luscious sci-fi.

In your seemingly chaotic compositions, there is also a lot of irony going on. Do you see it as a productive tool?

I love irony but if there's too much of it, it can become really annoying. So, I think that irony alone is not the most productive tool, unless compassion, empathy, and warmth is used alongside it. I appreciate it when warmth and irony are presented in balance.

Many of the characters in your universe are animals: giant dinosaurs, dogs, cats, snakes. It seems like your work brings out the most animalesque, instinctual, raw sides of these creatures, would you agree?

Can't argue here. I use the image of animals quite often to point to human "things" that at times make being human embarrassing, especially considering how we like to think of ourselves as the kings of nature. Animals rely on instincts and rawness to survive. In theory, humans could be a bit more refined in their choices.

And what's with the poop chain that connects some of your ceramic sculptures?

It's the never-ending chain of shit that binds us for all eternity. We are all linked to bigger or smaller messes, whether we want it or not. But of course, I have a soft spot for tiny droppings of rabbits, goats, and deer. They're so pretty. I used to own rabbits, so they provided me with an endless supply but that's no longer the case, so I go and find the droppings in the forest with my child. I love it, it's so relaxing to me.

You also showed me a picture of a seal skeleton you found at the beach. Have you turned it into a sculpture yet? Are you interested in death?

Yes, the seal became a work, titled *Short Story*. A transparent plastic suit stands next to the seal skeleton. The work looks at the relationship between humans and animals, that is, their unequal power balance. Here, animal is represented by death, human by garments. The suit evokes the power of uniform and the choice to support the system rather than to consider what is best for the soul. The transparent quality refers to the tale of *The Emperor's New Clothes* that ends with

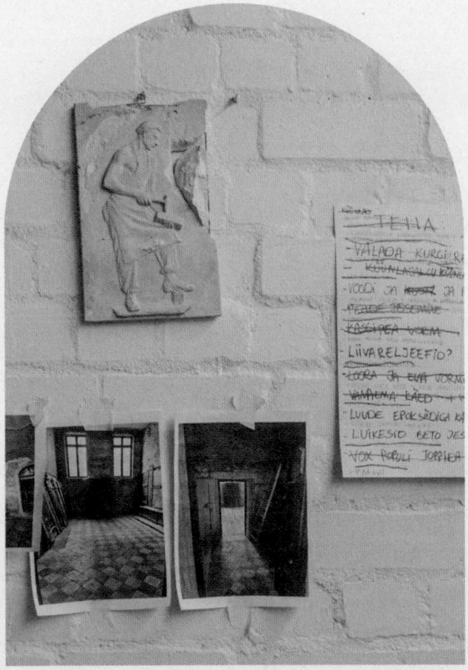

the realisation that it has all been a lie. And I am interested in death, yes. I have to admit that I'm afraid of death, although not dying myself but rather losing my loved ones. I'd like it not to be the case, I'd like to see it as a natural part of life, but in order to do so, we would have to live in a culture where death is not a taboo. I live in a place where death and ageing are not talked about and people have to experience it individually (through the death of their loved ones) and try to get used to it on their own. We all die.

And on the reverse side, did motherhood influence your practice? Is your son a source of inspiration? A collaborator? A critic?

It has been a tremendous influence. My whole world changed. In a positive way. It's good for your ego not to focus solely on yourself and your own issues. You concentrate and focus on somebody else's development and well-being instead of yourself — another small human being becomes the centre of your world. Goodbye egoism. I definitely feel I'm a better person than I was before. But to each their own. At the same time, it's difficult too, of course, worries of daily life and making art don't go together too well and once you have a child, all sorts of worries come at you like a torrent. There's only one artwork I've made based on my personal experience with being a mother. It's called *Doomsday* (a character that killed Superman). That was my first piece after I had a child. I made moulds of parts of my body, casted these on porcelain and constructed a human chandelier with multiple hands, heads etc. I was literally picking up pieces of myself and putting them back together. Until the age of three my child almost never slept and that was an incredibly difficult time in my life. But now he's often in my studio and even without my encouragement, he has become a sculpture enthusiast — with his untainted and absolutely limitless fantasy, he has become a great source of inspiration to me. His works can also be seen at the Venice Biennale.

Tell us about your project for the Estonian Pavilion at the Venice Biennale. What is your approach there?

My main aim is to give sculptures a central position. I want to create a little world in each of the exhibition spaces and hopefully, people find that inexpressible something that touches them at their very core. Without words.

You also found an amazing space for the pavilion. What was most exciting about it?

The space really does play a significant role. When I stepped into that space for the very first time, I felt such joy of recognition — something that does not happen too often in life. At least in my life. The space is a decaying church. Glory in decay is something that has a massive emotional impact at least on me. We were looking for the perfect space for a long time and when we finally stepped into Chiesa di Santa Maria delle Penitenti, I immediately began to see how my works should be placed in each of the spaces. There will be a number of my previous works on display but also new ones that I have been thinking about and planning for years. There, everything started to acquire a natural flow. The space made me excited and gave me a will to do things which I have not felt for a long time. I truly like the space. There is a strong contrast between the ceremonial atmosphere and decay — it is simultaneously beautiful and inevitable.

If you could choose an exhibition setting, what would it look like? A white cube gallery space, or an industrial rougher context? Somewhere outdoors? I saw your dinosaur outside, in front of an old industrial complex in Tallinn. Was this the first time you were confronted with a public space? Have you overheard any amusing comments in response to your work?

Because my studio is an industrial and rough environment, I inevitably feel the most at home in similar spaces and that would be my first preference as well. But that is also in my comfort zone and I do enjoy the challenge different spaces pose. I would say that the space is not an obstacle if I find something that triggers me even a tiny bit. It's more about the attitude. When it comes to works in public spaces, I have a couple more. People love the dinosaur, that is no surprise to me, of course... People are easily impressed. Soon a larger-than-life bronze cat with mice crawling in its hair I sculpted will be installed in public space in Tallinn. I made it just the right size, so that children and even adults can easily climb onto the cat. I'm so looking forward to seeing it. When I climbed on the cat myself and sat there, it was so comfortable and I really hope that it will make children happy, that it will become part of their childhood memories, just like a lion in a park in Tallinn was mine.

Did you study art in school?

Yes. I studied sculpture at the Estonian Academy of Arts. Did my BA and MA there. To be honest, I wanted to study printmaking but the father of one of my friends who worked at

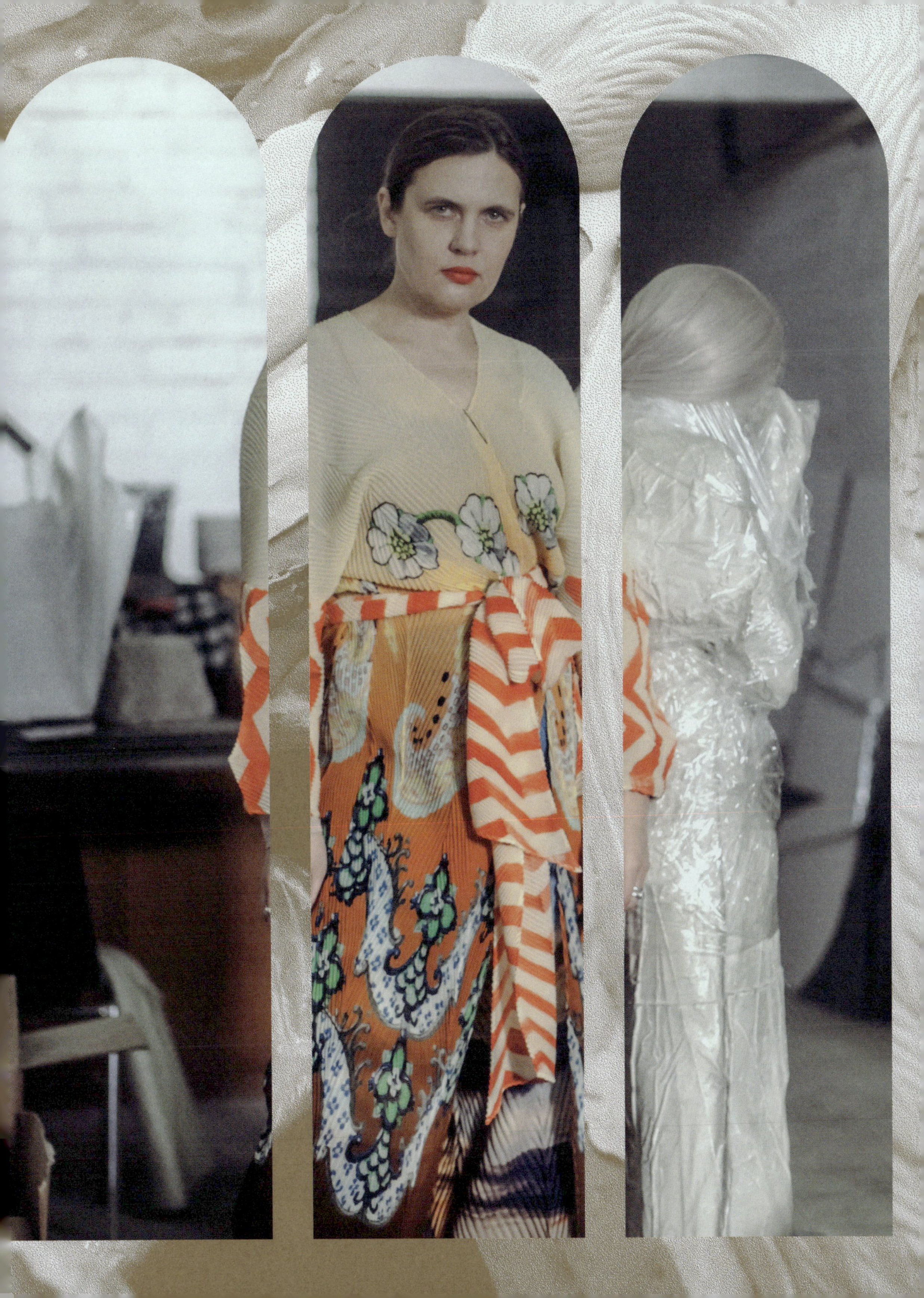

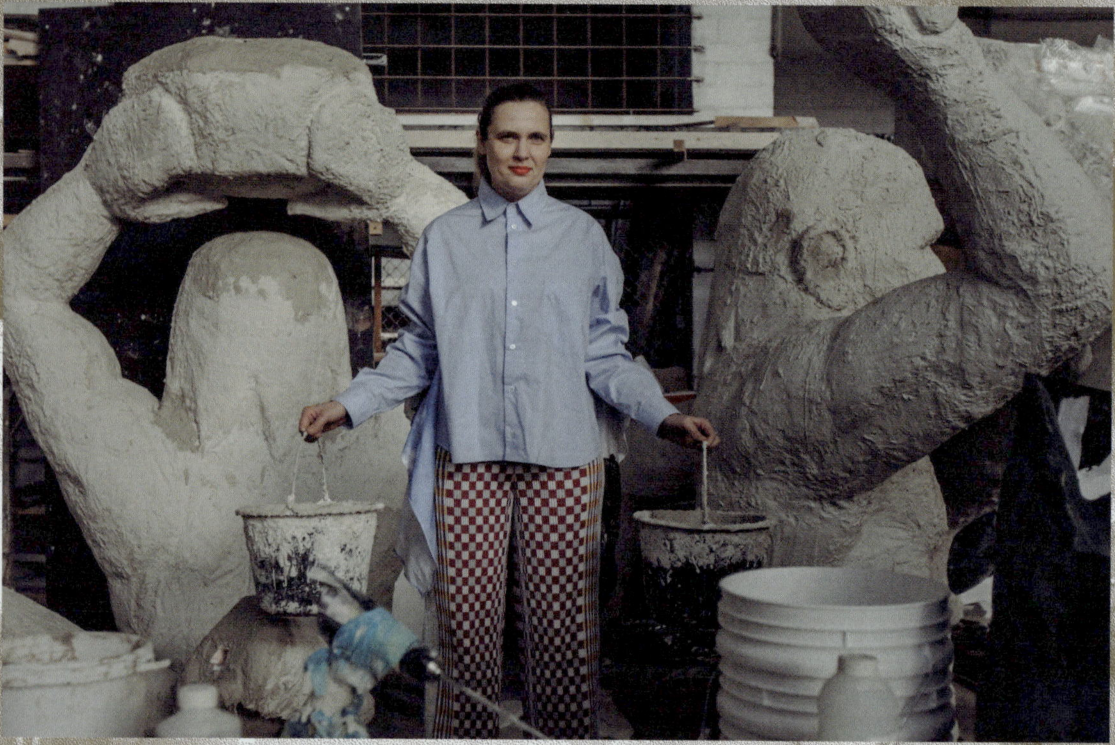

the academy said that all the girls who think they can draw want to study printmaking and the competition is crazy... Because there are a lot of those girls. He suggested I apply for a place in the sculpture department, because almost nobody wanted to apply but the department is also part of the fine arts faculty, so once I had been accepted, I could transfer from sculpture to printmaking. That was my little scheme. I very clearly remember that when I was accepted someone I knew told me that sculpture is such a difficult field and definitely not for women. I think that was the first time I felt a rush of spitefulness and I thought I'll show everybody that it is, in fact, for women. This is one of my defining characteristics — stubbornness. Sometimes it works in my favour, sometimes it doesn't of course. So, in the end, I stuck with sculpture, I made my choice out of stubbornness and curiosity, because I realised it's a field where you never get bored and the possibilities are endless.

Did you always want to be an artist?

I think I just didn't know I could be an artist — I had no idea what it means. But I did know that I wanted to study at an art academy, because that was the only type of higher education I was able to get through. I thought that was the place where people were normal — the kind of people I'd like to spend time with. Becoming an artist wasn't really a goal in itself.

Have you had any mentor or very influential teacher?

I think a broader understanding that sculpture is what I want to do and study was planted into my brain by the head of our department, Villu Jaanisoo. When he came to the department, a lot changed — he started inviting international professors and I realised sculpture is both a very difficult and a cool thing to do. He gave me courage and confidence and for that, I am forever grateful to him.

Who are the artists you admire and that have influenced you?

I have always been a shitty fan, ever since I was a child. I have never had a favourite band or a favourite artist. But I definitely admire my friends, who are also amazing artists — Jass Kaselaan, Kris Lemsalu, Art Allmägi. They have all influenced me in some way.

You have collaborated with other visual artists in the past, like Kris Lemsalu. How do you choose your collaborators and what do these collaborations add to your practice?

I don't choose anything. Things just happen to me because I'm a yes-man. That is, of course, my weak spot. I just keep saying yes to everything. But that has also brought a lot of joy, excitement, and work into my life. I can only dream of saying no, although I do try to practice that sometimes... Unfortunately, on my loved ones. The thing with Kris is that she happens to be one of my best friends, so working with her comes naturally. Sometimes I've helped her with her work and she has done the same for me. What I really enjoy in Estonia is that artists often help each other out. When someone is working on a bigger project, they ask their colleagues for help and I think that is truly beautiful. I've often worked together with Jass Kaselaan. Although sculpture is not always the focus of my creative collaborations. For example, I've taken photographs for several of Julia Heuer's collections. I've also collaborated with theatres on stage design projects and that has actually become one of my "other" jobs. In theatre, everything you do is a collaboration and that is always a good shift away from my time alone in the studio. On top of that, I also do sound collaborations. Me and my partner have a band. Sound has always been important in my work and now that I'm really focusing on it, I'm getting better at it. I strongly believe in collaborating!

Tell us about your working style. Do you go to the studio every day? Do you have assistants? Do you listen to music or audiobooks as you paint? What does experimentation look like in your practice?

Yes, I go to my studio every day thanks to the routine that having a child brought into our family. And that works for me. I go to work in the morning and home at night. I try to keep my weekends for my child but I don't always manage. At the moment, I have two assistants, Loora and Eva. When I need to do something, I can rely on Maria Luiga, who will definitely be a star architect in the future. The three girls are massively helping me with Venice. We are working really hard right now but when it's easier, I ask for their help when I need them. I think I work mostly intuitively and experimentally; I enjoy humour and I'm dedicated. My focus is on work and working. Through constant experimentation I find new approaches or unexpected forms but going to the studio regularly and being in tune with my practice is something I need — it propels me forward. But I'm also inspired by life, so listening to local radio stations, having conversations with people with studios next door to mine and unexpected found objects or pets also act as catalysts.

Do you work with sketches and drawings? Do you use any digital technology for your compositions?

Sure, I do. But I mostly doodle. I don't consider myself much of a drawer. But doodling does help with setting ideas. Especially when I'm working on a larger exhibition. In that case, I usually work with an assistant, who helps me with placing all my squiggles into the space... Sometimes it helps me to understand how everything goes together... Colours and volumes.

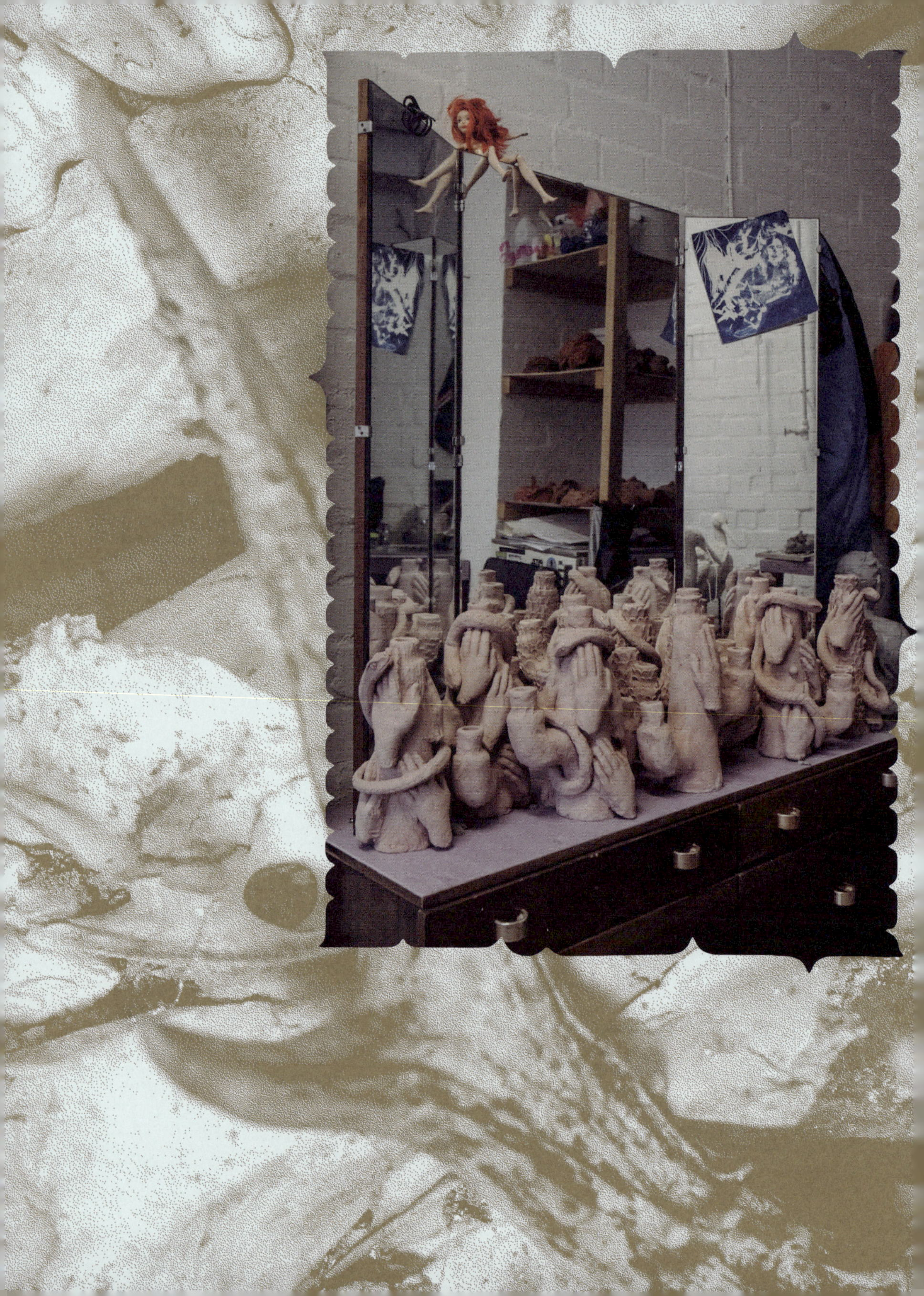

What is your home like?

My home is a place I would never want to leave, I always miss it. And I like it more and more. This has been one of my biggest dreams in life and because it came into my life through hard work and even suffering, I feel no shame in saying that I am very happy and proud of my home.

How did the pandemic influence your practice?

That is something I don't really want say to out loud but okay then. The thing is — I'm an incredibly lucky person to have a country house on an island and I'd like to spend all of my free time there. I don't have much free time, though. When the pandemic started, I was on the island with my family and it so happened that my best friend's family was also there and then the island went into lockdown. Nobody could leave. And we were there over a month. I had none of my work stuff with me, everything was postponed. And I just let everything go. I'm afraid that was one of the happiest times in my life. I observed how spring came, little by little. I was watching the grass and my child grow. That was a time for myself, something I hadn't had for so long and I really needed it. I also felt guilty in my bubble of happiness, because a friend of mine was living in New York and there, her life was completely different from mine, which was so in sync with nature. She had depression and I was content and happy... Totally unfair, I know, but that's how it was. When we were allowed to leave the island again, I was full of energy and soon after made one of my biggest and strongest exhibitions, *Return to Innocence*.

If you could move to another city, where would you go?

There are so many cities I have never been to, so I don't want to make any bold claims. I'd love to see all kinds of places but moving is another thing. When life offers me something, I accept but... I don't know, I don't really have a preference, personally.

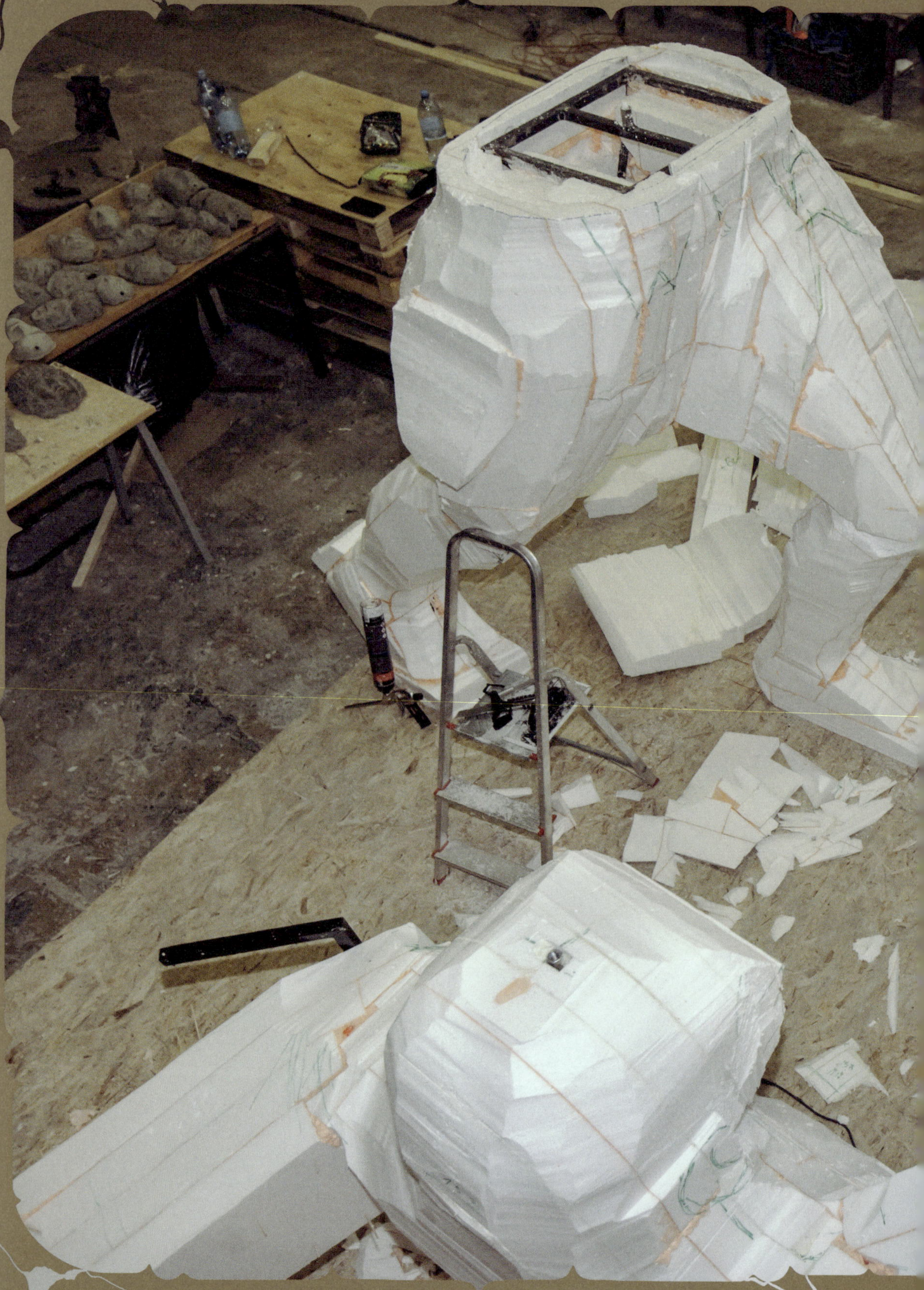

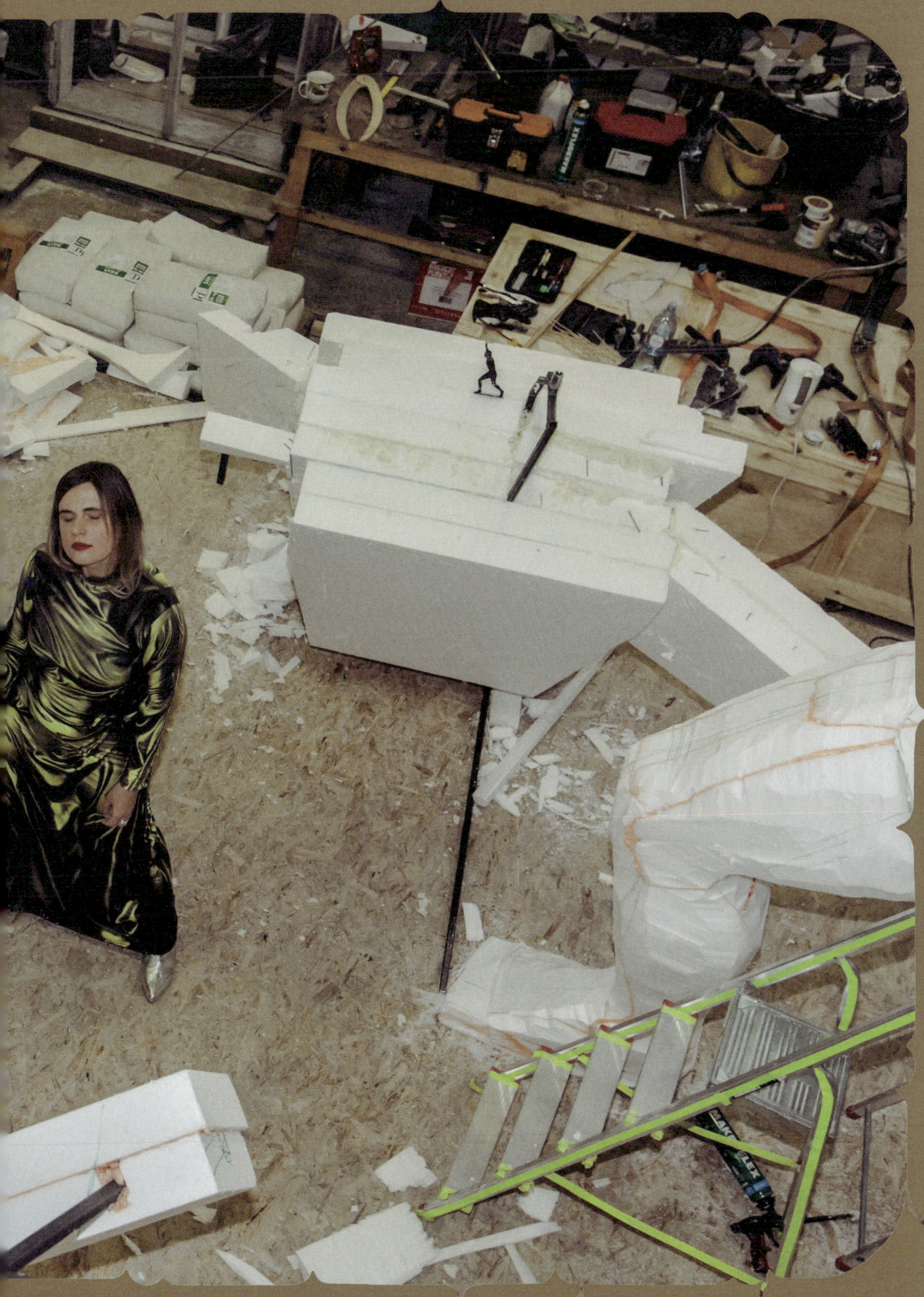

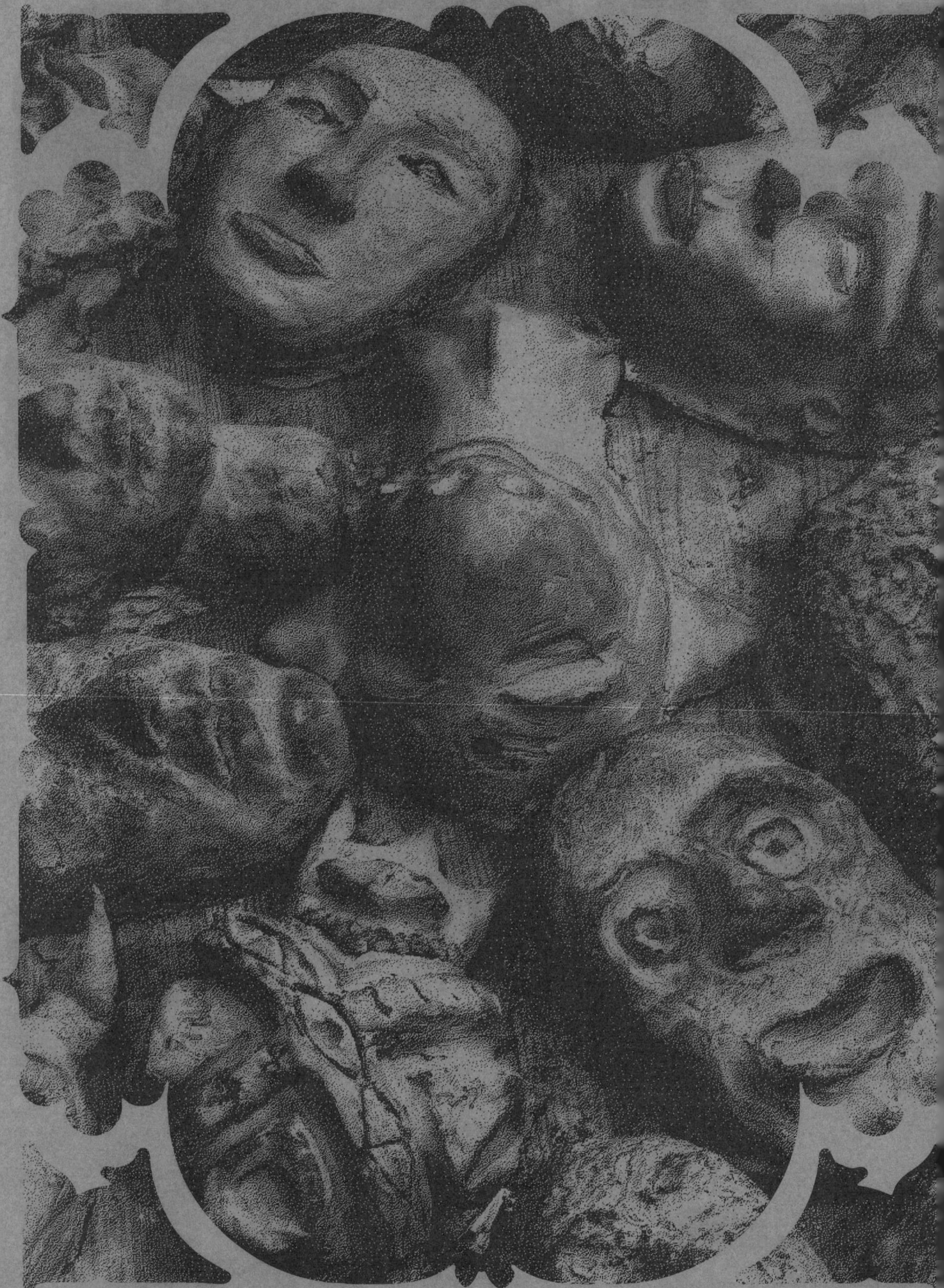

Eero Epner

THE EQUINOX TURNS DAYS ON THEIR DARKER SIDE

(Pööripäeval keeratakse päevale mustem külg peale, an old Estonian saying*)*

Edith Karlson's delicate formative years took place in the late-Soviet period of the 1980s, when Estonia was still a part of the Russian empire, or, as it was known at the time, the Soviet Union. In the early 1990s, the stale atmosphere of the congealed empire was replaced by dramatic social collapse followed by widespread destitution and existential crises. Eventually, this gave way to the relatively brutal invasion of capitalism, the turbulent changes from which eventually calmed into a petite bourgeois welfare society resplendent in its superficiality and desire for hygge.

The ebb and flow of these tumultuous trajectories alongside the dynamics in Edith Karlson's personal life (becoming a mother, starting a family, aging) have considerably shaped her artistic vision, which is expressed mainly through sculpture and installation. Occasionally works are presented as single objects, other times as dramatised exhibition narratives, while in the hinterlands of Karlson's oeuvre we find lo-fi melancholic songs containing lyrics which conjure surreal situations, and claustrophobic stage design for apocalyptic works of theatre. Karlson's work is not autobiographical, rather it is existential. It looks at the human experience from a general vantage point, or, to be more precise, it seeks out the dark creatures and shadows of the past which lurk beyond the edges of human experience.

Karlson began exhibiting her work around fifteen years ago after graduating from the Department of Sculpture at the Estonian Academy of Arts. Her exhibitions included animals and humans and, in the years which followed, an increasing number of hybrid blends have appeared, mixing mass production and mythology by juxtaposing large roughly surfaced beasts (snakes, dinosaurs, animal bones) with highly polished, cute, kitsch little animals (puppies, bunnies, kitties), fears with jokes, and bodily fluids (blood, piss) with sacrality, brutality, and gentleness. At the core of Karlson's work with hybridity seems to be the conviction that both people and animals are united by intense primitive instincts, and returning to that very primal level allows Karlson to work through her own existential fears and tensions which originate both from her childhood and her projected long life expectancy. A room padded with clay hashed with claw marks, as if someone has desperately tried to escape (*Interspace,* 2015) can be seen as the culmination of this early adulthood angst of the artist, age thirty two at the time.

Karlson continued observing herself through this world of animals, people, and hybrids, struggling with questions of beauty and violence, anguish and freedom, birth and death, until the latter became one of the most significant themes of her art to date. Death is present in its corporeal, raw, and bodily form (Karlson often brings animal bones into exhibition spaces) but also in less direct ways (extinct dinosaurs, an army of grieving women, or placing an old wooden sculpture into dark space as if it were a body). Death is among Karlson's core obsessions, however her work with death has very little to do with current political situations and a lot to do with social sensitivities and the brutality of Medieval art, which looked death straight in the eye in an attempt to constantly remind itself and the world of this thing called vanitas. Getting older and becoming a mother, which paradoxically highlights the process of aging even more, as nothing reminds us of our mortality more than seeing your children grow at an incredible speed — this is the basis of Karlson's work. Her sculptures depict, remind us of, and make us notice, the rapid passing of time, the omnipresence of death, and the sad poetry of it all.

HORA LUPI

The prologue to this exhibition began a couple of years ago when Karlson had a solo show titled *Return to Innocence* at an abandoned former electrical plant, now a contemporary art museum. The exhibition, with its title borrowed from a pop song by Enigma, began with a space in which the artist had arranged clay portraits of her contemporaries in a wall containing numerous alcoves, all of which were lit to evoke a sense of the sacred. The floor was covered with clay bricks and the shadow of a church window was cast onto the floor, despite the space having no windows. In the next space, clay candleholders containing electric candles were exhibited alongside a centuries old figurine of Christ, covered with dirt of the ages, that looked up to the sky from underneath his protective glass box. In the exhibition space on the second floor, a bedroom resembling a motel was set-up where under the gaze of a crucifix nailed to the wall something was constantly moving under a blanket, while on the highest floor, the visitor was welcomed into a celestial atmosphere by white plastic

storks, plaster flowers on a wire stem, and optimistic music that could also be heard in a small dark chamber, where a wooden corpse was laid.

This existential narrative brought the sacred into Karlson's work more strongly than ever before, and a paradox we all are probably familiar with was highlighted: it is increasingly difficult to sense and even more difficult to believe in the metaphysical dimension, although the desire for it has not decreased, on the contrary. For the Venice exhibition at the church of Santa Maria delle Penitenti, Karlson has developed and expanded upon the previously described narrative and desire.

The mythological title of the exhibition, *Hora lupi, or Hour of the Wolf,* refers to the moment before the dawn, the darkest time in the day, in which the majority of people are born and will die. This is the high hour of transformation, a moment of flux and shift of self-perception, where, in among everything else, hybridity becomes possible. In today's world, where hybridity has been branded as capitalist adaptation, Karlson shows a kind of hybridity that is dark and comical. The eeriness of her work is not grotesque or off-putting, rather it alludes to the artist's desire for the eerie — or, to be more precise, the desire for a total hour of the wolf, where all self-perception blurs and states alter.

The exhibition is structured as a dramaturgical narrative, although for us as viewers only fragments remain of the original whole. We witness moments, details, and motifs woven together in a somewhat incomprehensible manner, yet the fact of their interconnectedness is undeniable, signalling in their fragmented being what we have already known for a long time: complete narratives are a thing of the past, we can only pick up the last remains of the narrative from the wasteland of oblivion, and in our misery, reconstruct something that once was but is no more.

Here, the church plays a key role. It is not only a spatial decoration or a partner in dialogue but an environment that makes up a hybrid whole together with Karlson's work. On the one hand, of course, the church does emphasise the drive towards sacrality that Karlson's characters display, which is necessary, since the characters themselves are in no way aware of their drive towards sacrality. Karlson's characters do what they do just because they do it and there is probably no point in trying make sense of it or find greater morals in it. They, too, are struck by unexpected miniature dramas caused by their inexplicable drives, yet it is in this kind of unpreparedness and surreal impulsivity that cracks and fissures appear in Karlson's incomplete worlds and through these, the craved redeeming light shines through. This light does not shine on reason, logic, morals, and political correctness. Rather, it shines on inaptitude, shamelessness, and true lust for life. This redeeming light

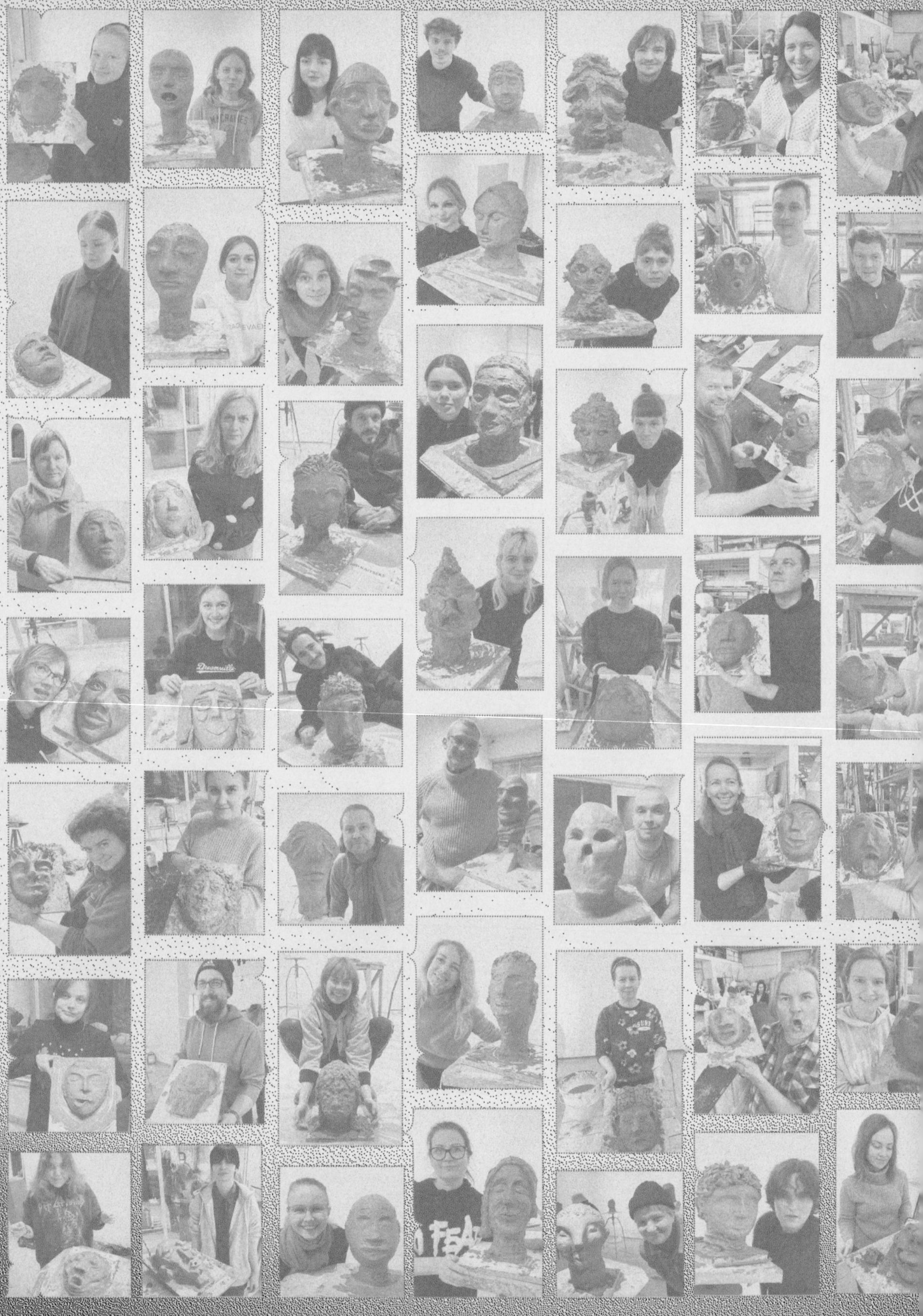

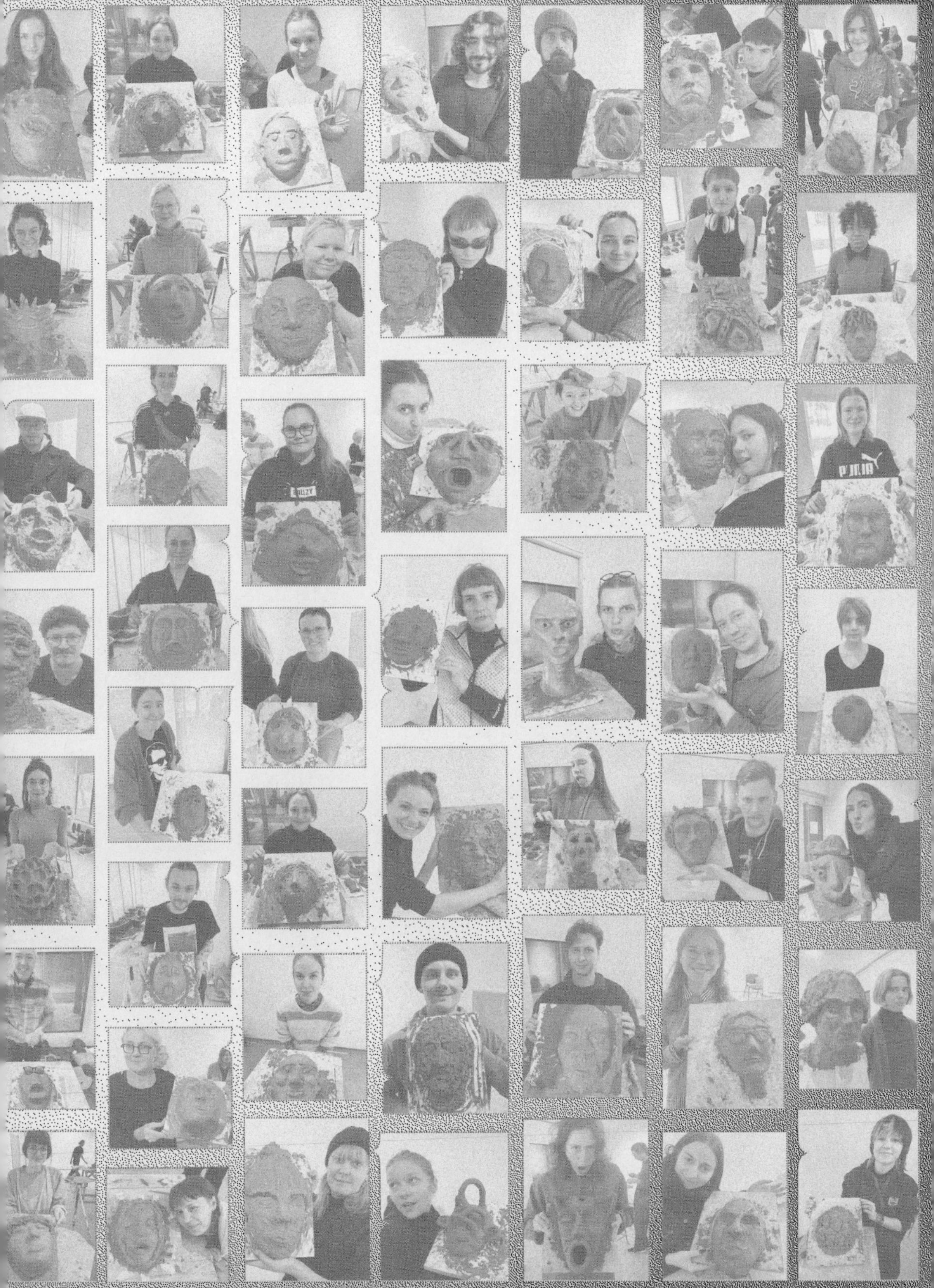
PUMA

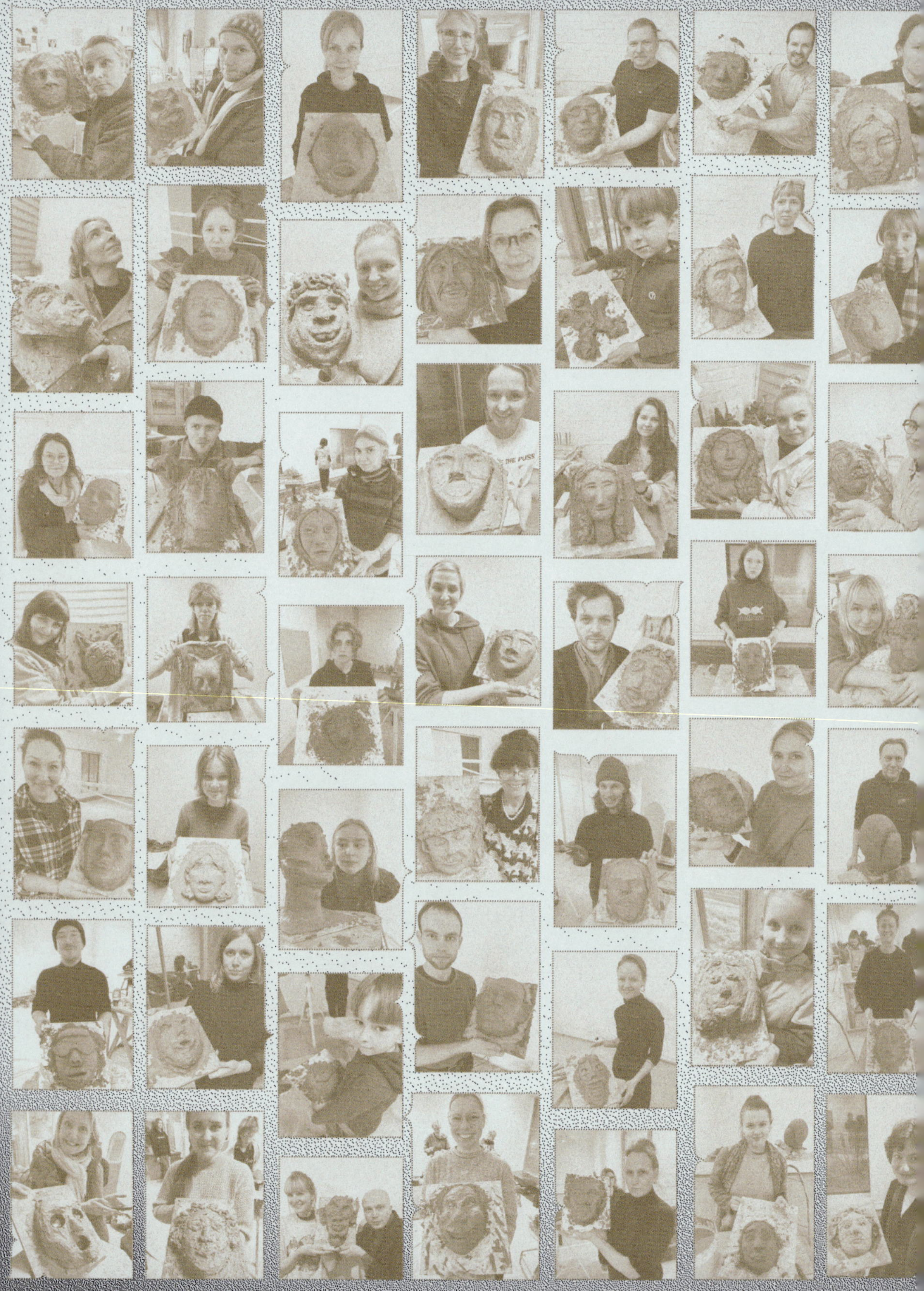

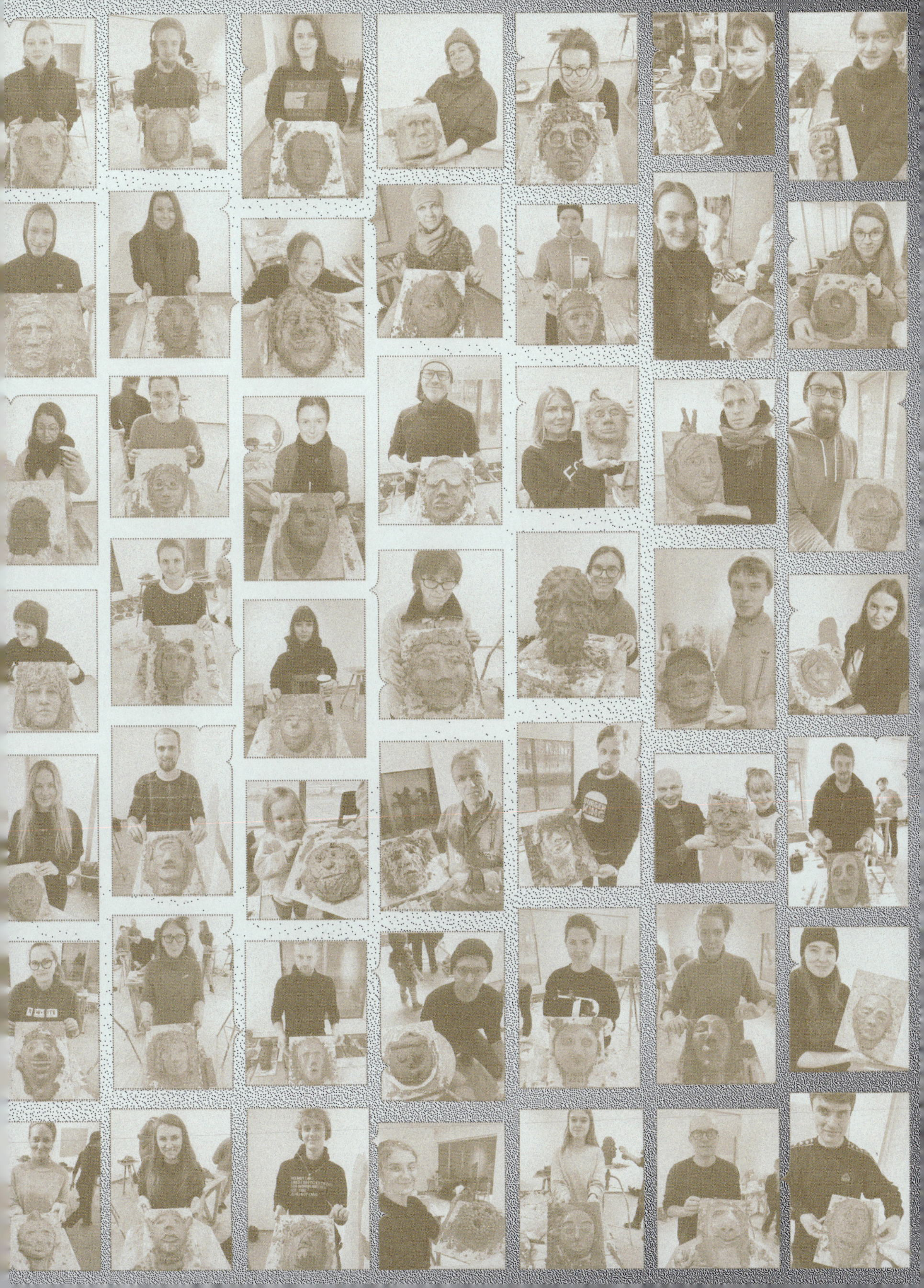

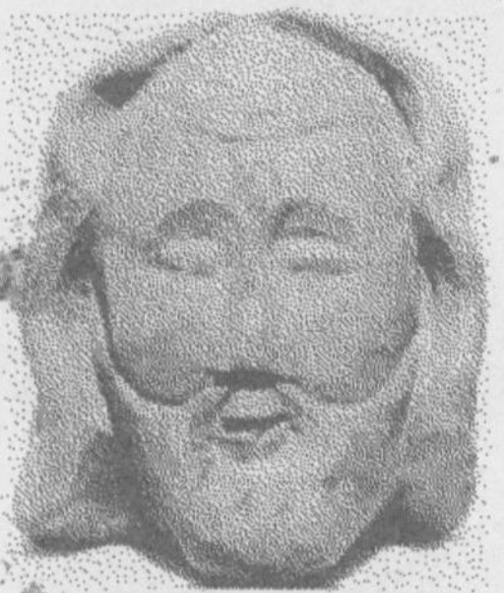

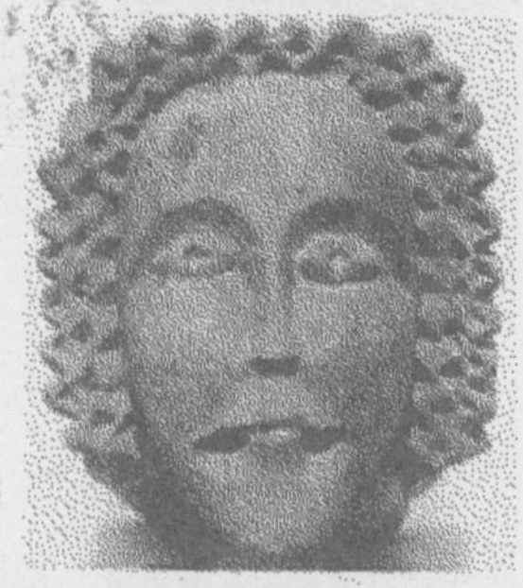

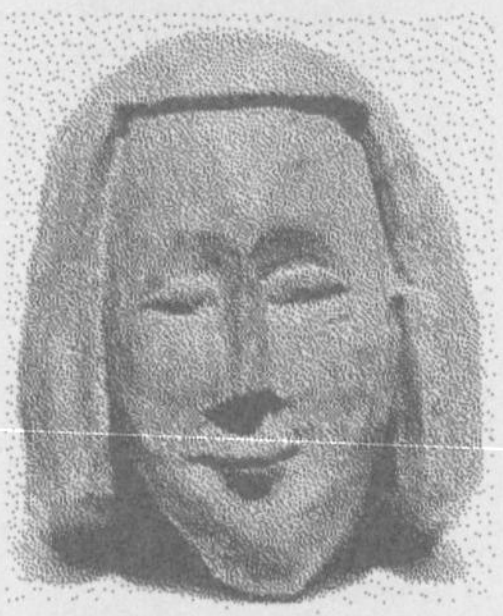

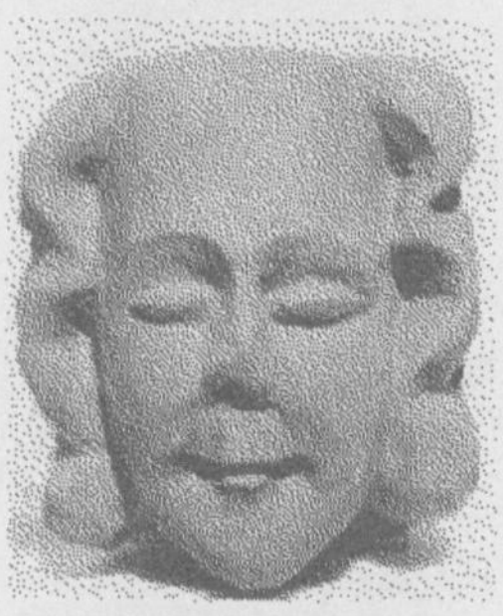

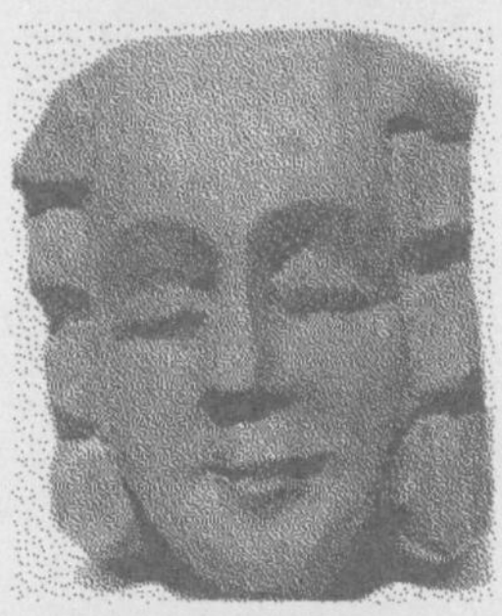

bleaches the bones of animals, caresses the swollen faces of giants, warms the bed of a small dog condemned to solitude as the human bed beside it lies empty, and searches through the church, standing in silence and naked: forgotten, abandoned, discarded.

FORGETTING AND REMEMBERING

The caved in floors, the squeaking of stairs, and the silent crumbling of plaster have been left untouched by the artist. This attachment to dust and love of fractures is poetic in its melancholy and critical in its poetry, reminding us that despite the orgy of information that surrounds us, the collective amnesia only deepens. Forgetting the way Karlson does it, however, is physical, and smells of dust and canal water, returning to its original meaning: to forget means to look and see, to touch but let go.

This is what the clay heads in the exhibition space also testify to. These heads are self-portraits, created by dozens of amateurs: charming in their authenticity and roughness, free of artistic refinery and perfection. The way the surface of Karlson's works is modelled always carries a special meaning, as their robust look and seeming clumsiness, brutality et cetera speaks to a similar kind of impulsivity and lack of refinement as can be seen in the dramaturgical arcs of her exhibitions. For years, Karlson mainly worked with concrete; more recently clay has been added to her arsenal, foregrounding the visceral quality of her sculpting.

These blasphemous clay heads are inspired by the Medieval terracotta sculptures at the St. John's Church in Tartu (the second largest city in Estonia). At one time, there were thousands of these, making it a unique collection of sculptures. There is a lot about those sculptures that we cannot explain: when they were made and, above all, why such a tiny church (considering the scale of European churches) is filled with portraits of townspeople, placed so high up that only god can have a proper look at their faces. There are many hypotheses about the sculptures, including one by art historian Kaur Alttoa, who has suggested that these sculptures could actually be a plague memorial — depictions of a plague epidemic that were meant to capture ordinary lives for all eternity.

Karlson doesn't extend her work from this hypothesis, however it is interesting to mention as one possible interpretation as through it we can draw a parallel to our contemporary epidemic, Covid. Dozens and dozens of people participated at the workshops in Karlson's studio, everyone from children to entrepreneurs, from artists to state officials,

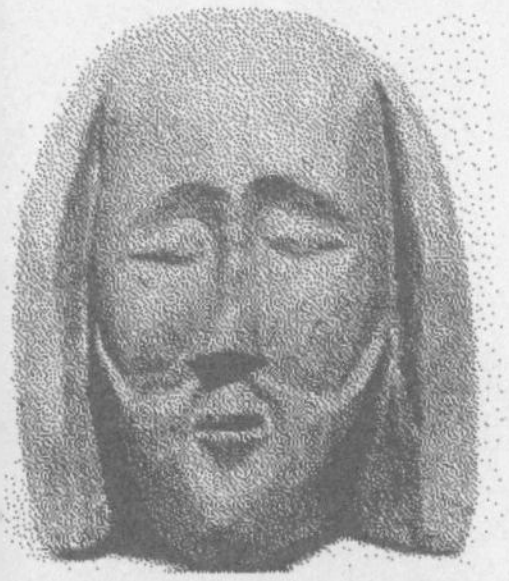

making up a contemporary gallery of faces. Karlson did not instruct the makers too much — that might have led to a sudden rise in mastery when what she needed was quite the opposite: genuine contributions by amateurs, strange expressions of creativity, dadaist interpretations of an intimate genre, the self-portrait. Materialised in clay, people's faces began to elongate, explode, crumble, distort, and contort, highlighting the unpolished impulsivity of our self-image. And now, having placed these contemporary faces in the abandoned church, they feel like a return projected into a future. We look at them the same way as we would those who have passed away a long time ago and walk on the endless battlefields of *memento mori* where the fighting continues over who will be remembered and who will not be. For some reason, in the eyes of eternity, these people are winners, they have been brought into the church and given a sacral halo, although the only thing that makes them remarkable is the fact that they are utterly common. They live for an eternity, yet they will be dead soon — just like the rest of us.

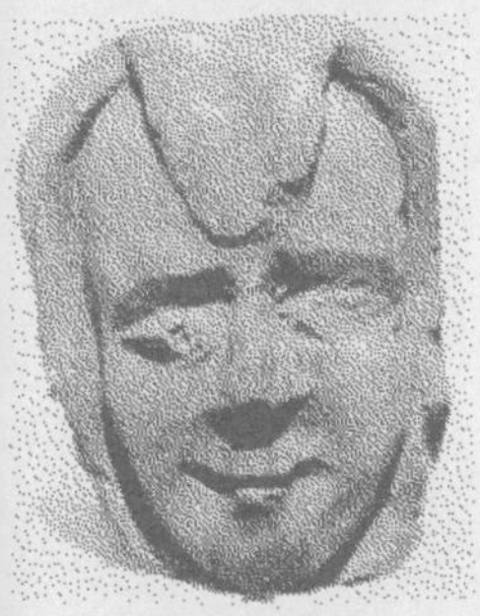

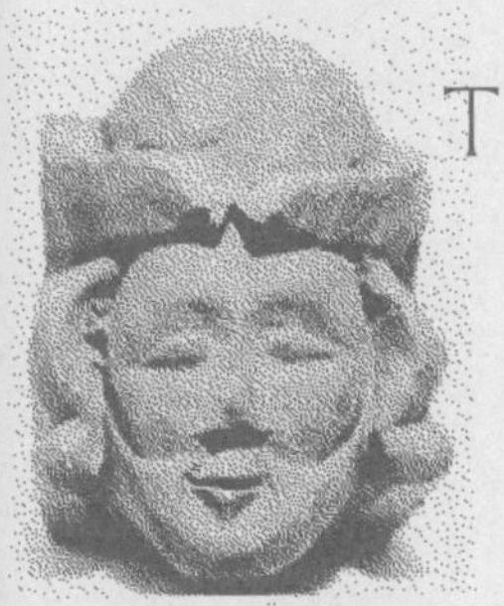

THE ROBUST AND THE SACRED

In the central space of Chiesa di Santa Maria delle Penitenti, under the watchful gaze of a crucified Christ, three giants tower, playing their brutal games. These figures, modelled on mass-produced Soviet plastic dolls, feel like elephants in a porcelain shop — in a clumsy, rugged manner, they trample around the sacred space, simultaneously out of place yet evoking empathy. In their lack of sophistication they too seem to have emerged from the depths of the hour of the wolf, a place where civilised man loses his dress shoes and polished manners and becomes a creature entirely guided by his primitive impulses and nothing more.

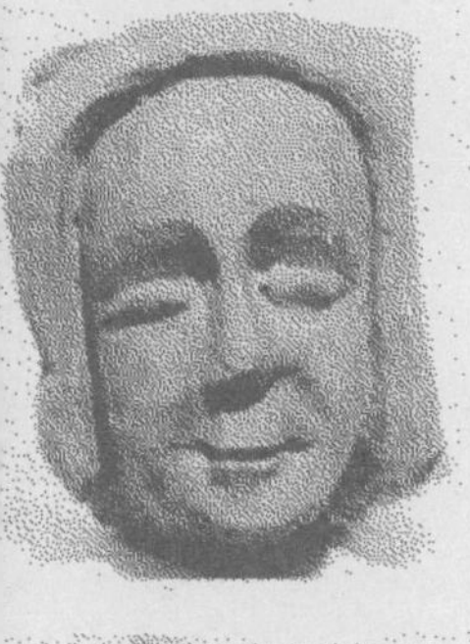

However, the space around these Neanderthals adds multiple additional layers to the artwork. The biblical snake slithering between the figures refers to the Fall of Man and the sacral space between them speaks of nothing else but sin and redemption, but let us remember once more that the church is abandoned, forgotten, and forsaken. The zombies of humankind have risen and are stepping into church, they look around and raise massive rocks above their heads — neither redemption or penitence has power over them here!

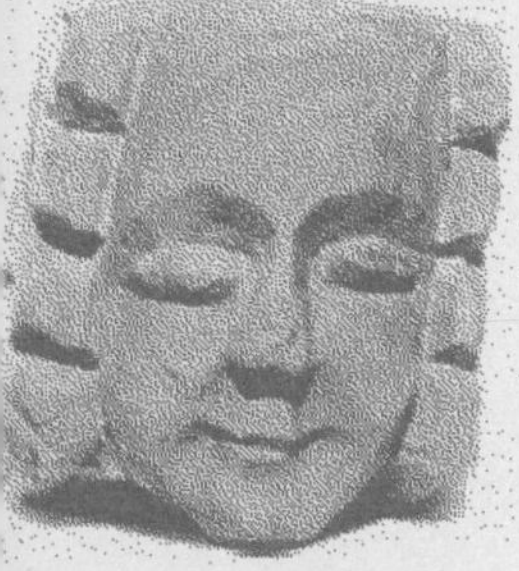

Moving from the main hall to the spaces at the side of the church, we meet an array of miniature dramas: a flock of storks has flown into the room but hasn't found a way out again; grieving women cover their eyes with their hands, as if trying to hide their tears for eternity,

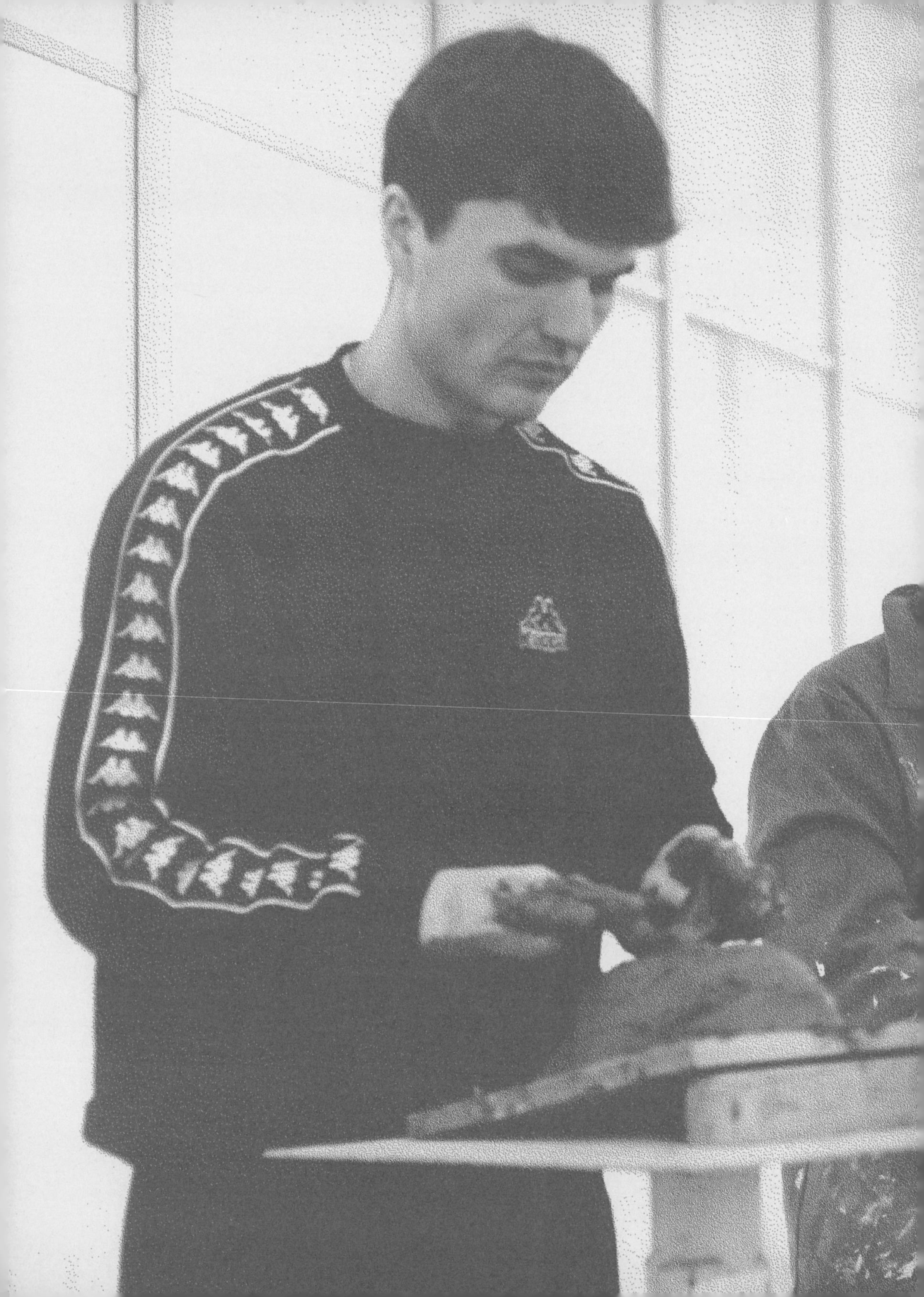

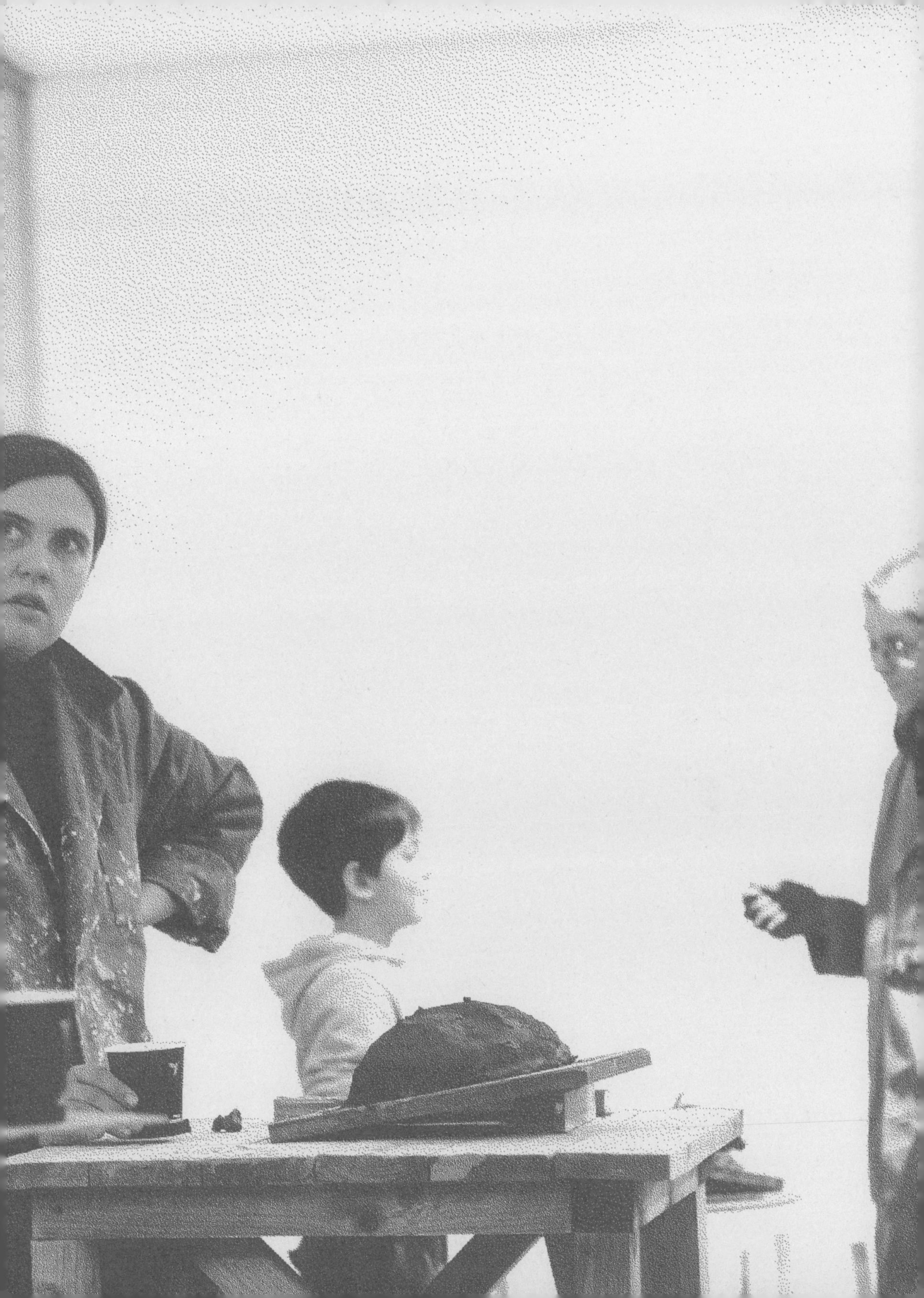

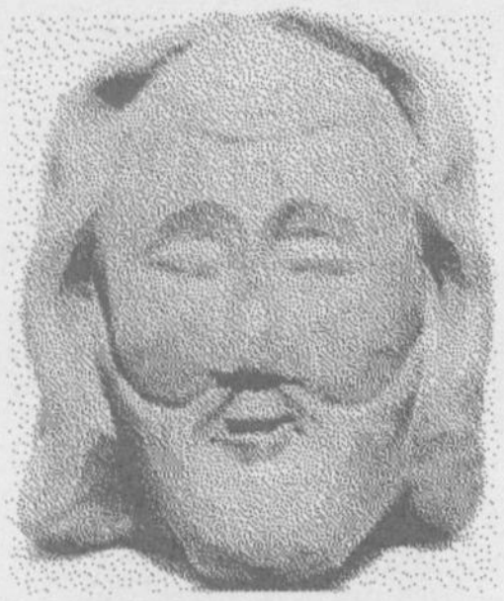
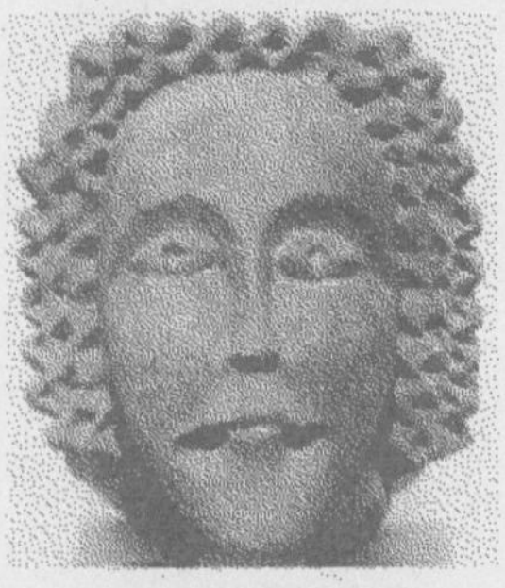
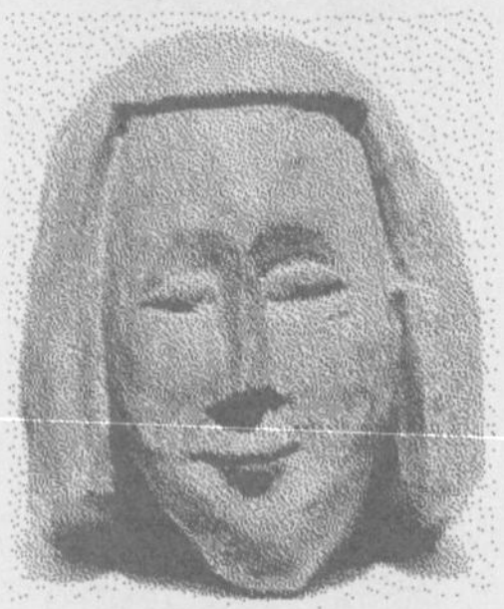
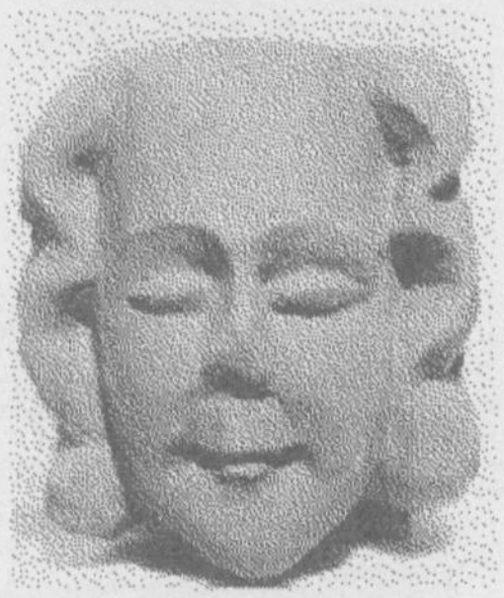
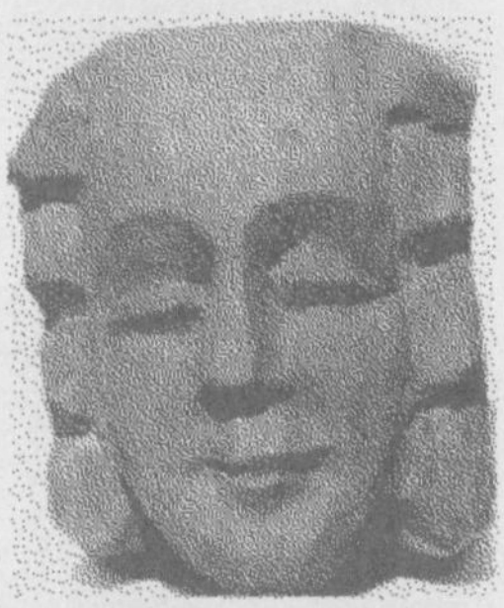

so that they would never need to see the world again; hidden in a cupboard we meet small repulsive statues akin to sneering demons; a tiny masterless sanctified dog, whose trail of paw prints mark its eternal wanderings akin to Ahasuerus and who could be seen as a metaphor for man, awaiting for the return of god in his abandonment; and hybrid *weremermaids* reclining around the hole in the church floor filled with water from the canal. There is a repetition of threes in the *weremermaids,* the Neanderthals and the crying women — this sacred number wanders around the exhibition just like the dog in its little room.

Among and in-between these miniature dramas, the artist has snuck in countless small details — leftovers of sculptures, church-like lighting, barely discernible sounds. We move from room to room and look at the personas hiding between marble walls and colourful paintings, funny in their primitive being, yet alluring in their genuineness and bluntness. Bodies with coarse, tactile, visceral surfaces. Beings capable of feeling enough shame to hide their genitals under animal hide but not enough to keep themselves from throwing stones at others and so tying violence and play, brutality and laughter together — as it always goes.

While in the main hall, the sacred and the strong merge in expressions of raw impulses and brutality, in the smaller side spaces Karlson is more gentle and poetic, building the following narratives around death, grief, and longing. The demise of a lost flock of birds in the auxiliary part of the space sings of Karlson's melancholy. This sadness pushes through unpolished clay surfaces and clay heads that have been cracked in the kiln, through the abandoned Christ and forgotten dog, through the *weremermaids* placed on the caved-in church floor, as if waiting for the final collapse, yearning to fall back into the Venetian canal like a human into amniotic fluid. At the same time, this is a push towards something fundamental, primal, genuine, natural, sincere, and authentic, this call becoming more urgent the more Karlson realises its impossibility — and she is acutely aware of its impossibility. The urge-driven Estonia of her childhood has become a polished society, anarchists have become bourgeois, Eastern Europe has become Western Europe, and violence has become boredom.

The three crying women, whose hands have ben modelled after those of Karlson's grandmothers, bring together the timeless and the temporal, the quotidian and the sacred with an exceptional sensitivity. Grief is among the most genuine and impossible to fake impulses which Karlson is seeking: unyielding sadness, boundless sense of emptiness, and a feeling of everything ceasing to exist. The surrounding church addresses grief on a mythological level, the main hall is filled with references to a Christ who was killed but he, at least, rose again —

there is no such hope for the human, pushed into a dimly lit auxiliary space. The crying women have been left godless, just like the dog in the room next to them, as for them, death is finite, total, and complete. Or is it? Does the church not make us see the work in a different light? Is the possibility of resurrection, a chance for reincarnation, the potential of revival not present in the work, bestowed by the church?

TENSION AGAINST THE WORLD

This is also how Karlson moves through other spaces on the ephemeral borders of hope and hopelessness, ignorance and acceptance. The poses of the three *weremermaids* next to the collapsed hole in the floor with the water undulating in the canal below allow this composition to be interpreted as one of grieving creatures (or, perhaps, as hedonistic tourists). As hybrid creatures, they are children of the hour of the wolf, born in the deepest moment of darkness, their transformation has been completed. The pseudo-Christian bas-reliefs, many-headed creatures, breastfeeding fathers covered in golden leaves, the ogling eyes of clay heads, the coolness radiating from the walls of the church, the empty bed, the tongue of the snake around a rough candlestick — Karlson's fragmentarium is a kind of bestiary, a collection of bastard creatures, mixing poetry and humour, abjection and desire, sincerity and irony, brutality and mythology in this ambivalent amalgam but, above all, it moves on plains where reason in its puniness is not allowed.

So, we can interpret Karlson's work as holding a certain tension towards bourgeois world, something which the artist and her generation sharply sense, because everything that, in Western societies, had been the norm for decades (if not for centuries), unexpectedly changed for them. For that generation, other worlds became possible, and they have experience of them, from lethargic childhood summer days where everything stood still to cruel social cataclysms that brought about existential borderline situations, such as epidemic poverty, dispossession, or weekly hunger. The brutal struggle for survival is familiar to Karlson, her generation experienced that in their teenage years and perhaps we can see the echoes of both this almost Darwinian principle and the superficial welfare society that followed, in her work today.

Similarly, Karlson's work does not stand outside current political contexts — the war in Ukraine and the methodical destruction of nature does not inspire faith in the capability of the civilised human to make moral decisions. Is it then not equally moral, or even more moral, to return to an innocence without morals, because in that scenario people are who they are, free of pretence. Would this make them better than they have managed to be thus far?

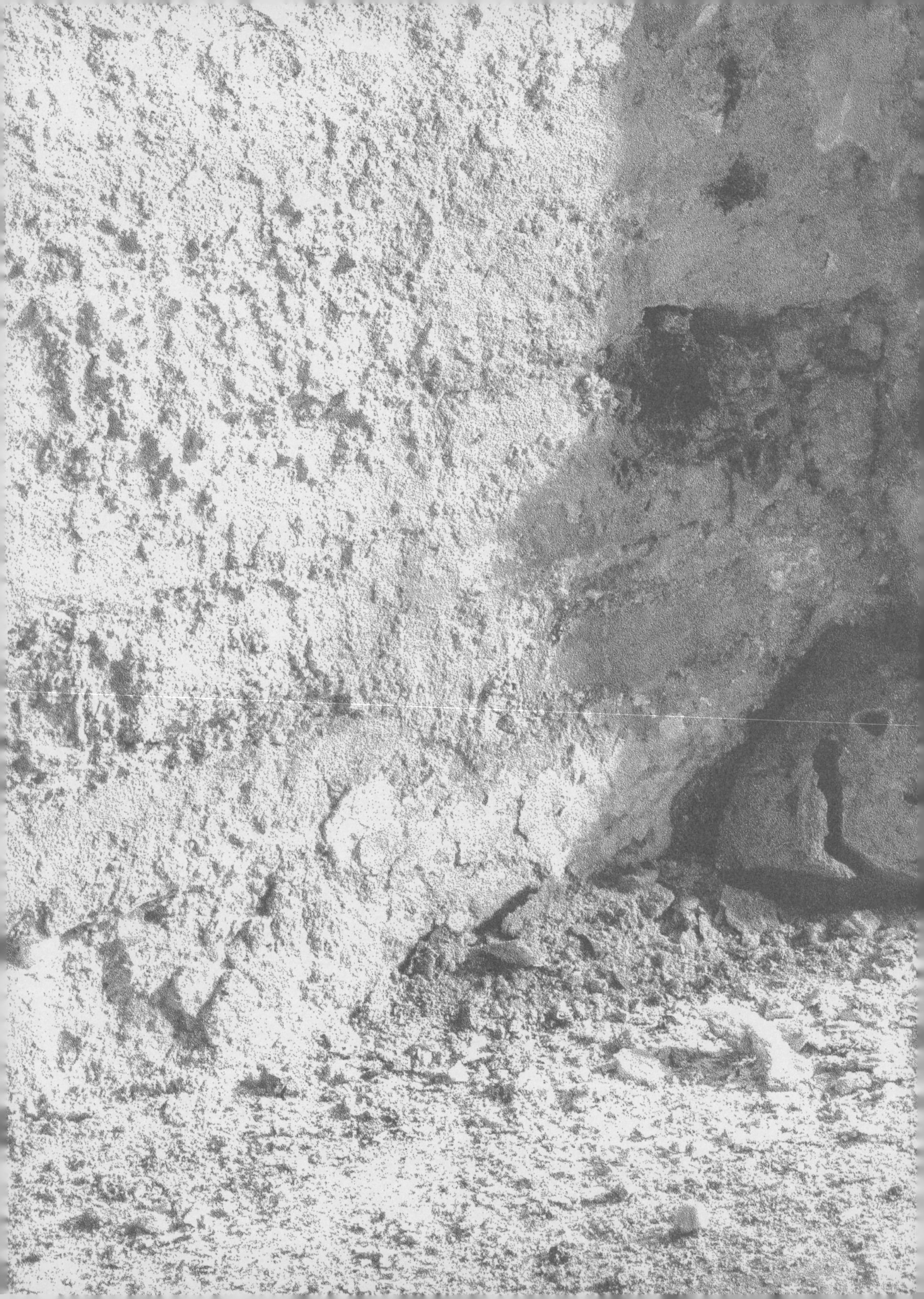

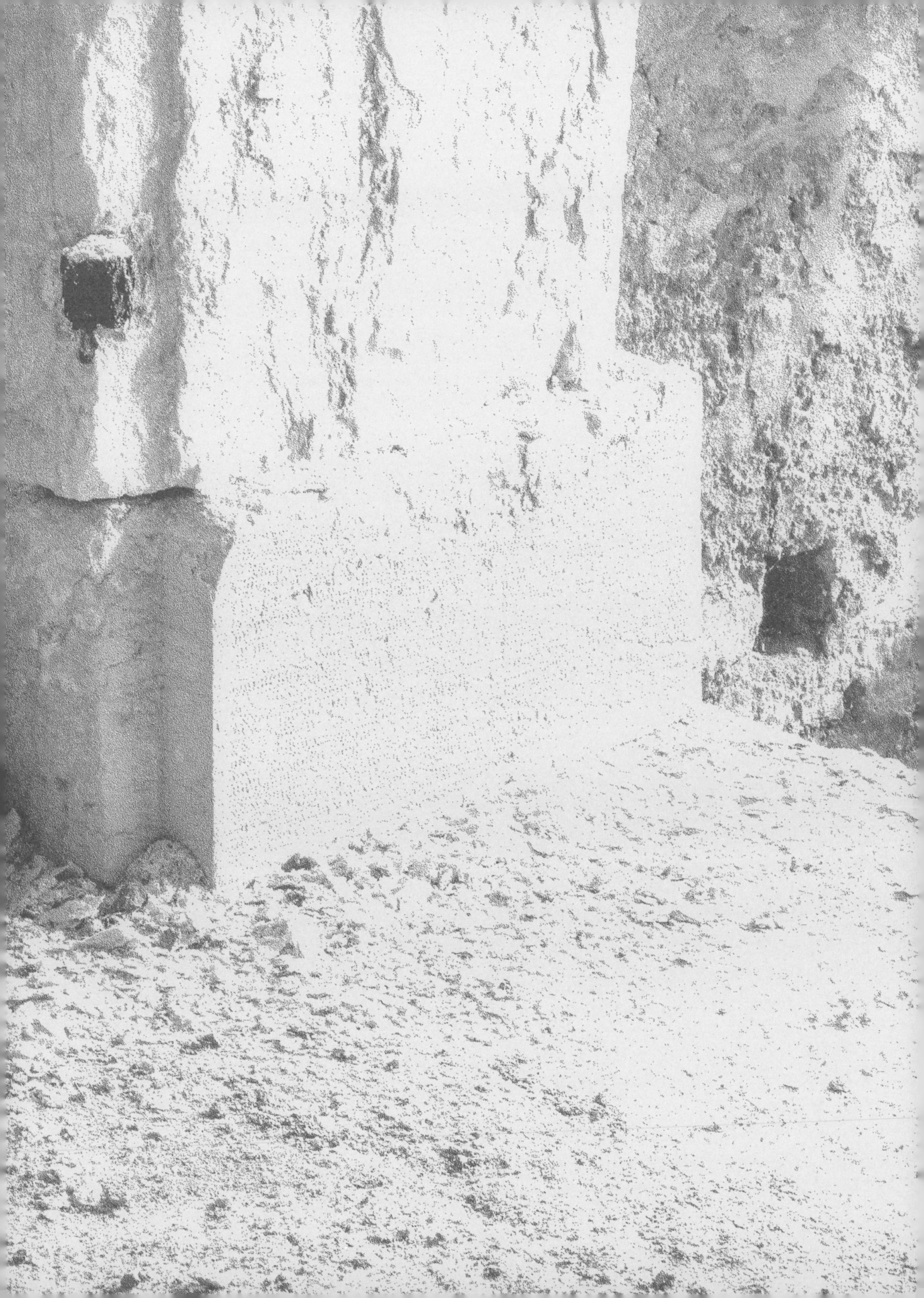

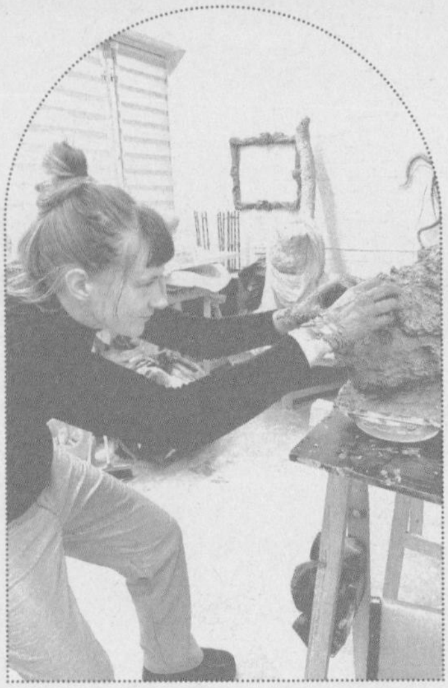

However, on a broader scale, the field Edith Karlson's work operates in is not unlike that of fairytales — it does not try to explain the world but to mystify it. Instead of awareness you get the unconscious, instead of mannerisms, impulses, instead of daylight, twilight, instead of order, dust, instead of logic, metaphysical yearnings. It could be said that this is how art always operates, but the meaningful intertwining in Karlson's work is idiosyncratic to her. She talks to the world in the way of folklore, by permeating humorous fragments, surreal characters, and mysterious atmospheres with epic themes like birth and death, and the creation of worlds in the midst of destruction. Karlson does not end up in a church with her existential dramas by chance.

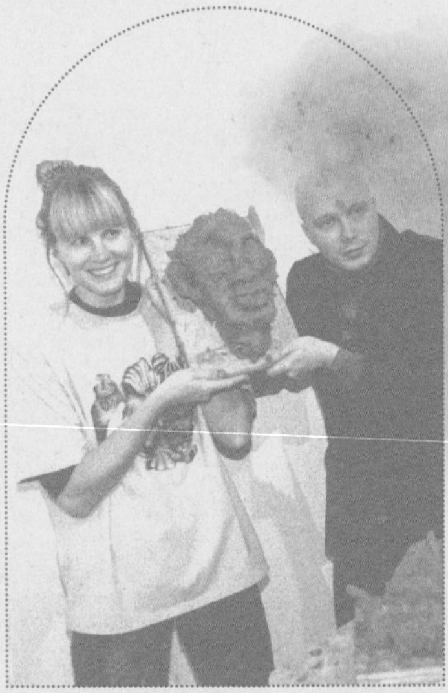

In Karlson's work, sacrality is something aspirational — or seemingly aspirational — as it is unlikely that her creatures are aware of the existence of morals, much less sacrality. Still, there is a drive towards an unknown sacrality that has nothing to do with any of the organised religions but everything to do with lust for life — a desire to reach a *heard* of existence, a place where, for some reason, everything vulgar turns poetic, dirt turns into a starry sky, everything physical to metaphysical, this not in a ceremonious manner but a rude, soiled, and physical one. Both birth and death, life and putrefaction are freed from the chains of human sentimentality — they cast off the civilised codes of conduct and all that jazz that frames our existence and become themselves once again. Death is death again. Sex is sex again. Grief is grief again. And life is life again. Crude, pure — and serious and sacred because of that.

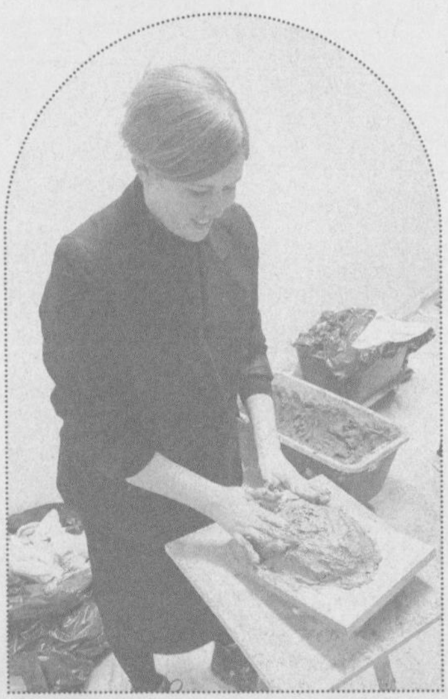

Many of Karlson's themes — cultivating a conscious naiveté, making the banal sacred and the sacred banal, valuing robust physicality, constructing spatial narratives, fragmenting mythological narratives and reusing these fragments in a pseudo-sacral context, the search for a true moral stance through a giving up contemporary morals, reverence for our animal nature, obsessively observing death and decay and so on — speak of the spirit she seeks and the clear axis upon which it is positioned. At the very heart of that axis seems to be a desire to relocate humanity in a place that once turned everyone who entered sacred, and in this forgotten and abandoned place, to deconstruct people to their most primitive drive to live and hold a deep lust for life until no social norms, masks, or morals can hide them, and then, facing that naked drive and desire, to ask if there is still something sacred there, or will everything go as it always does — that we, together with the church, will slowly sink in the water, fall back to where we came from. Back to the hour of the wolf.

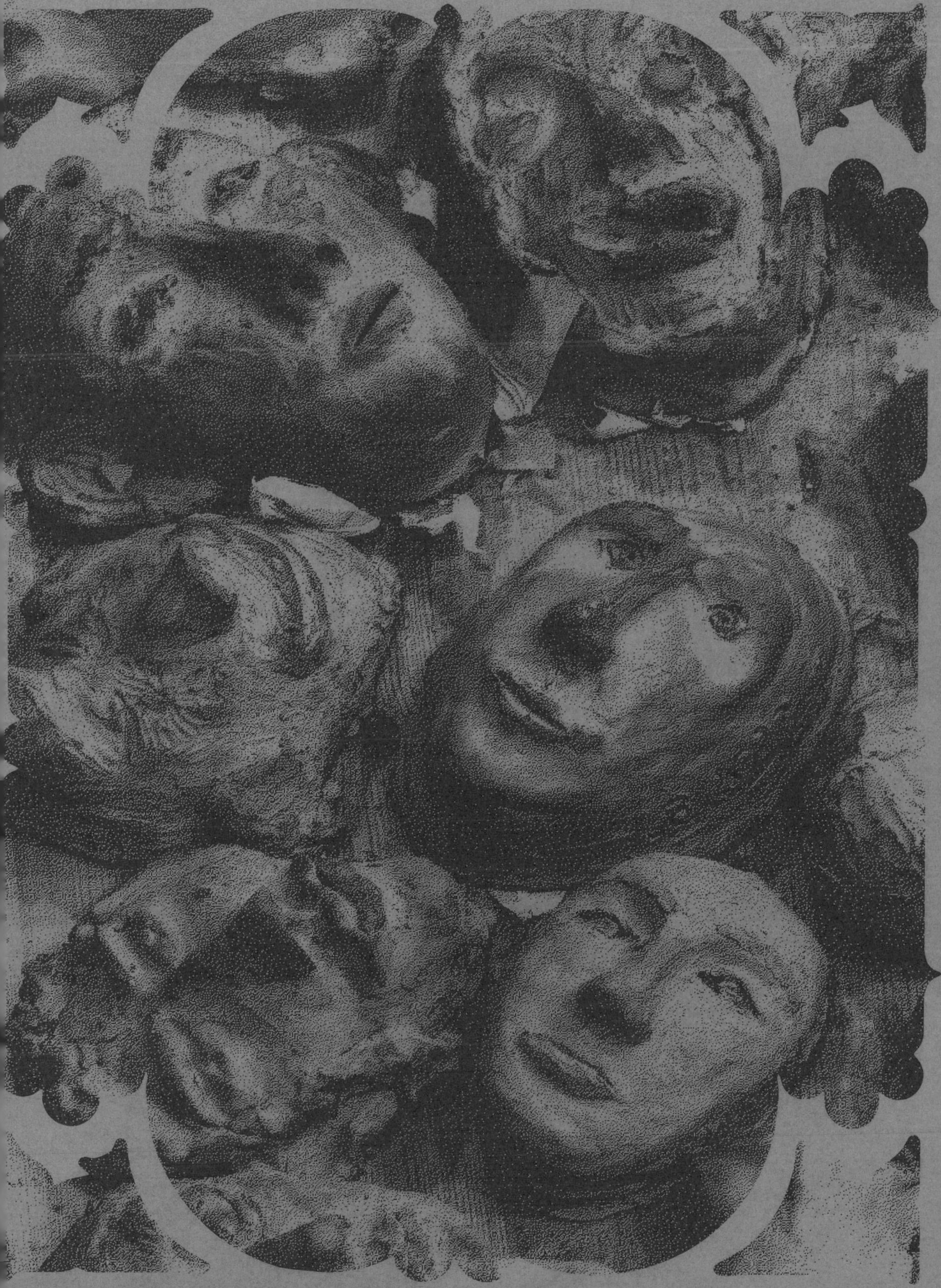

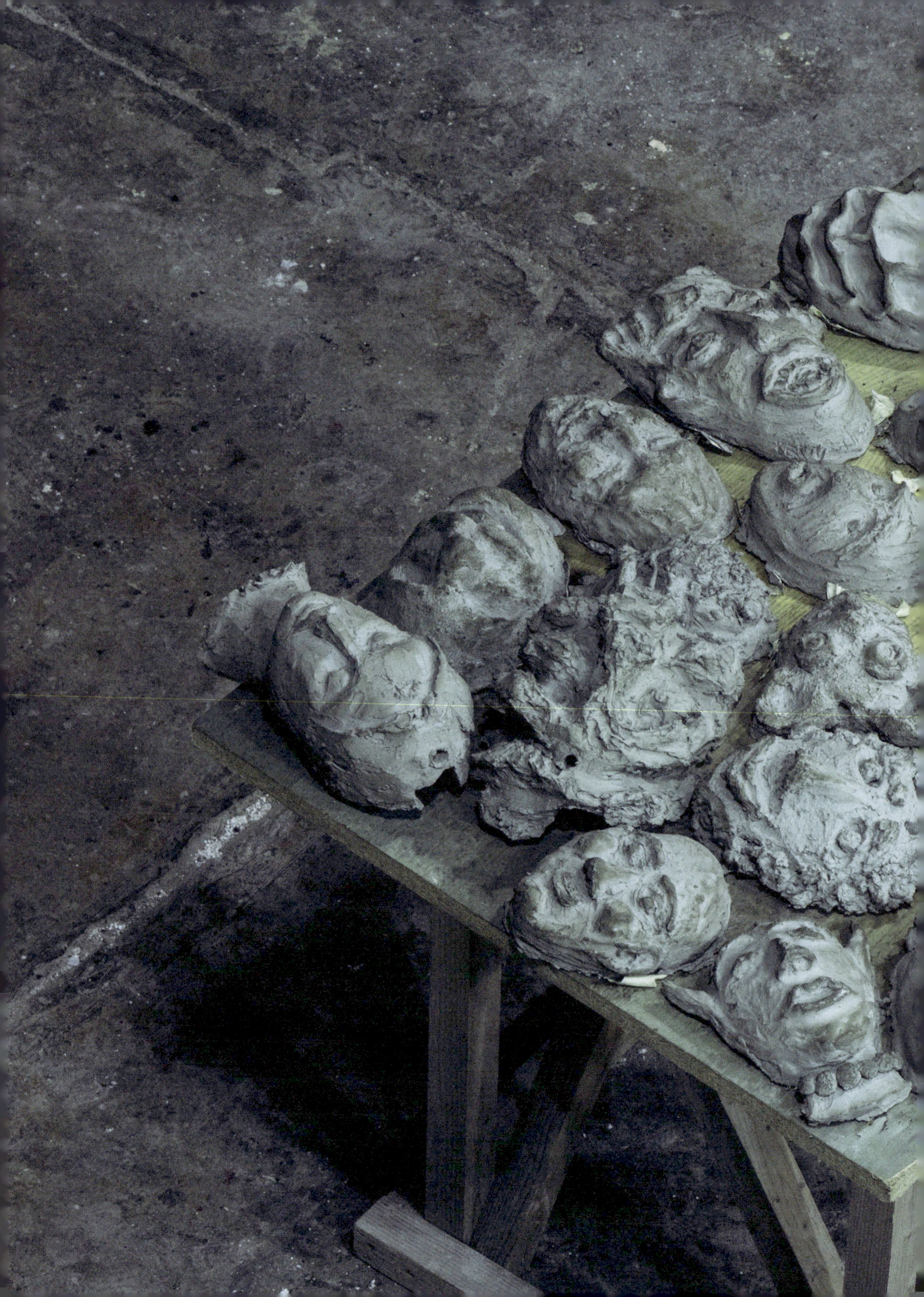

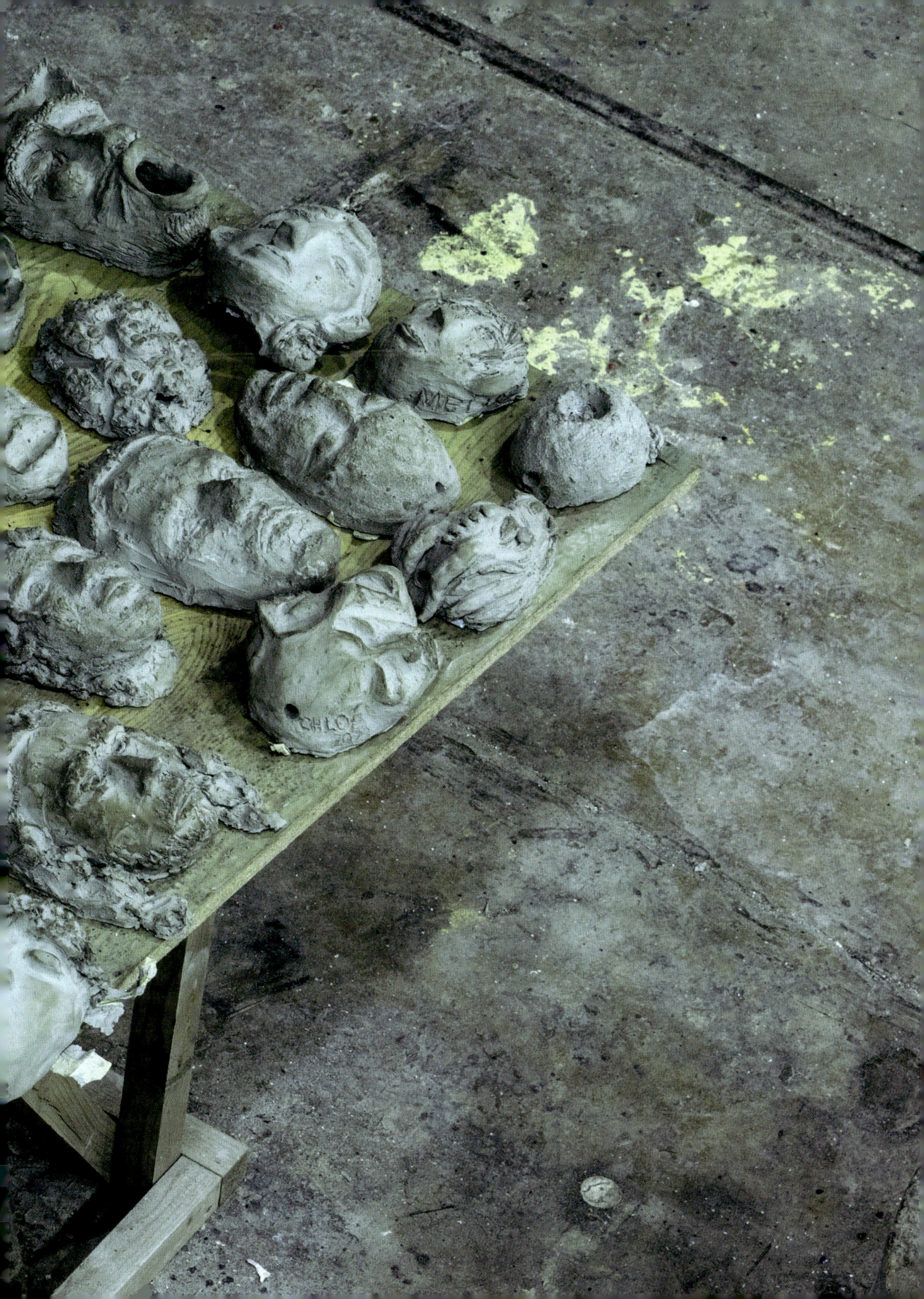
CHLOE

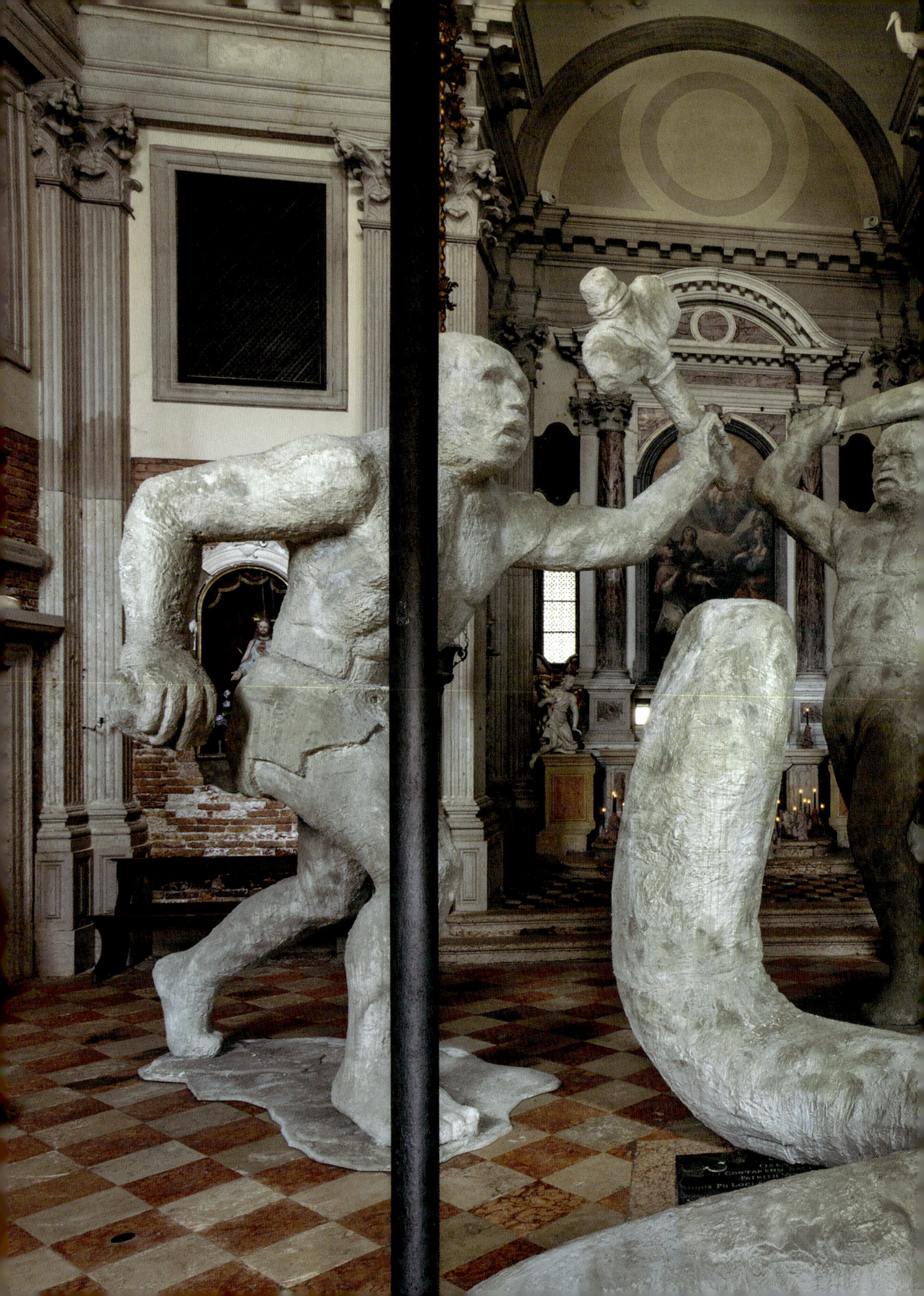

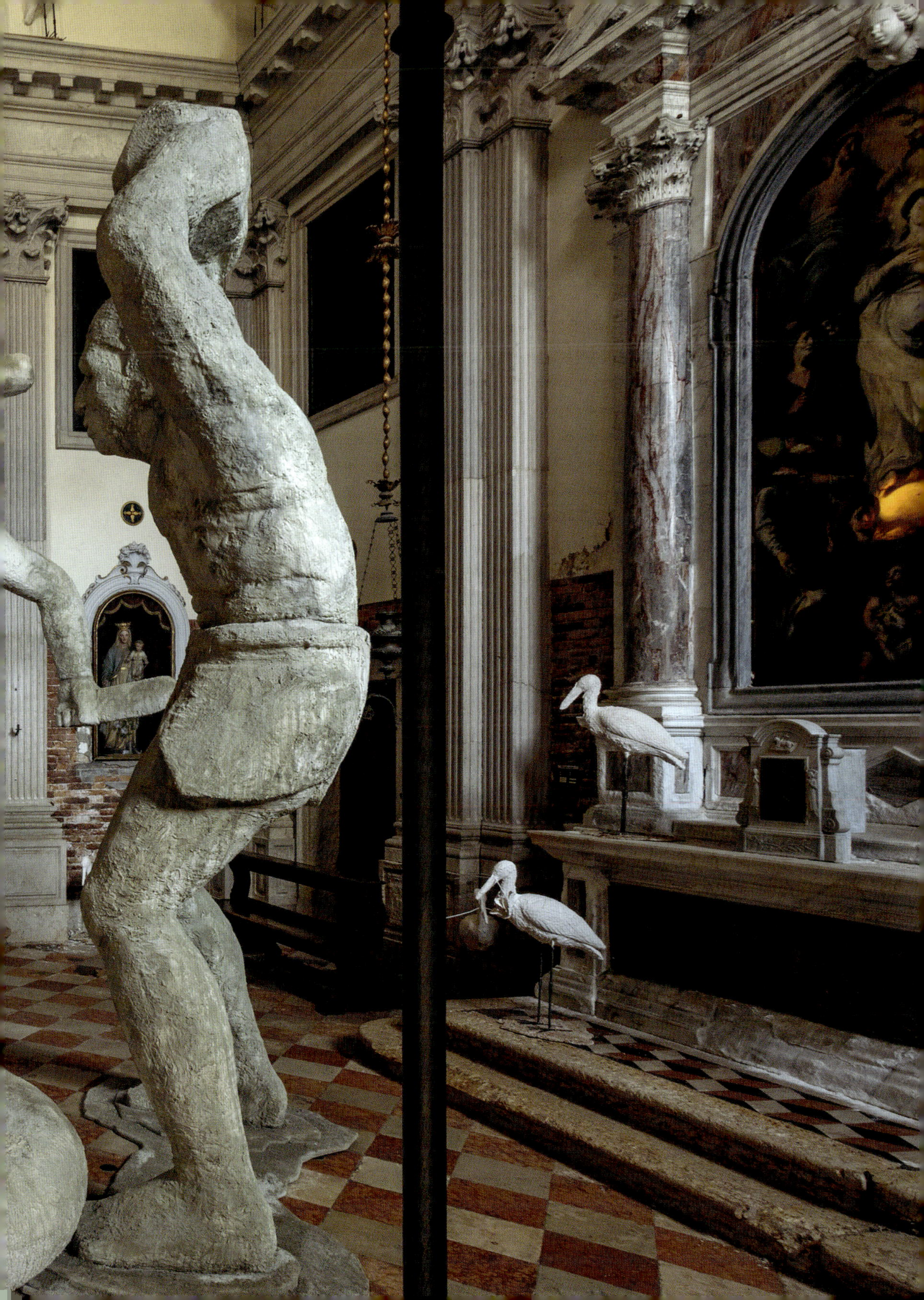

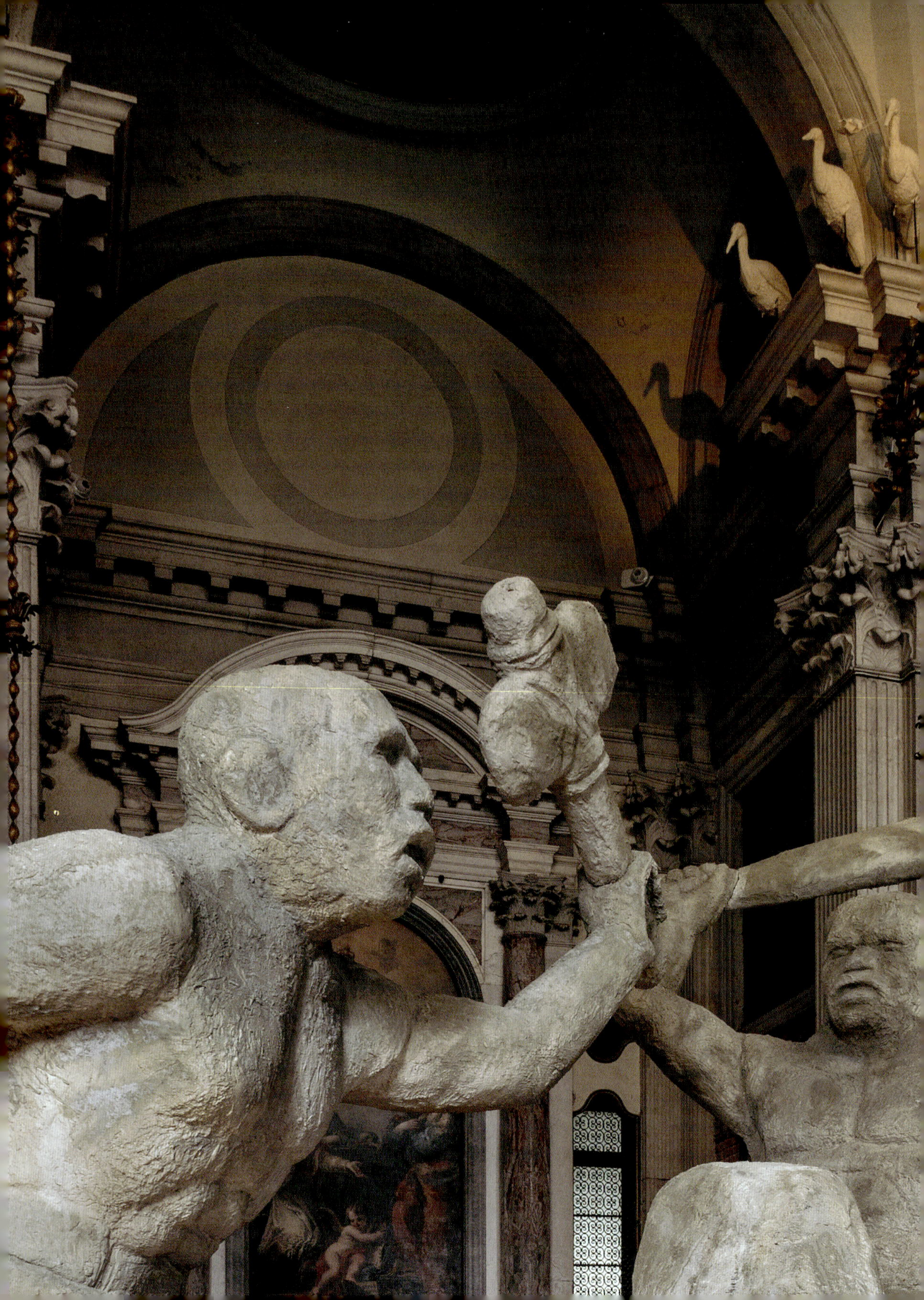

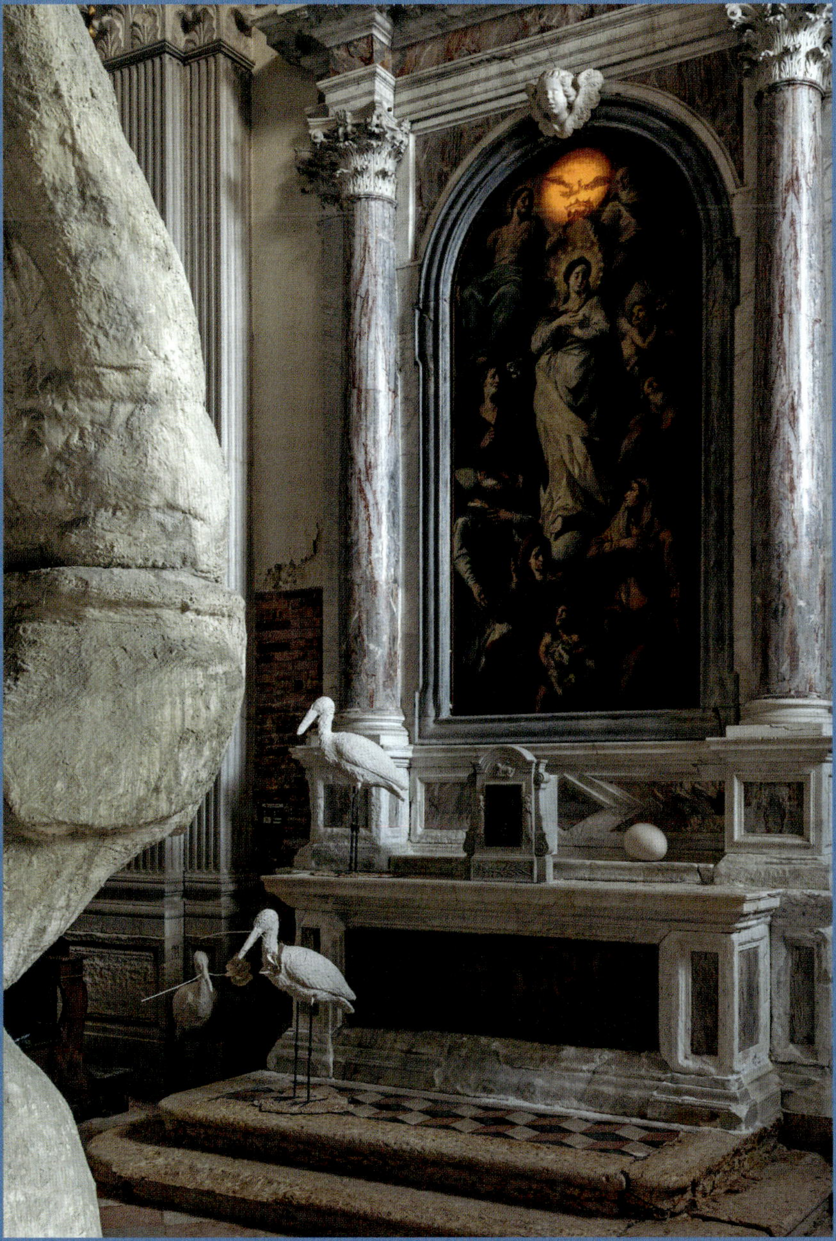

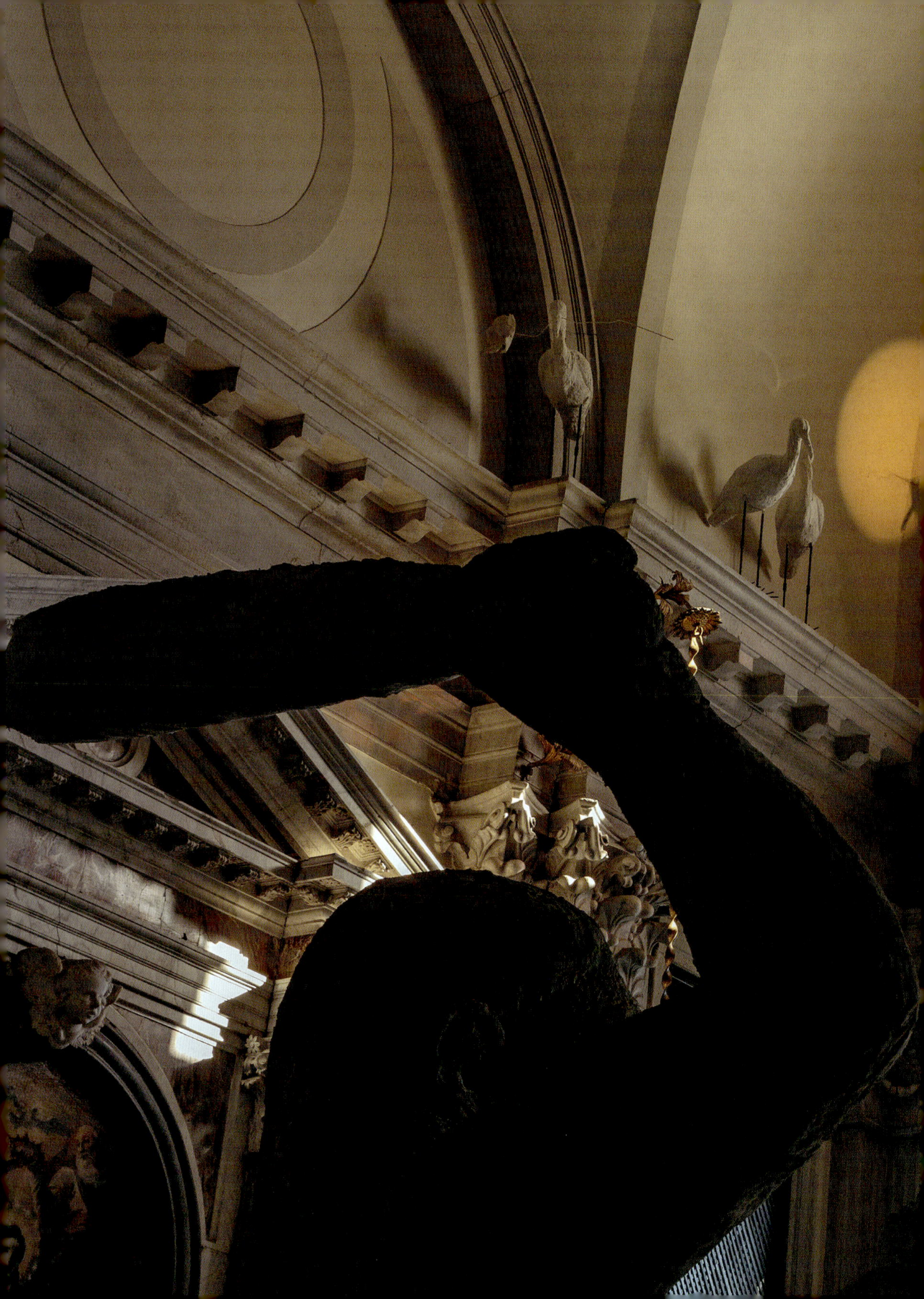

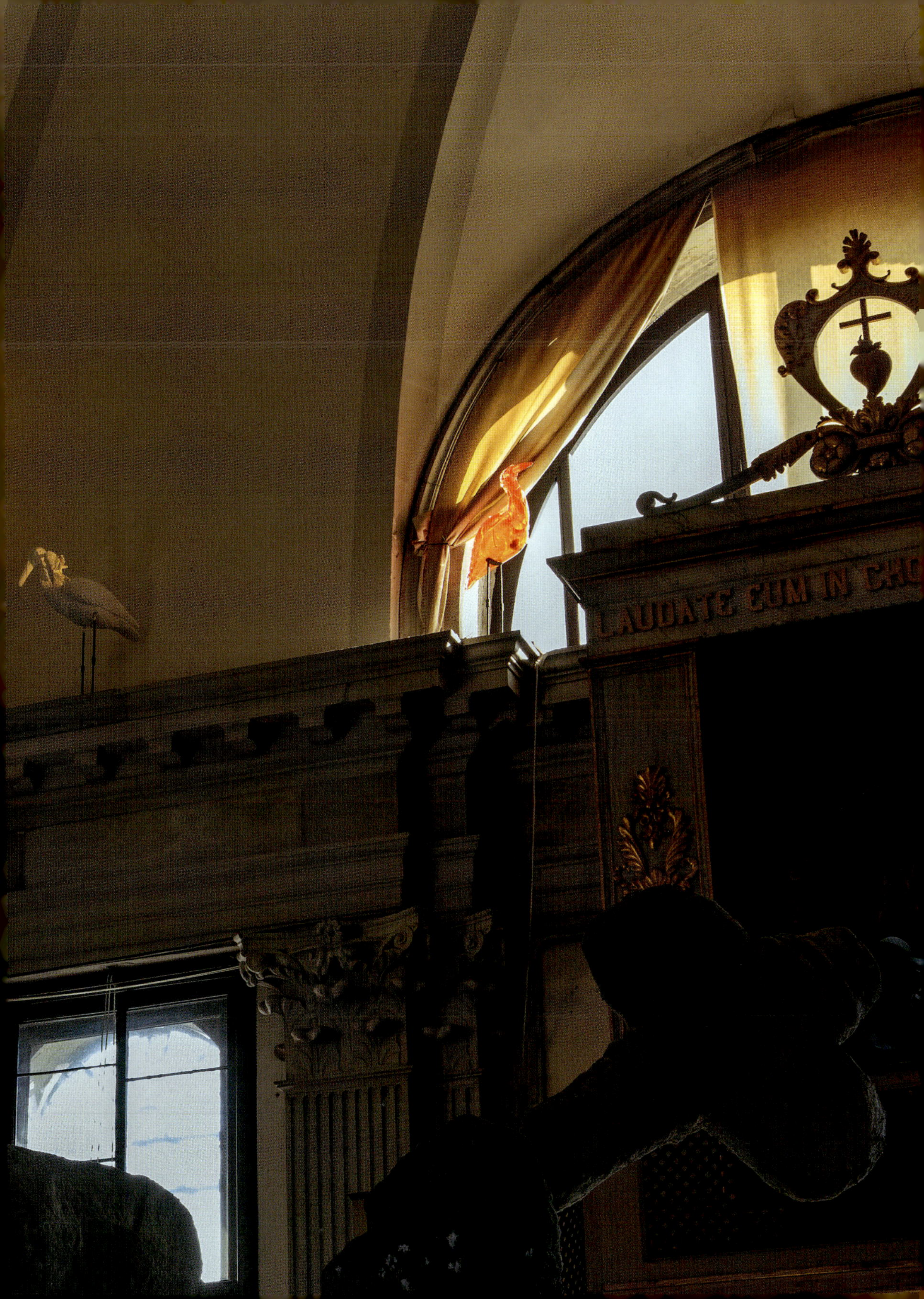
LAUDATE EUM IN

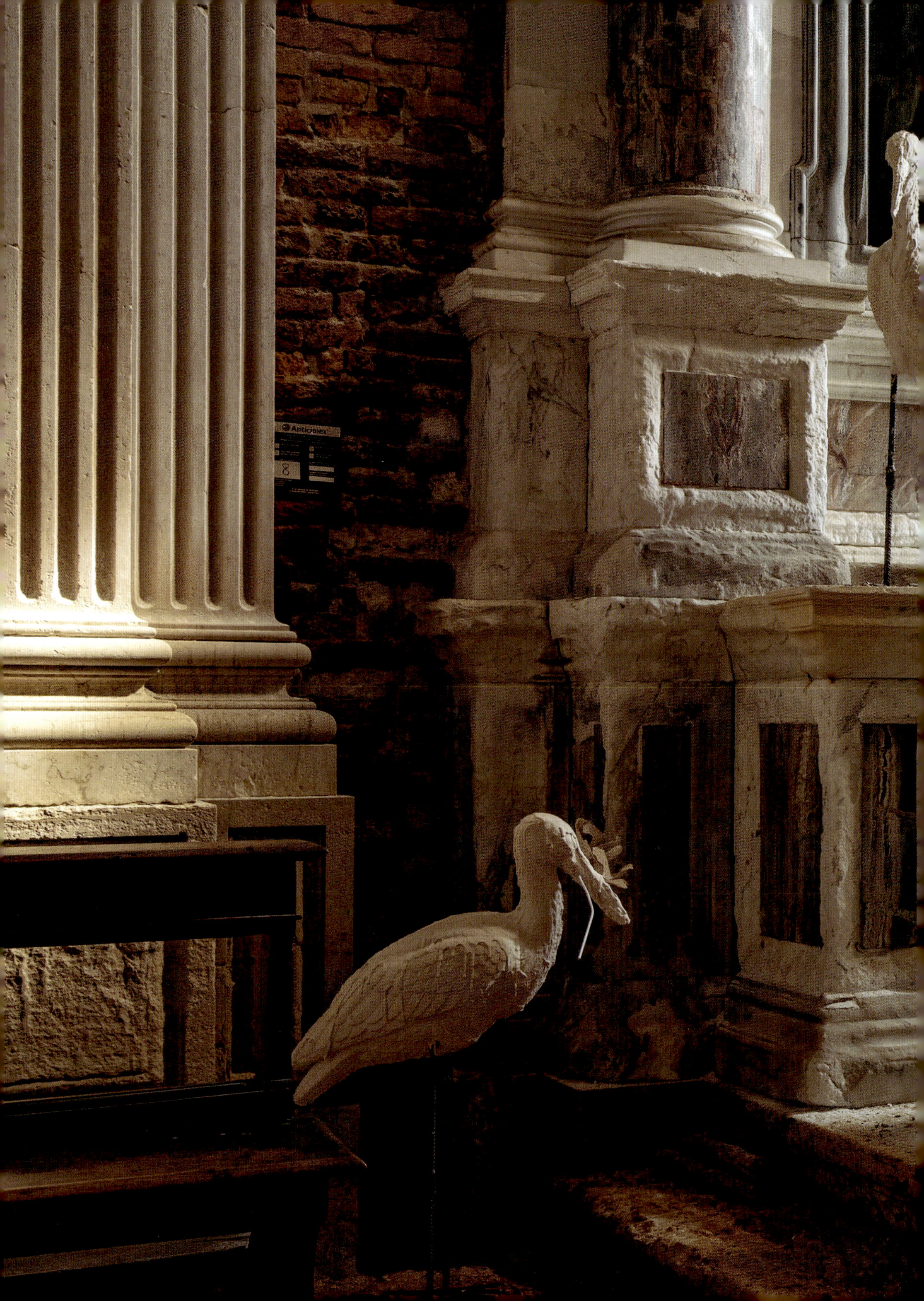
Anticimex
8

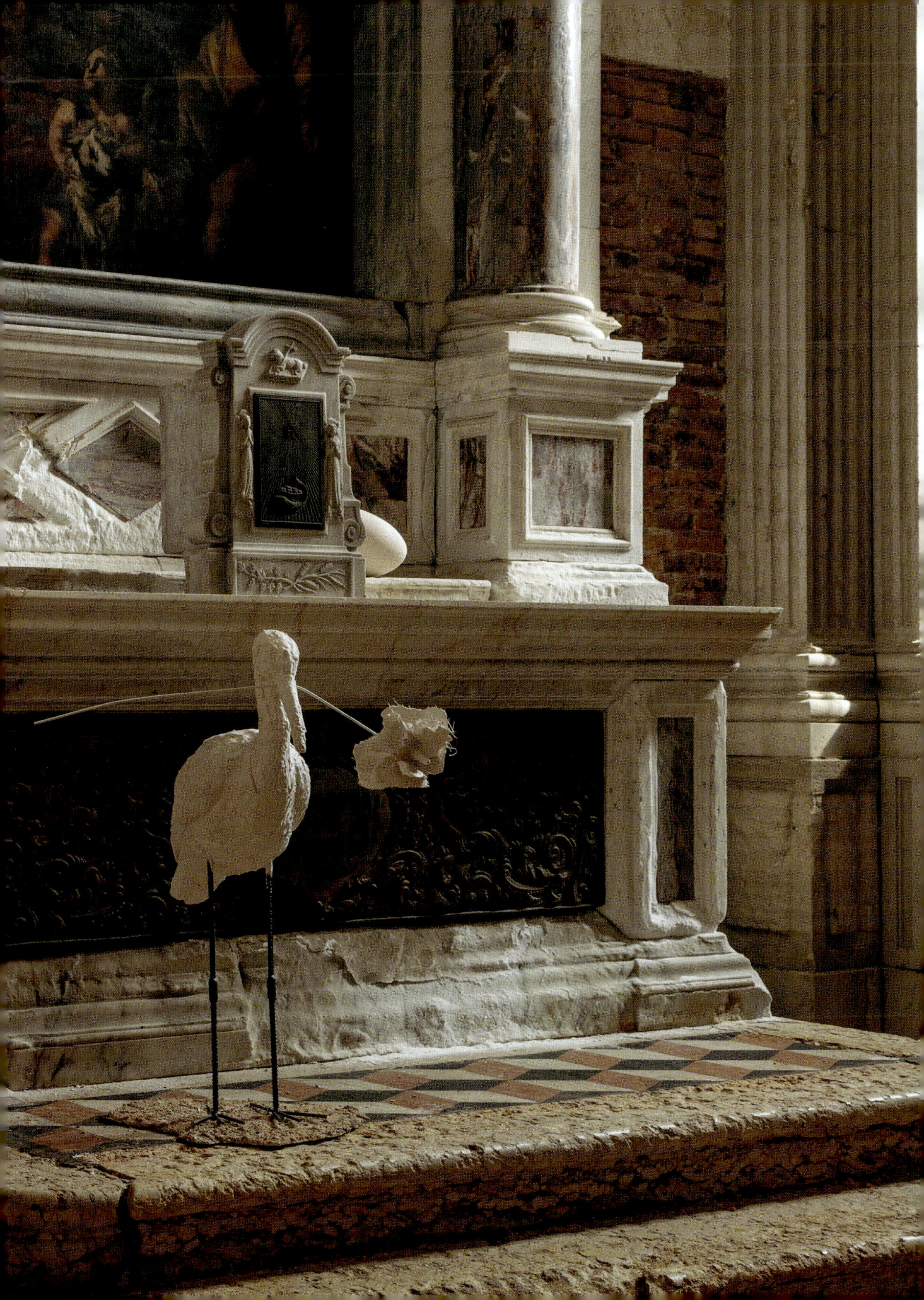

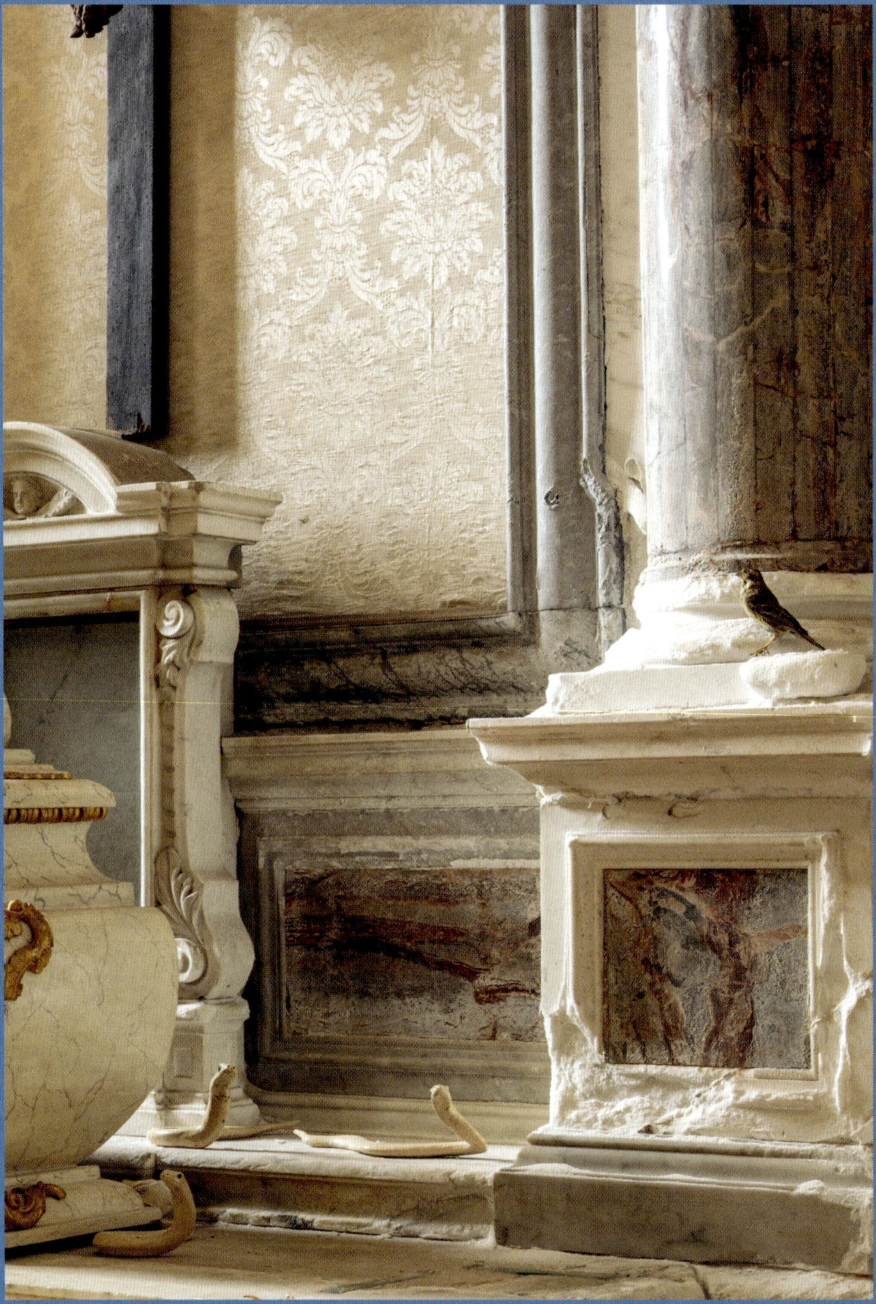

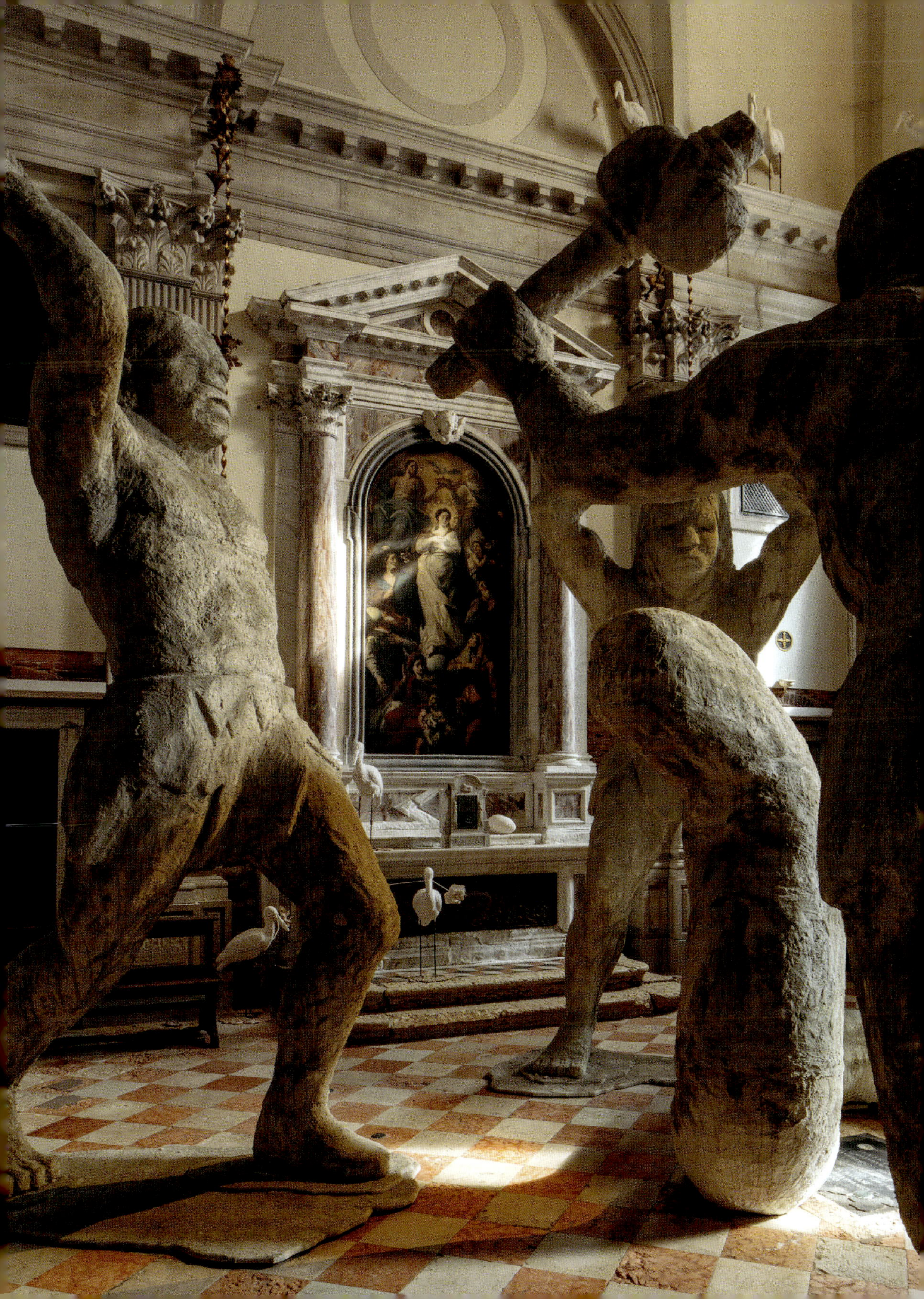

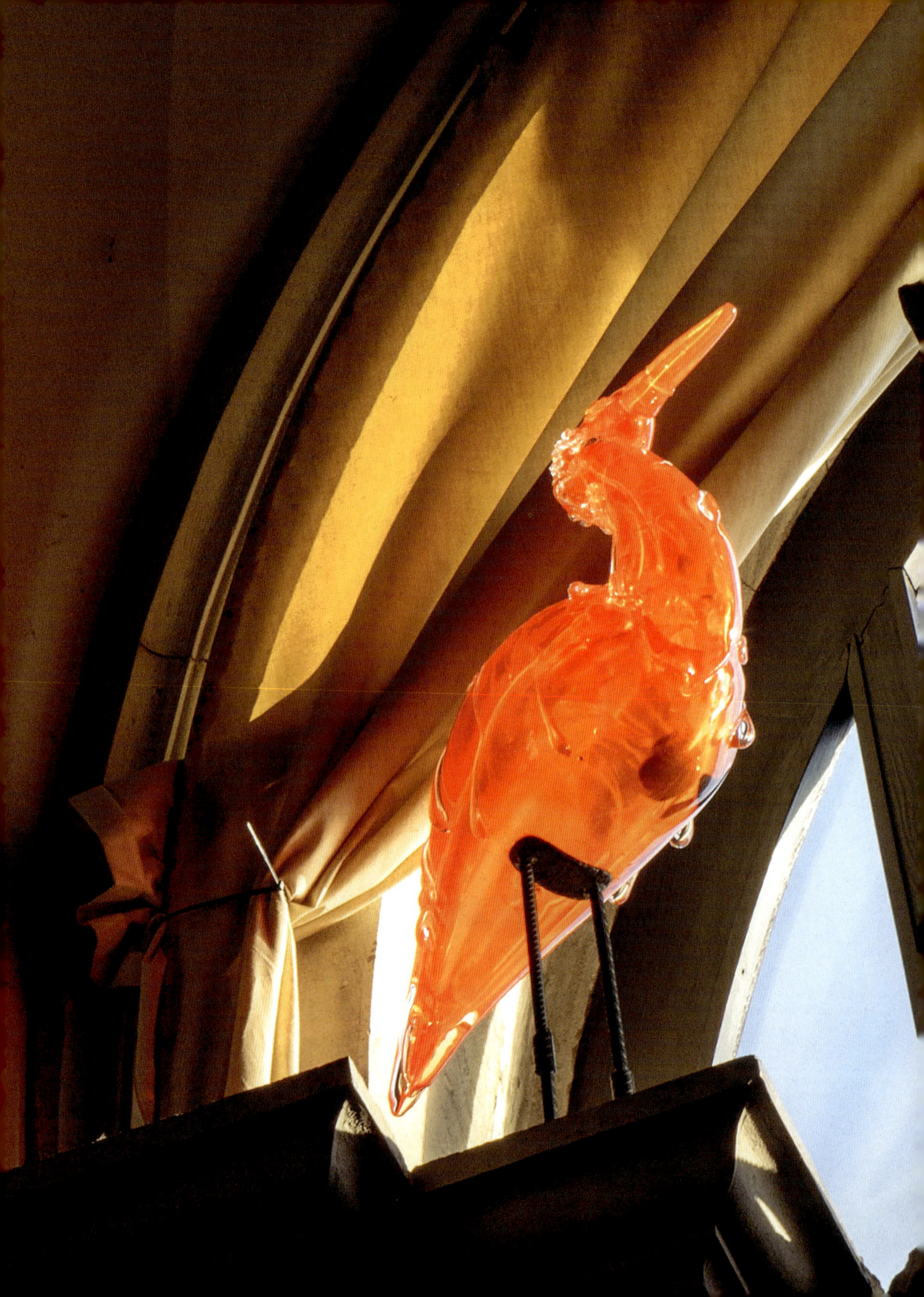

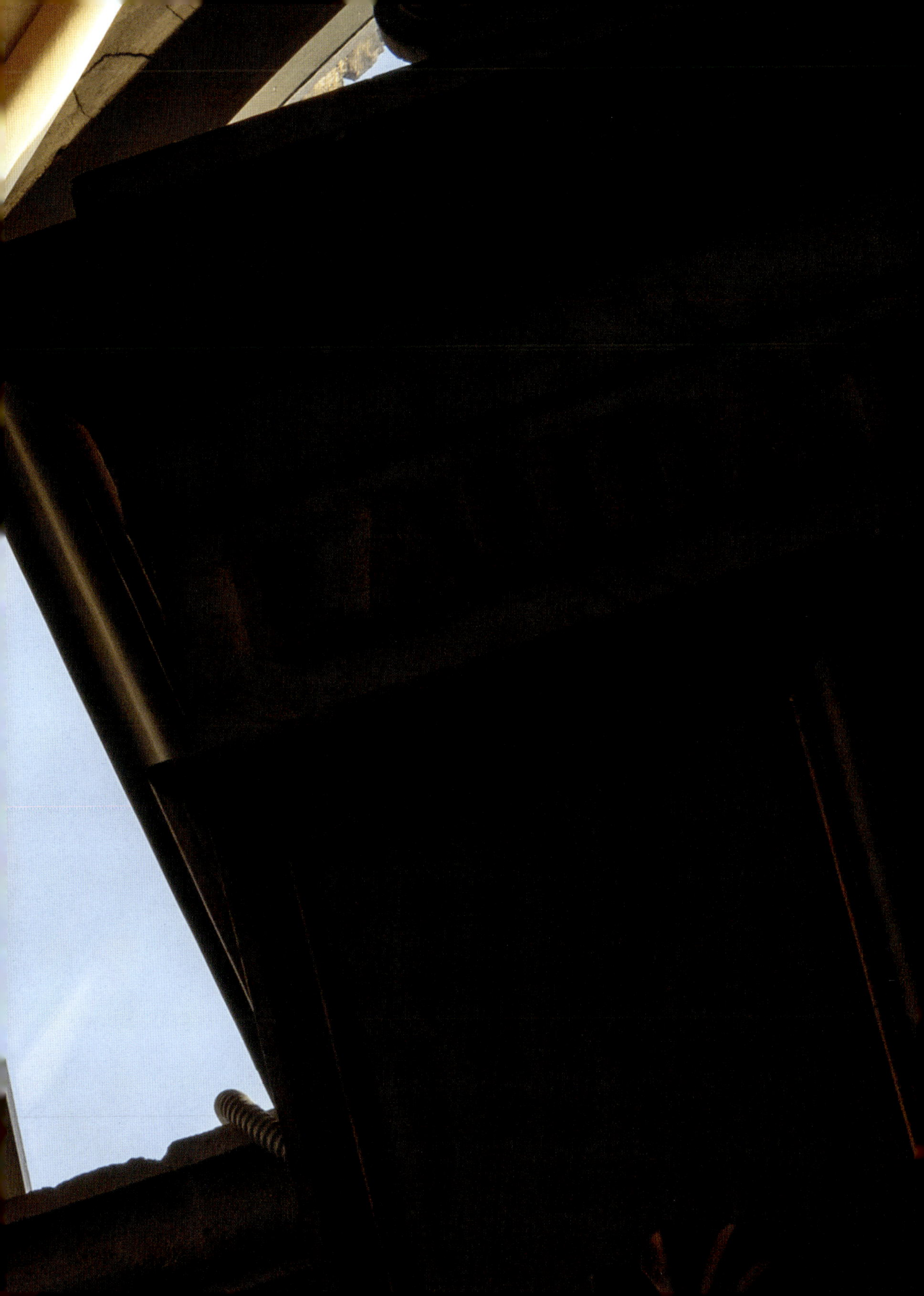

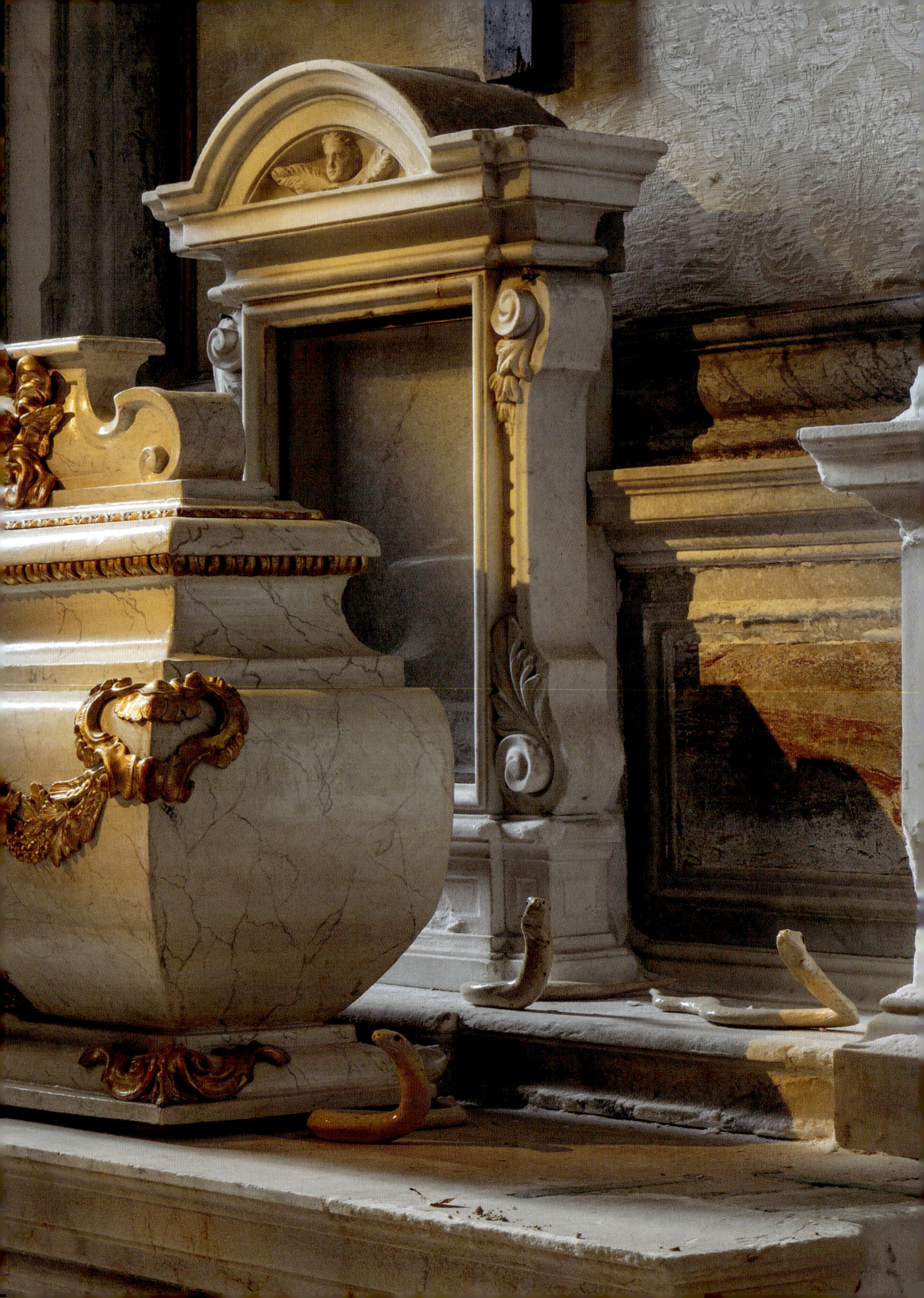

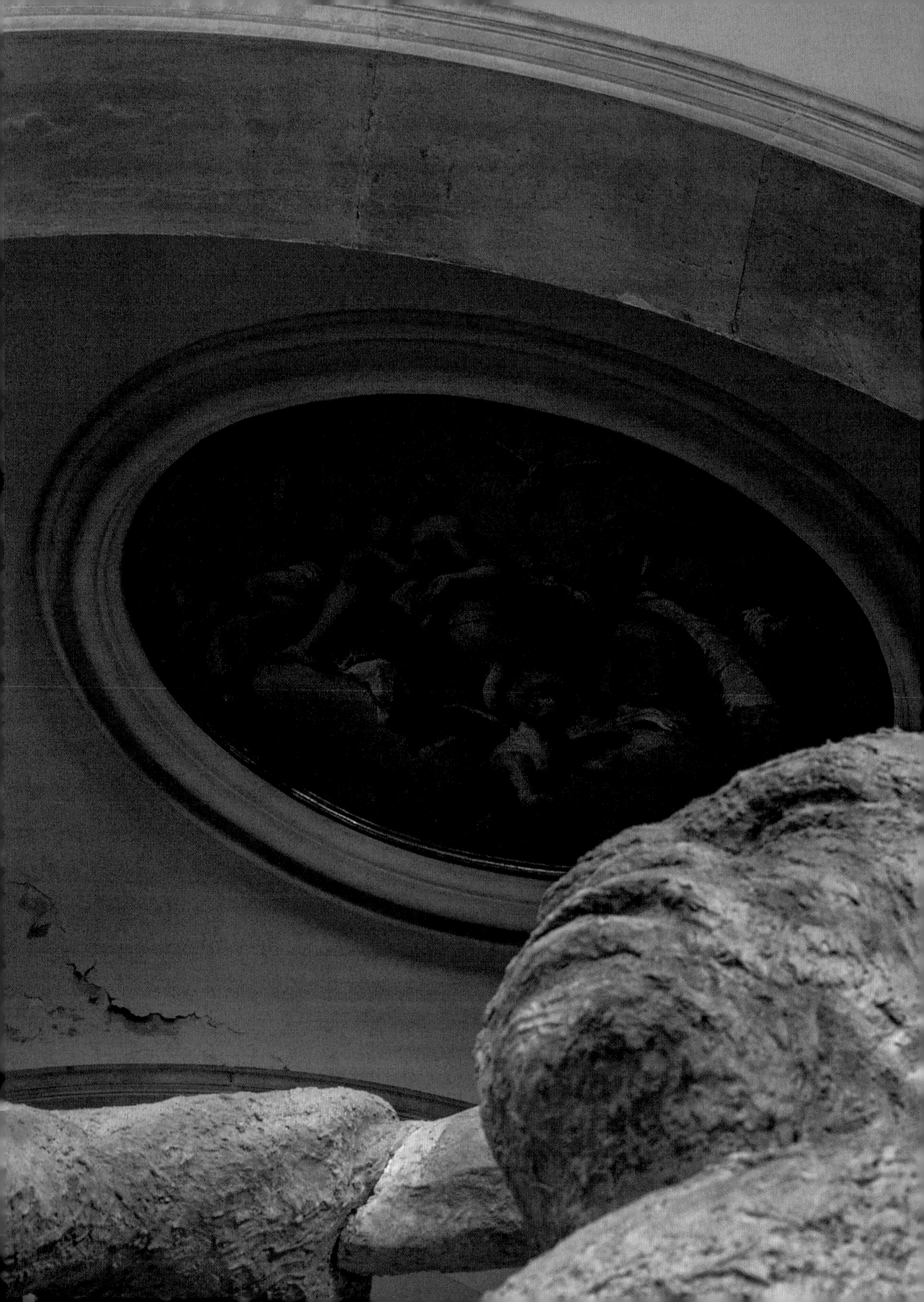

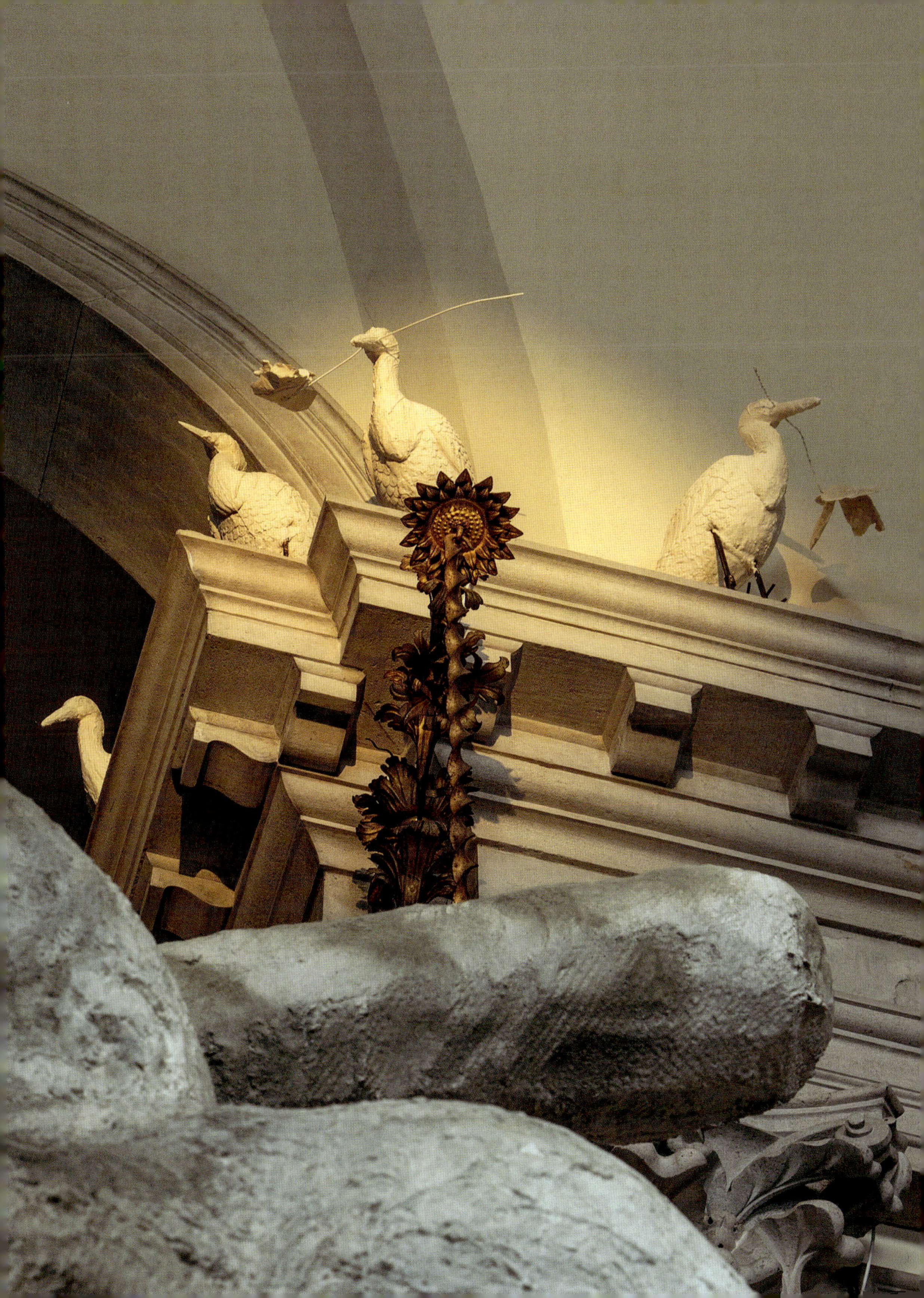

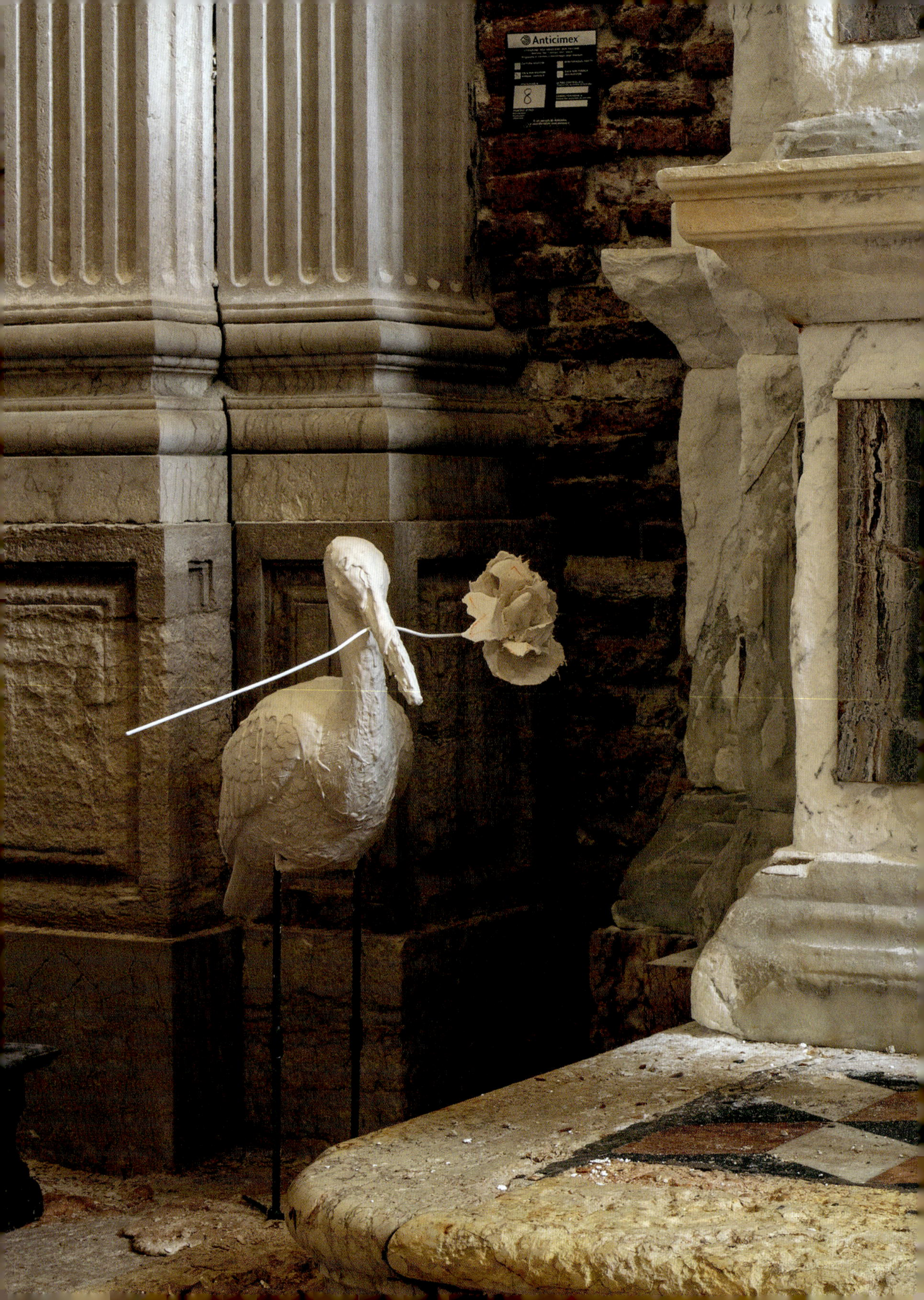
Anticimex

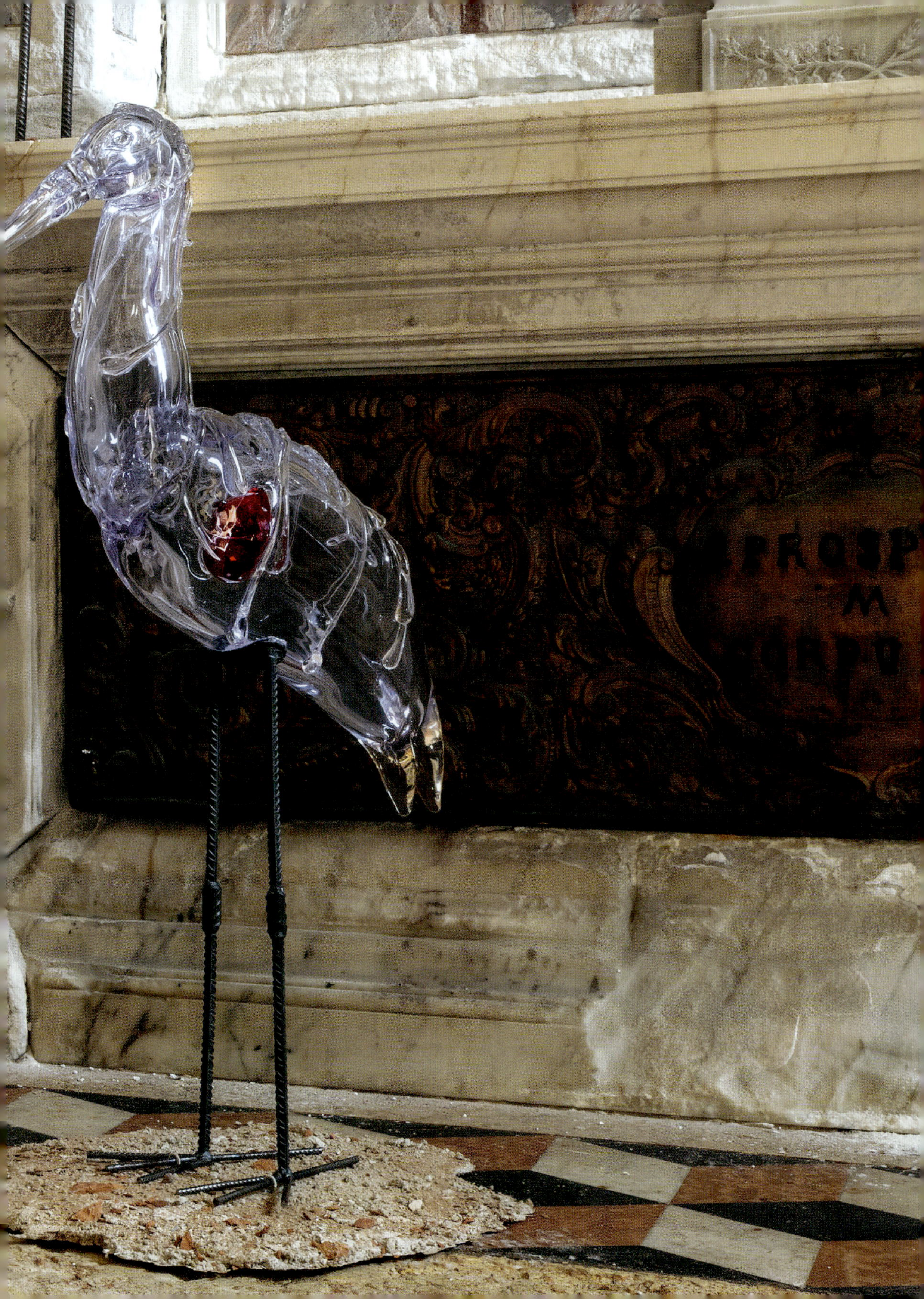

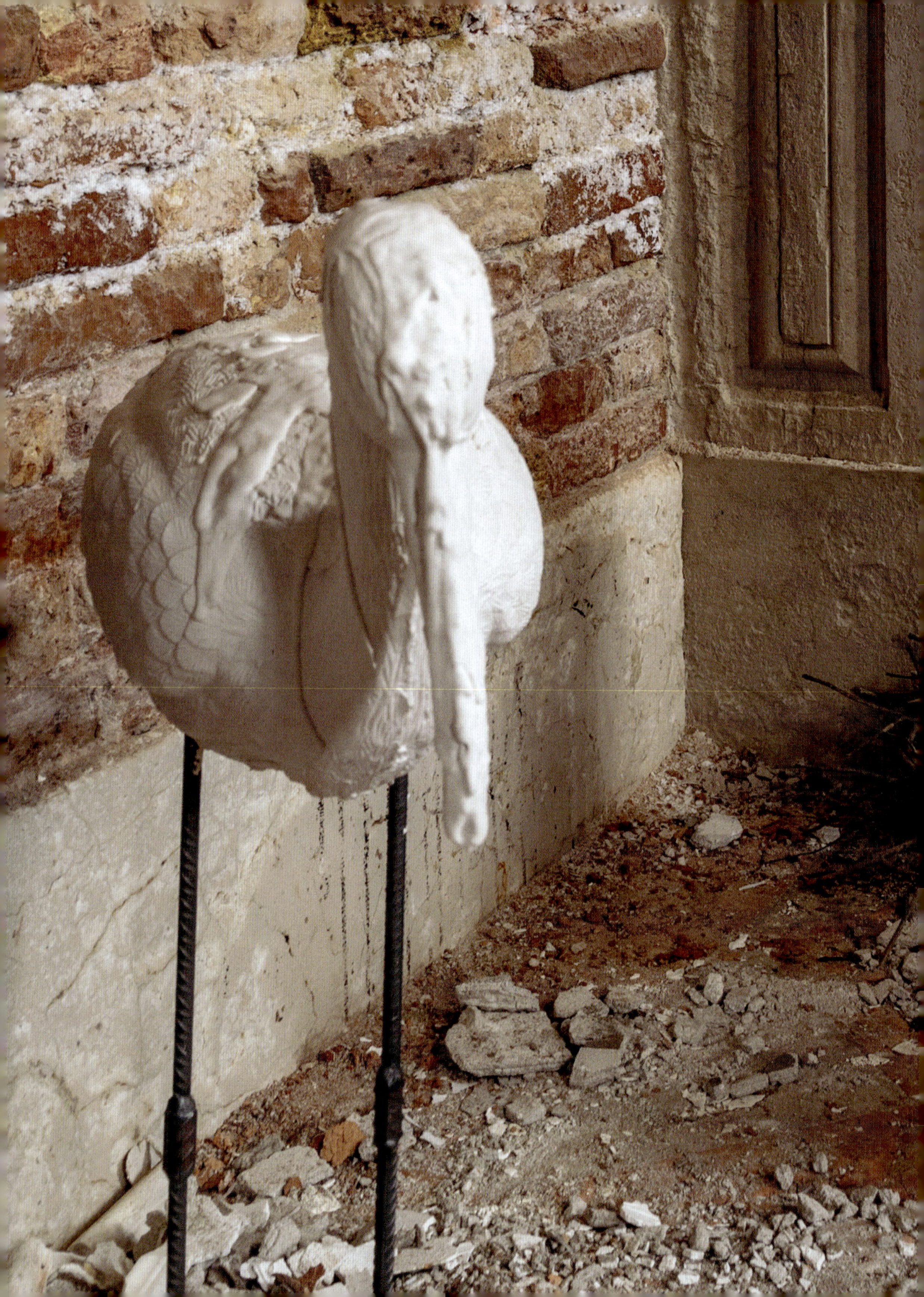

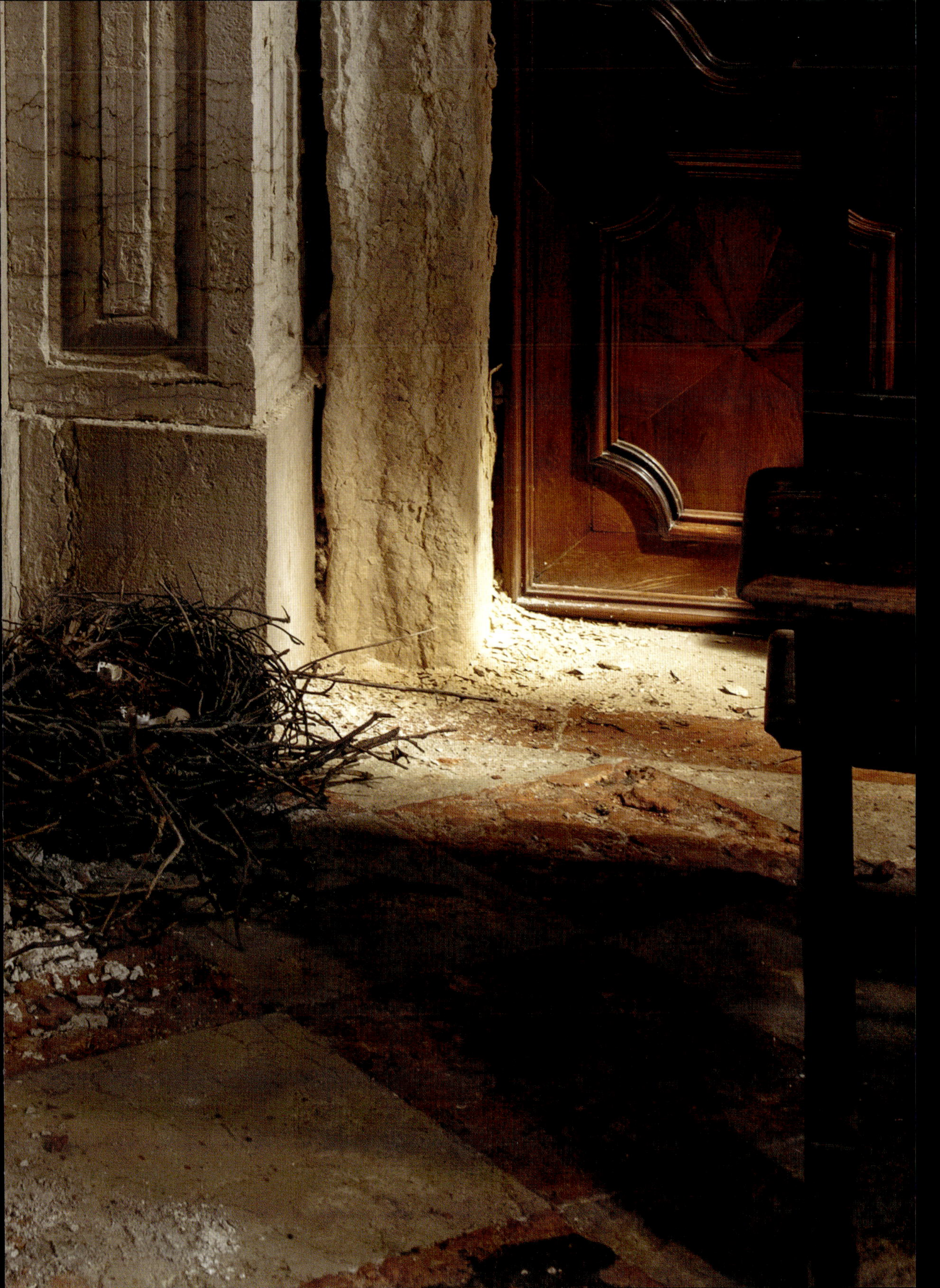

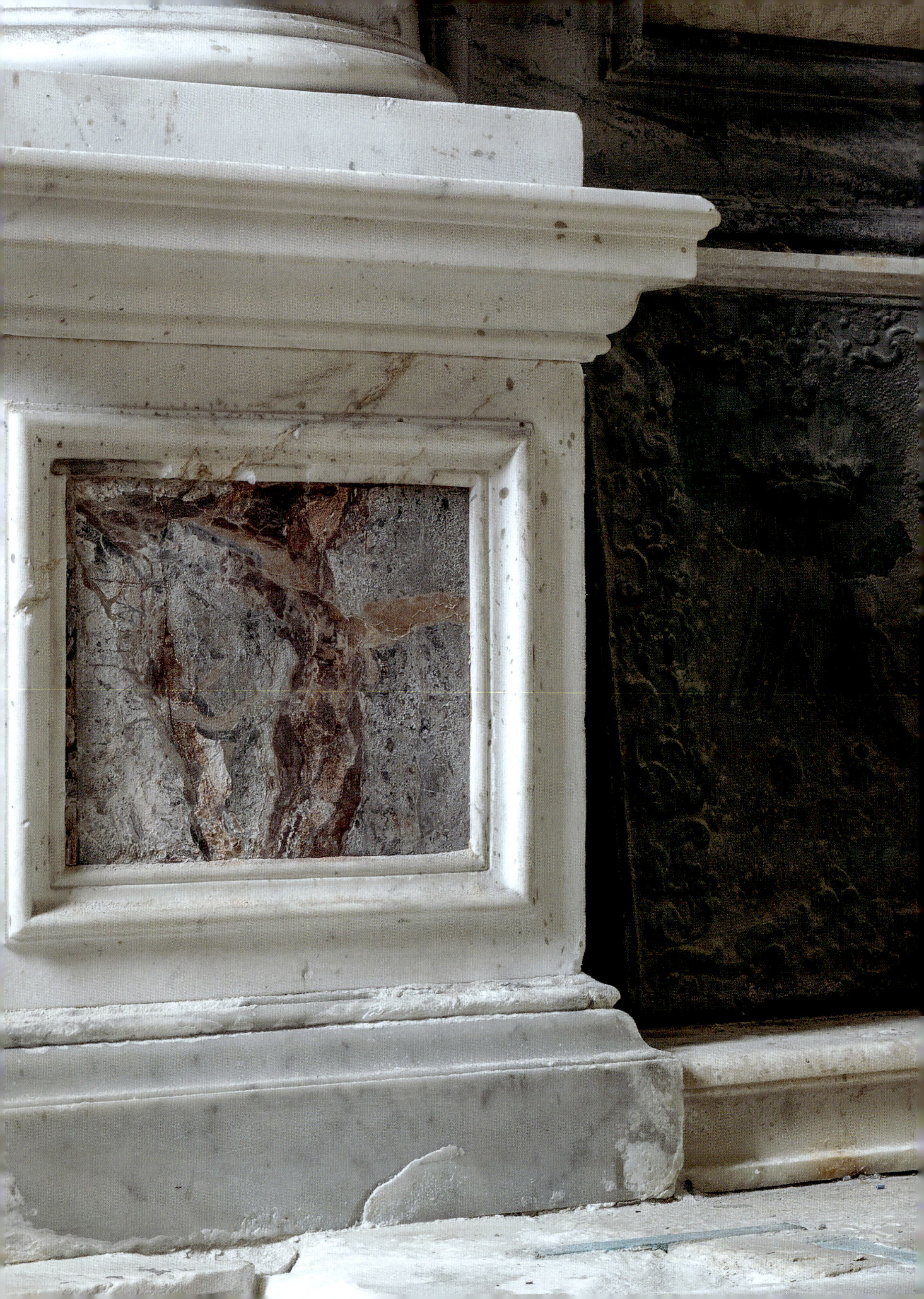

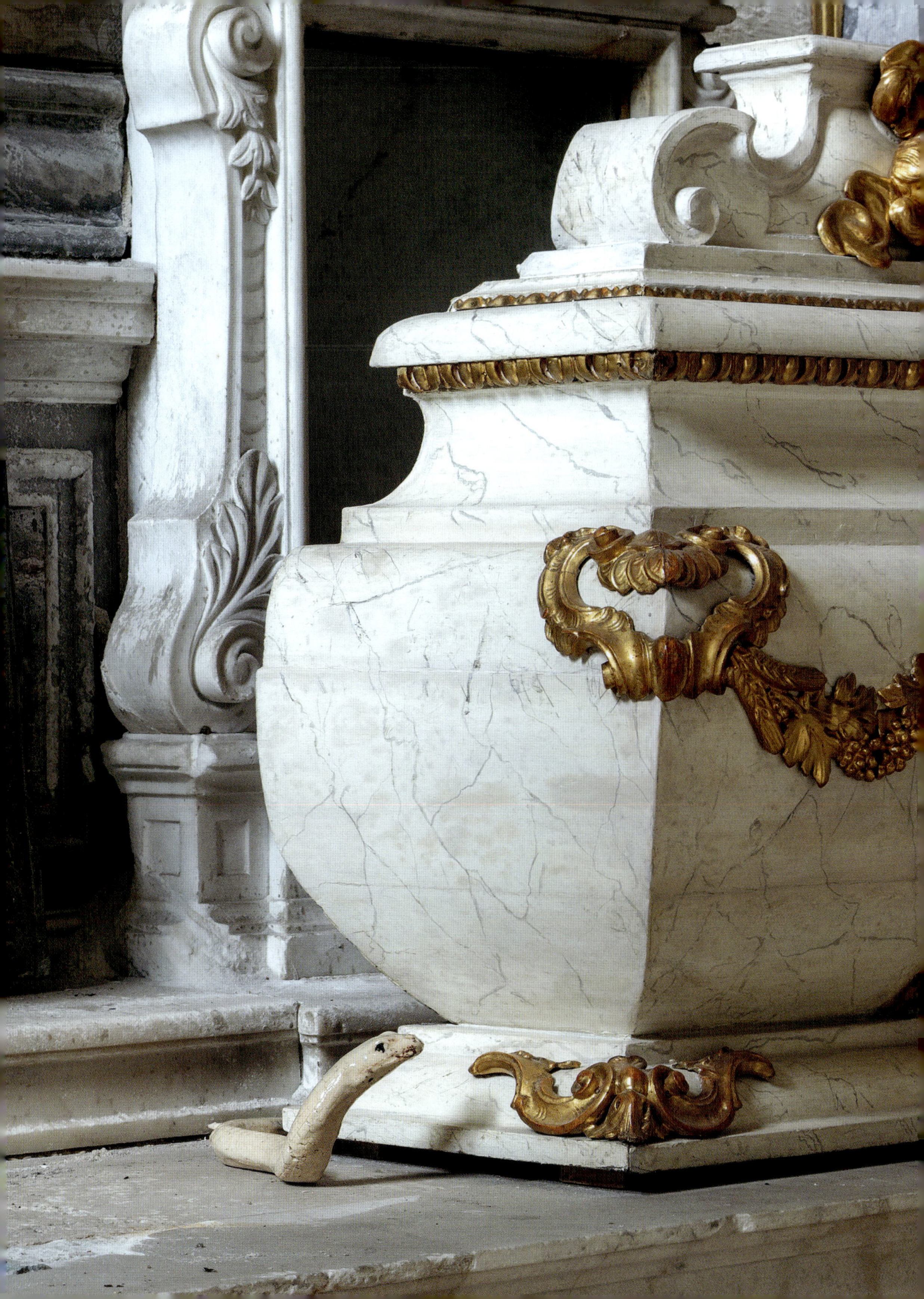

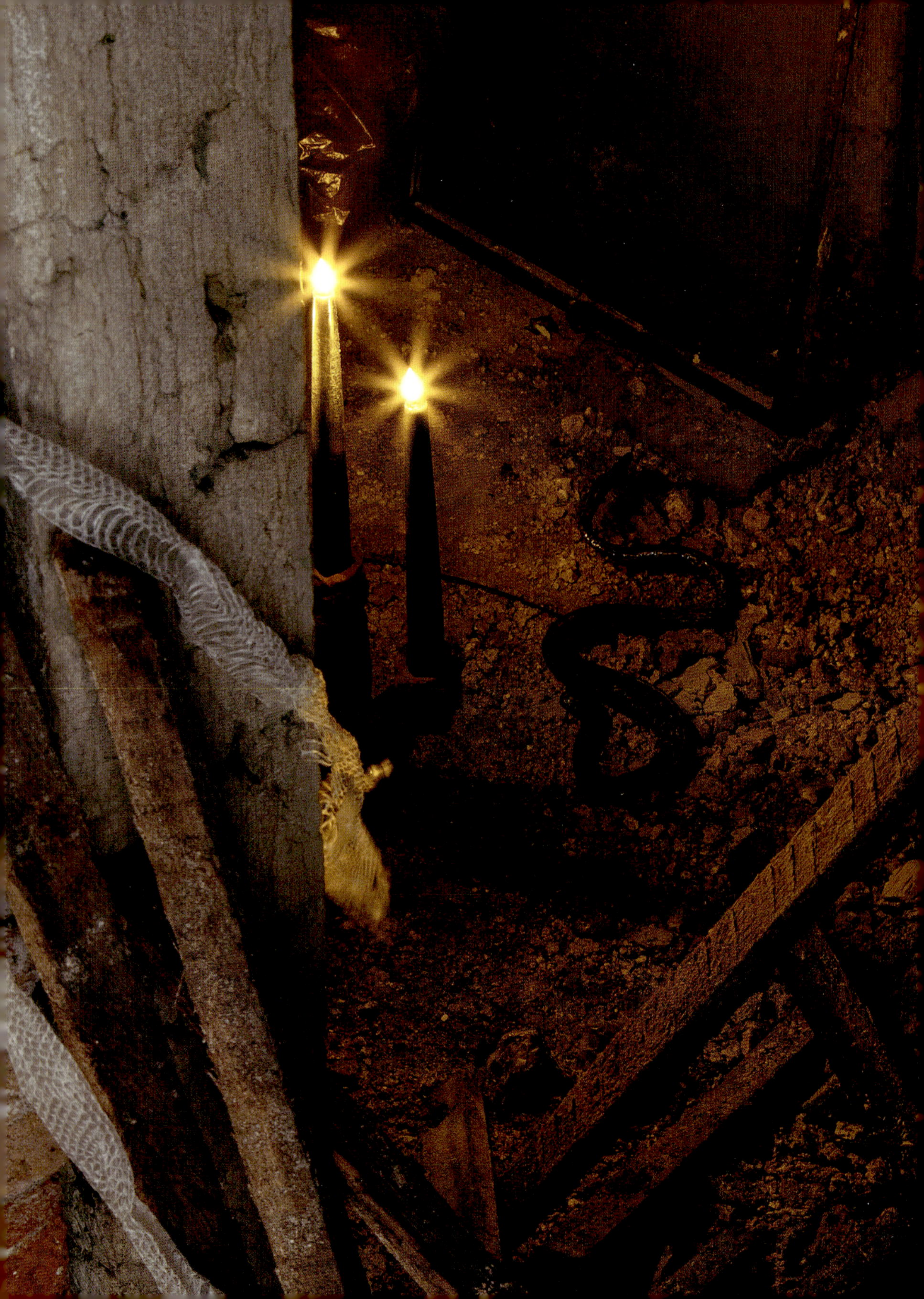

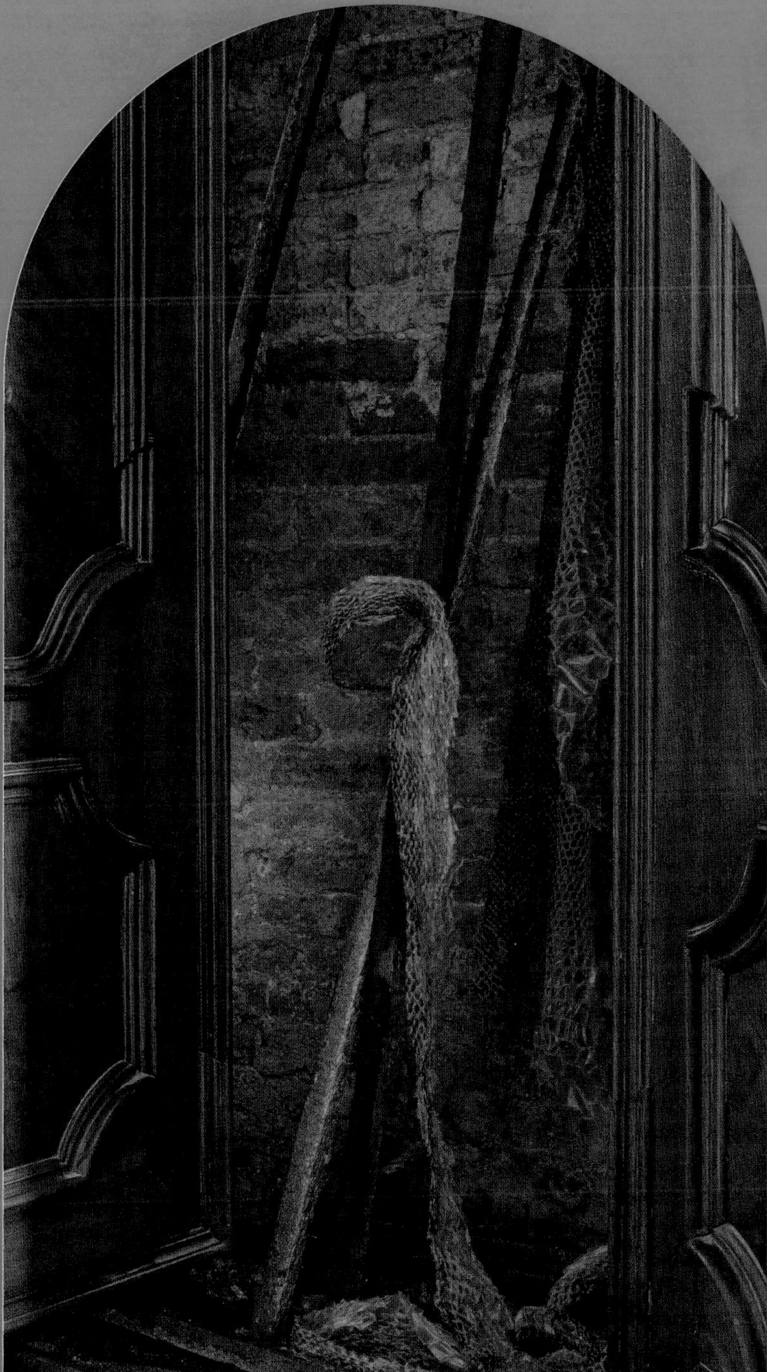

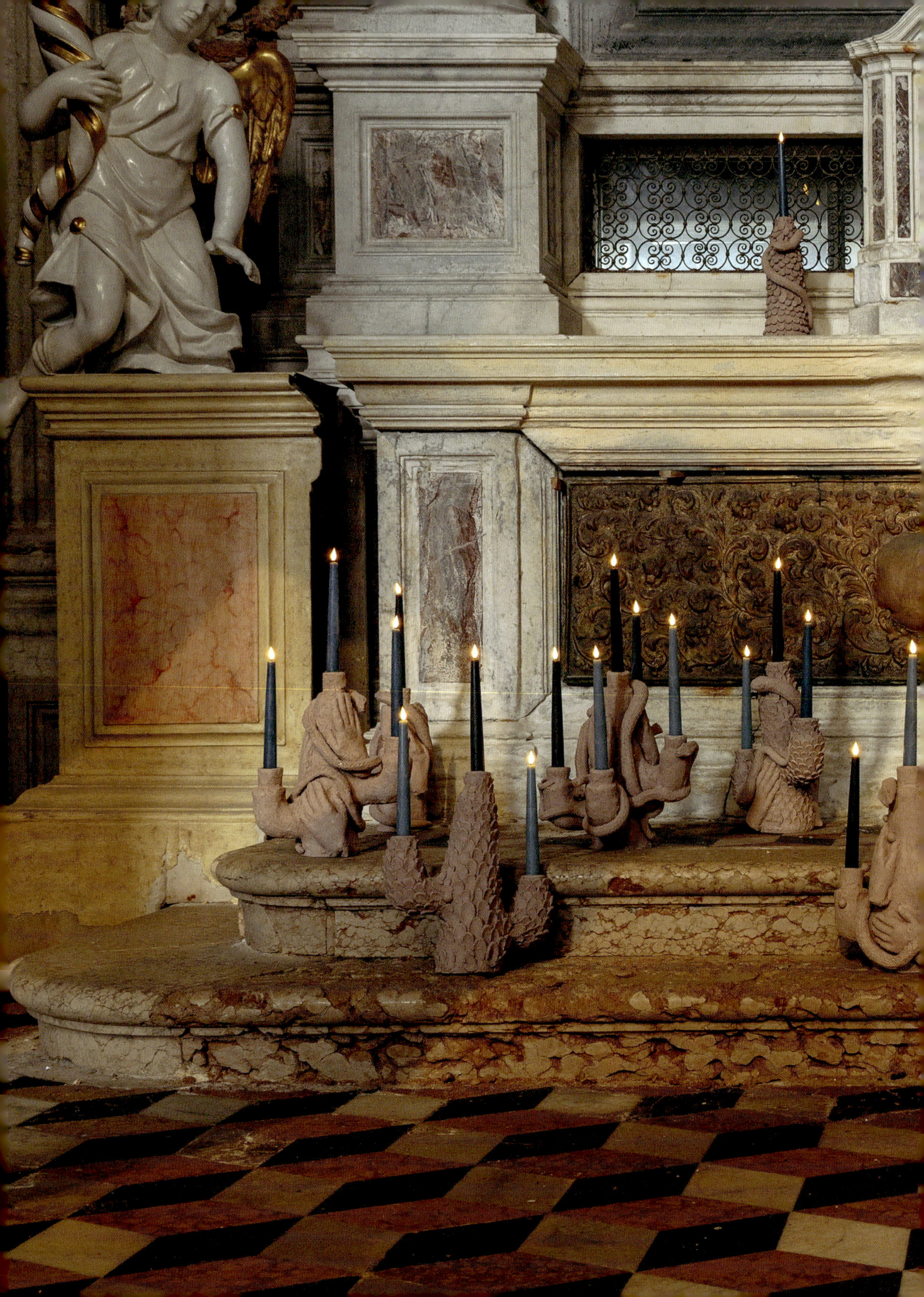

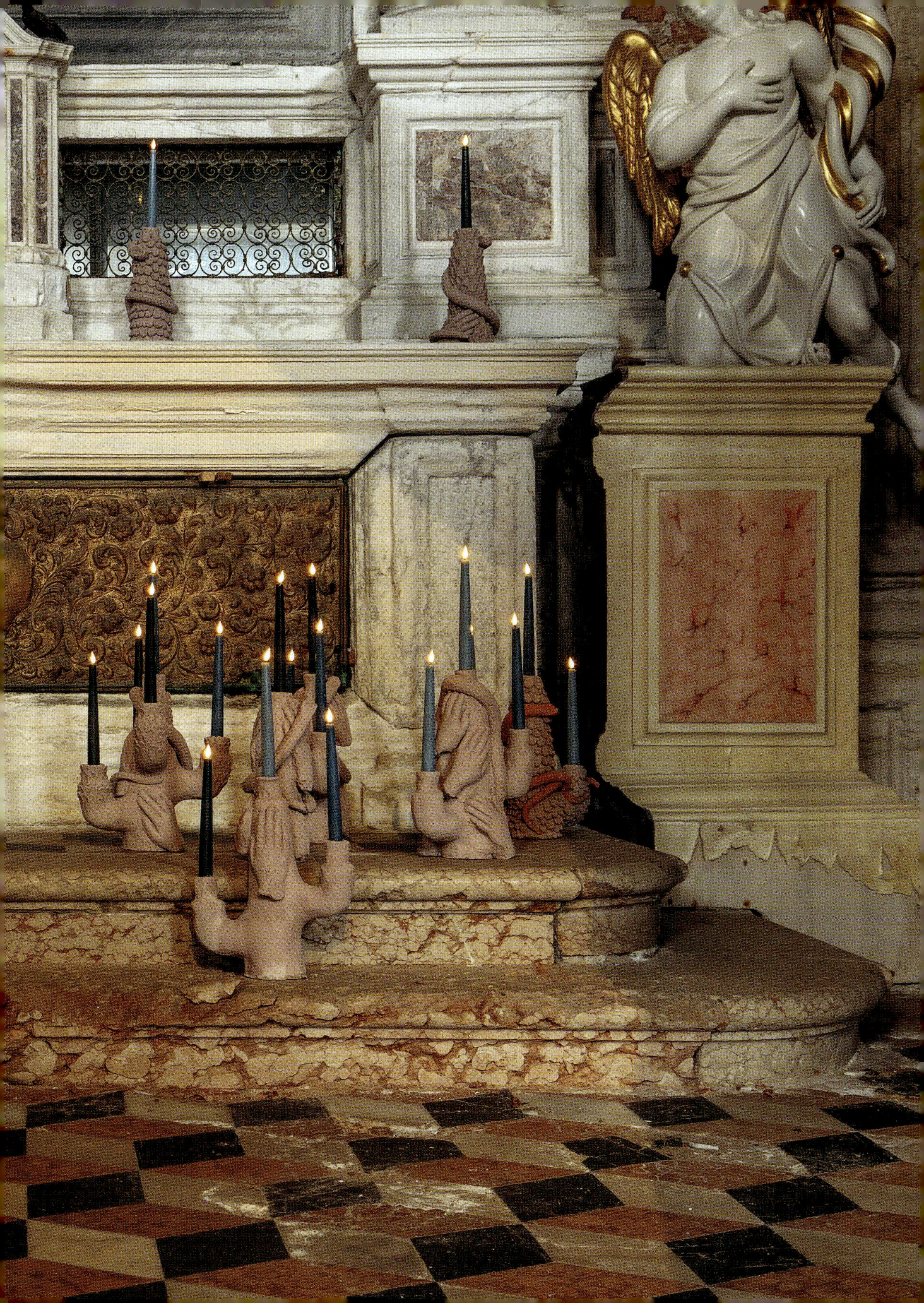

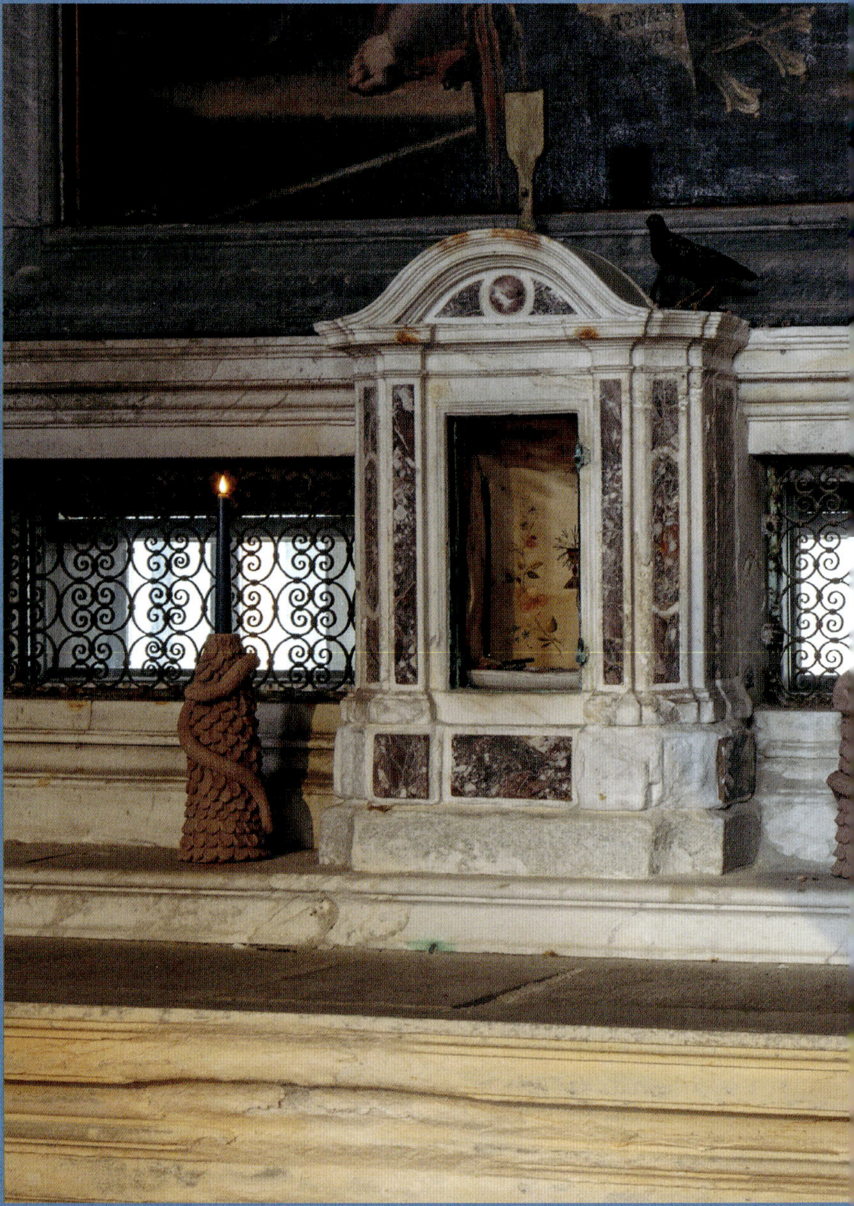

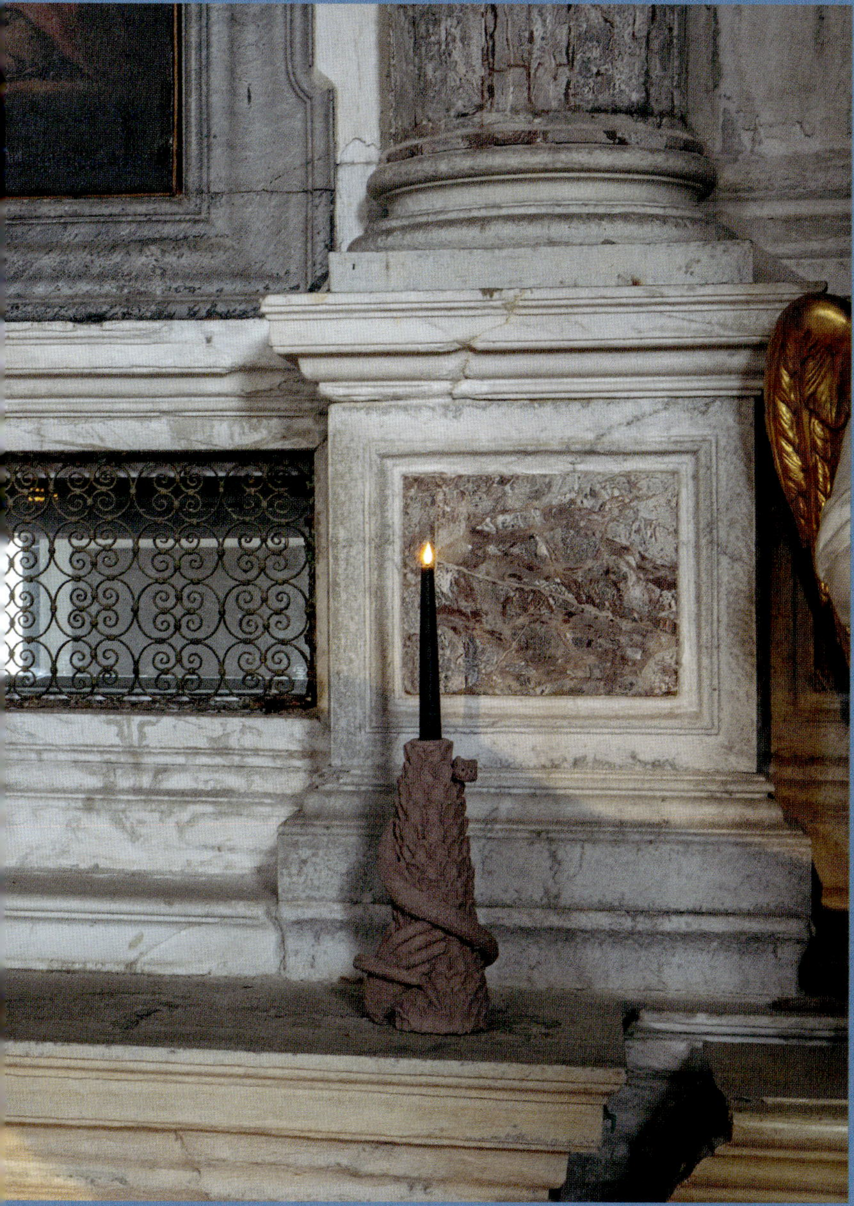

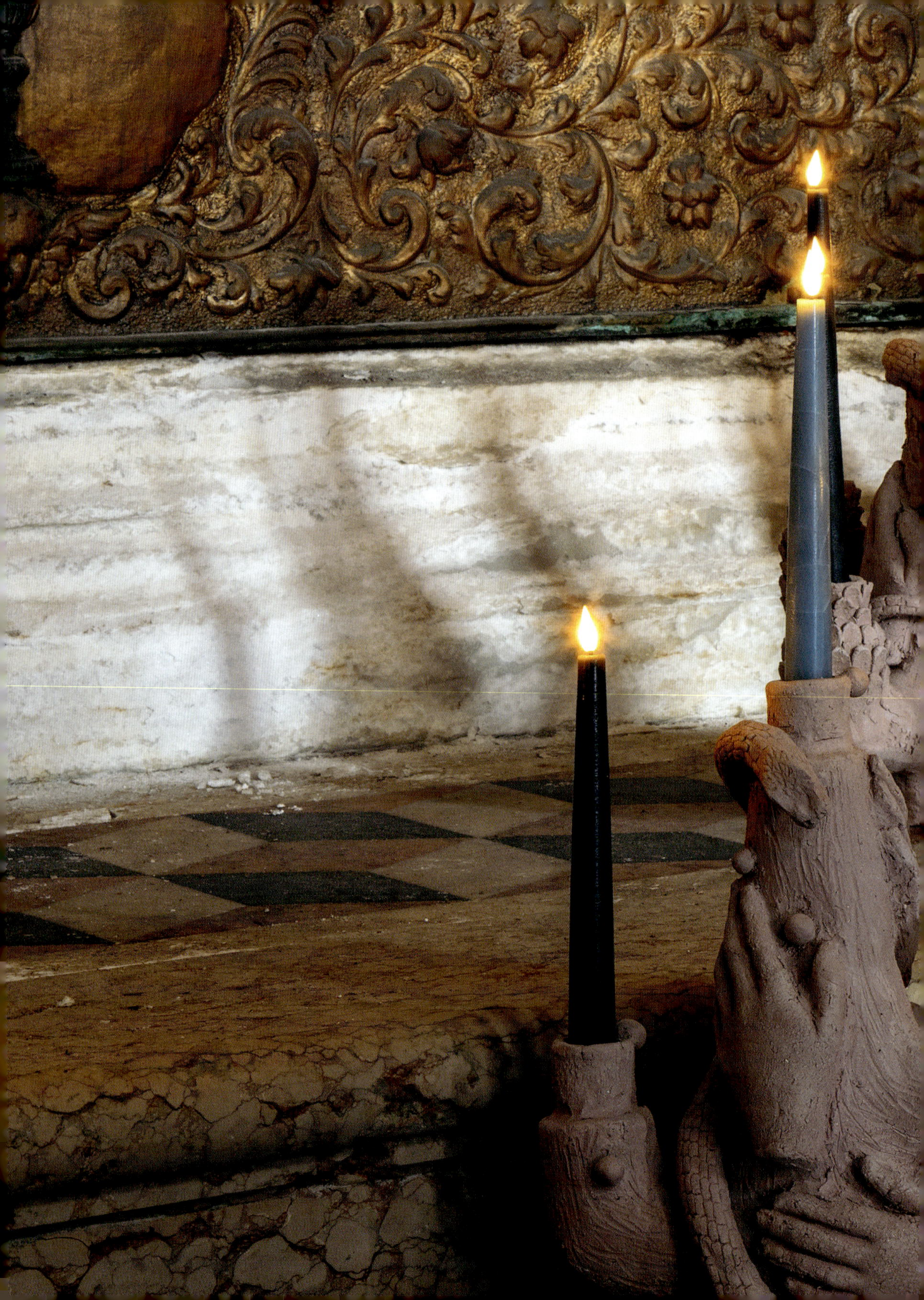

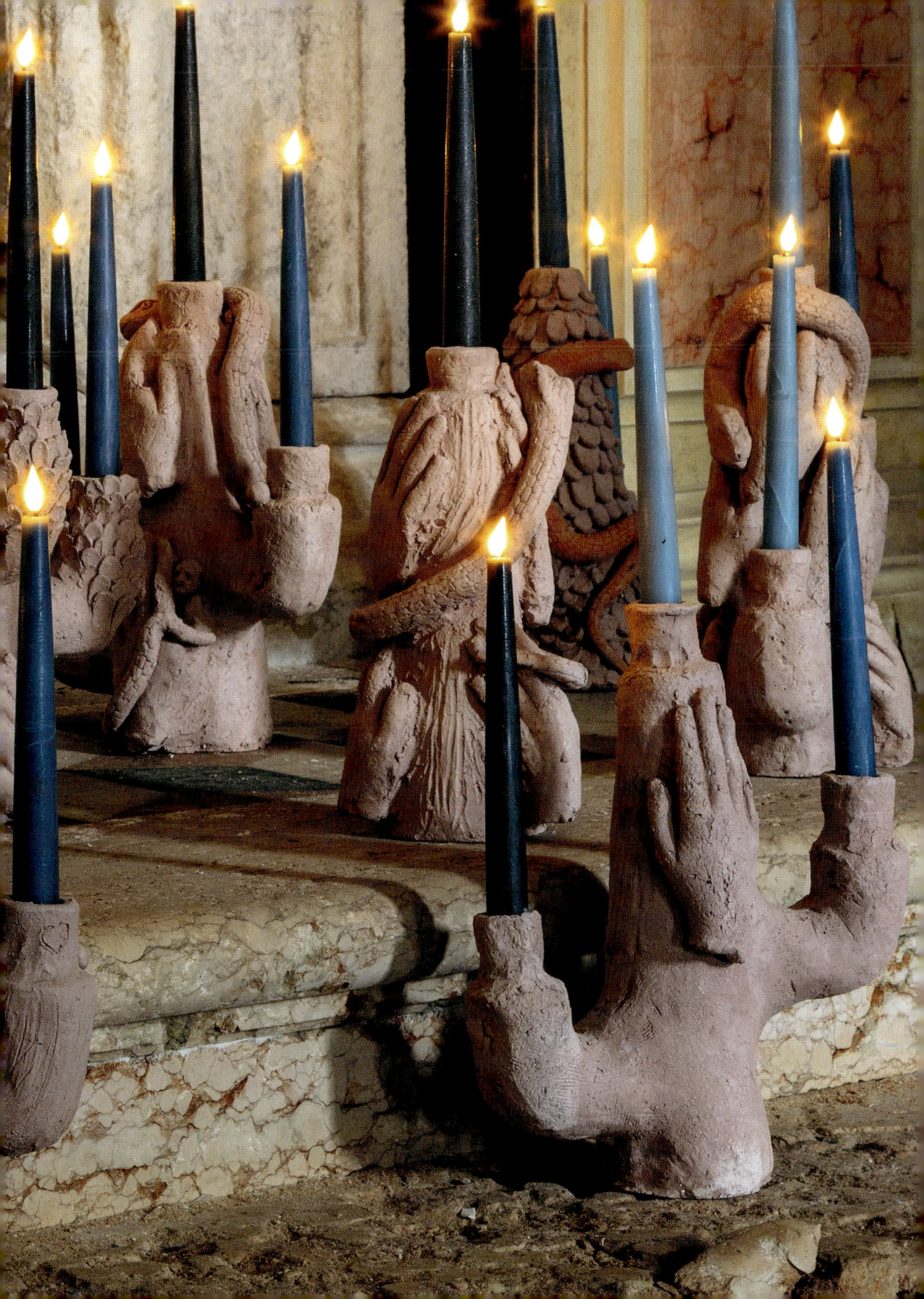

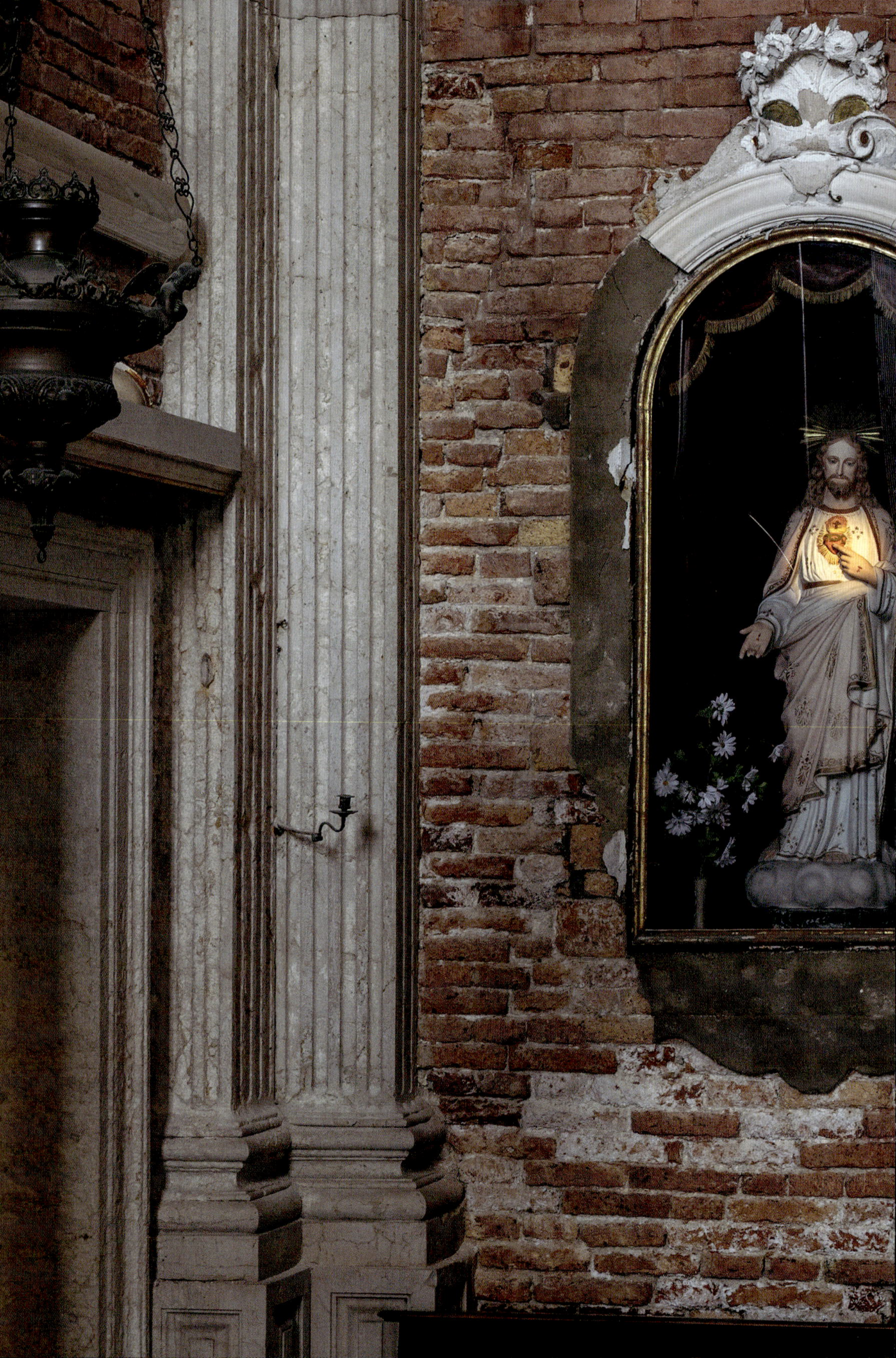

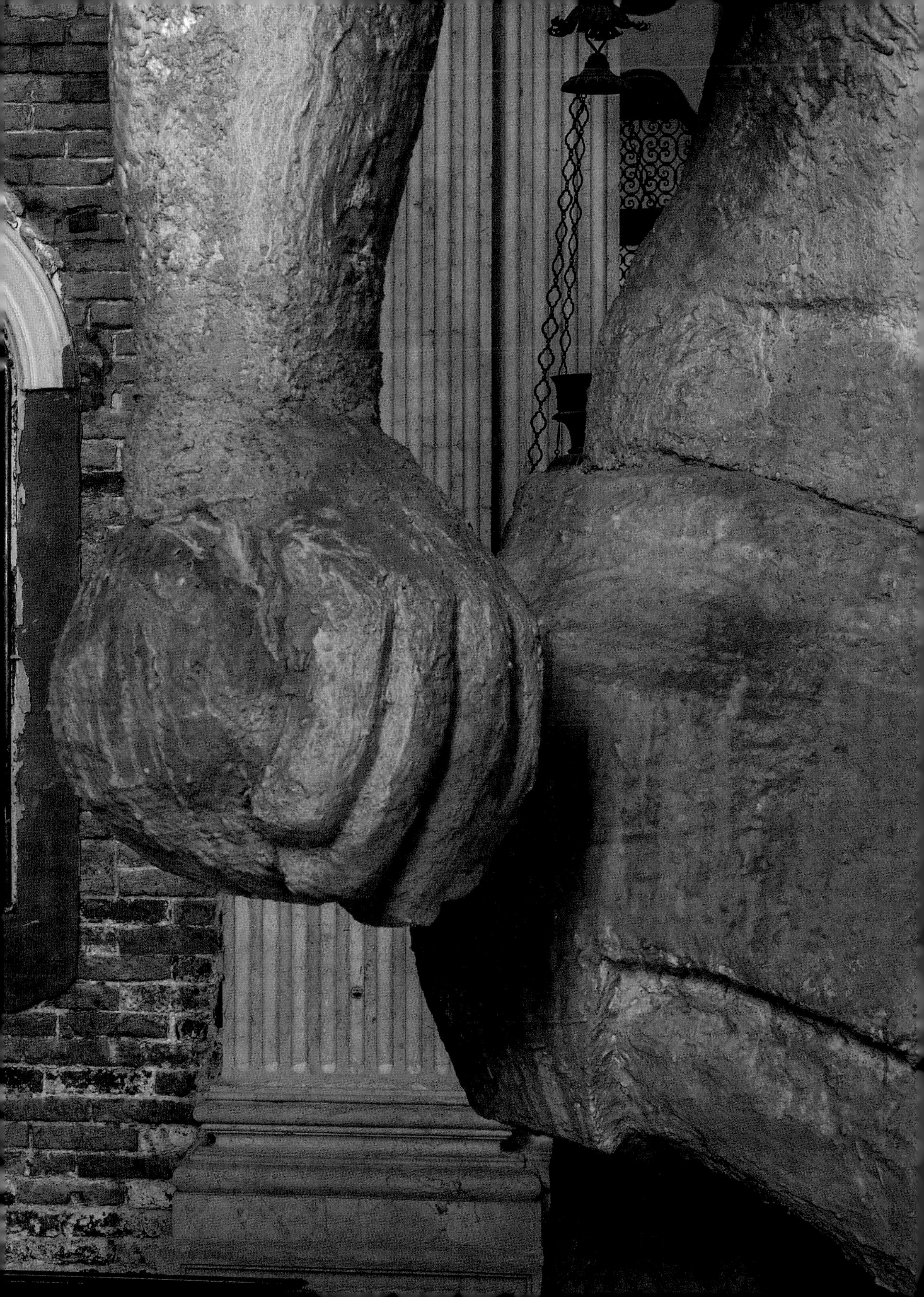

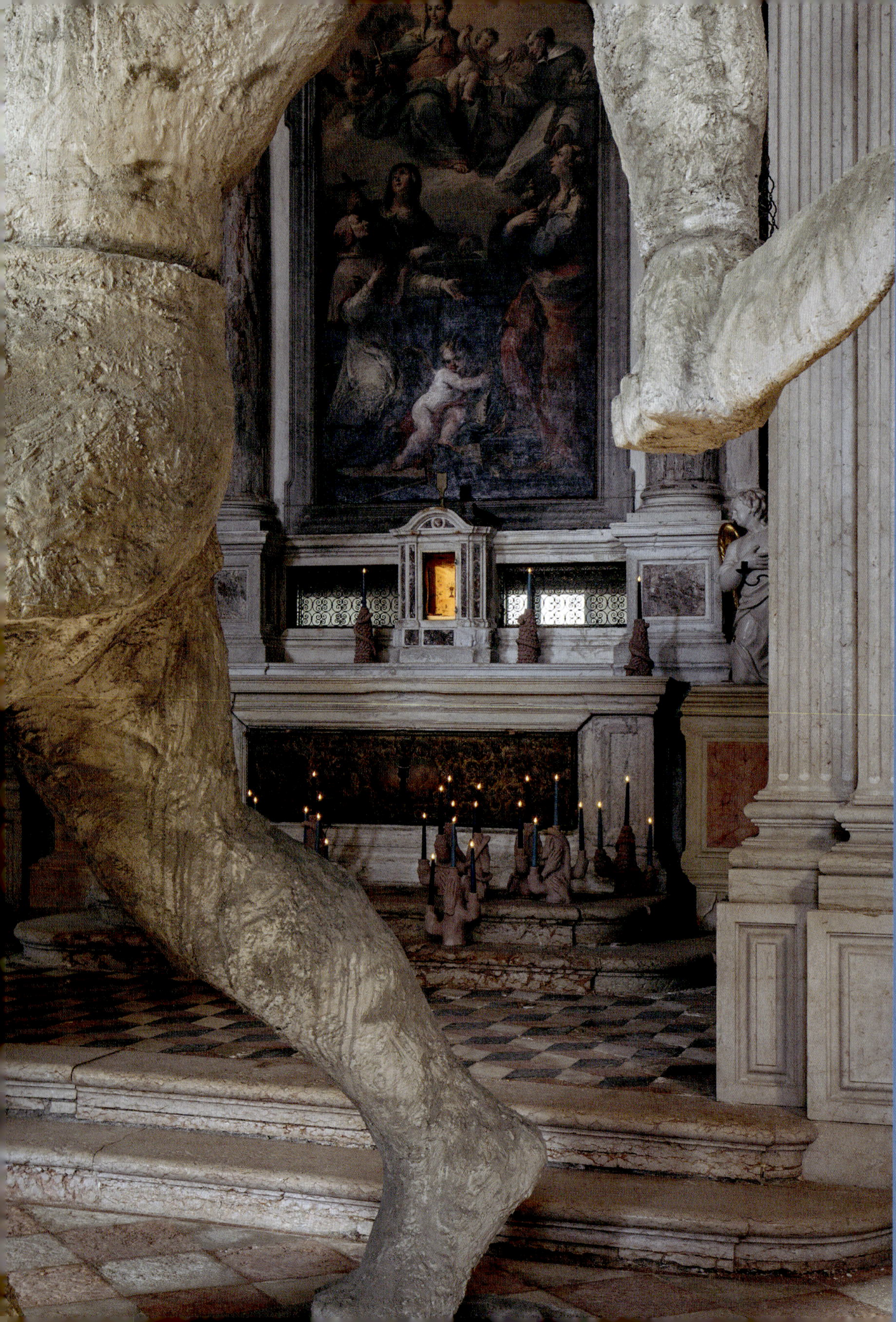

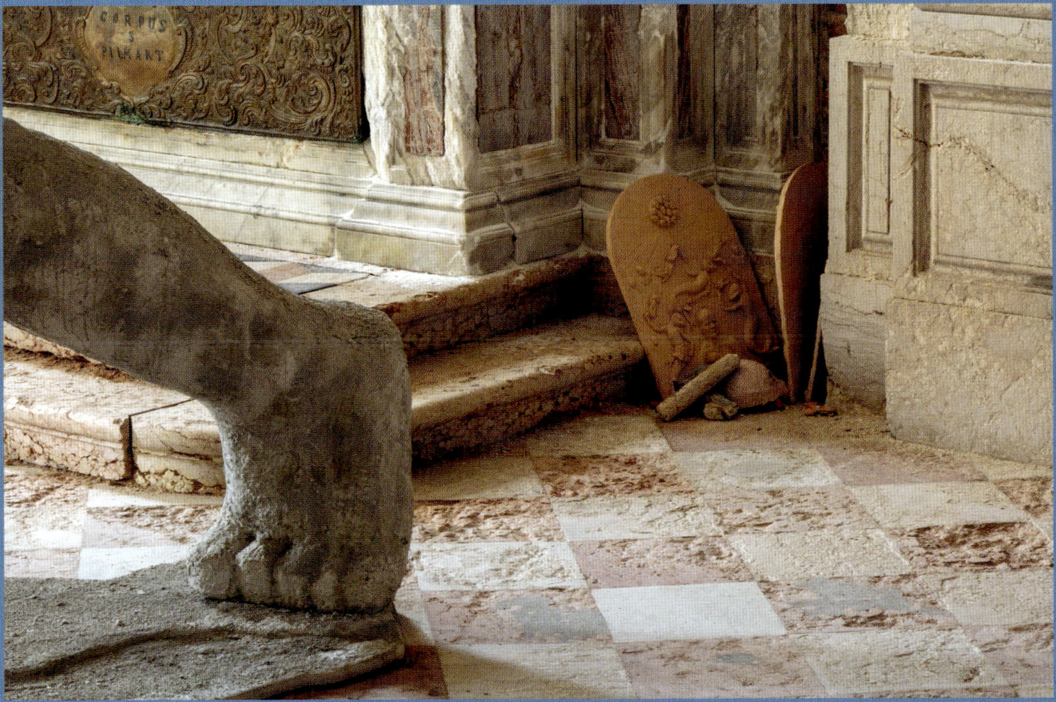
CORPUS
S

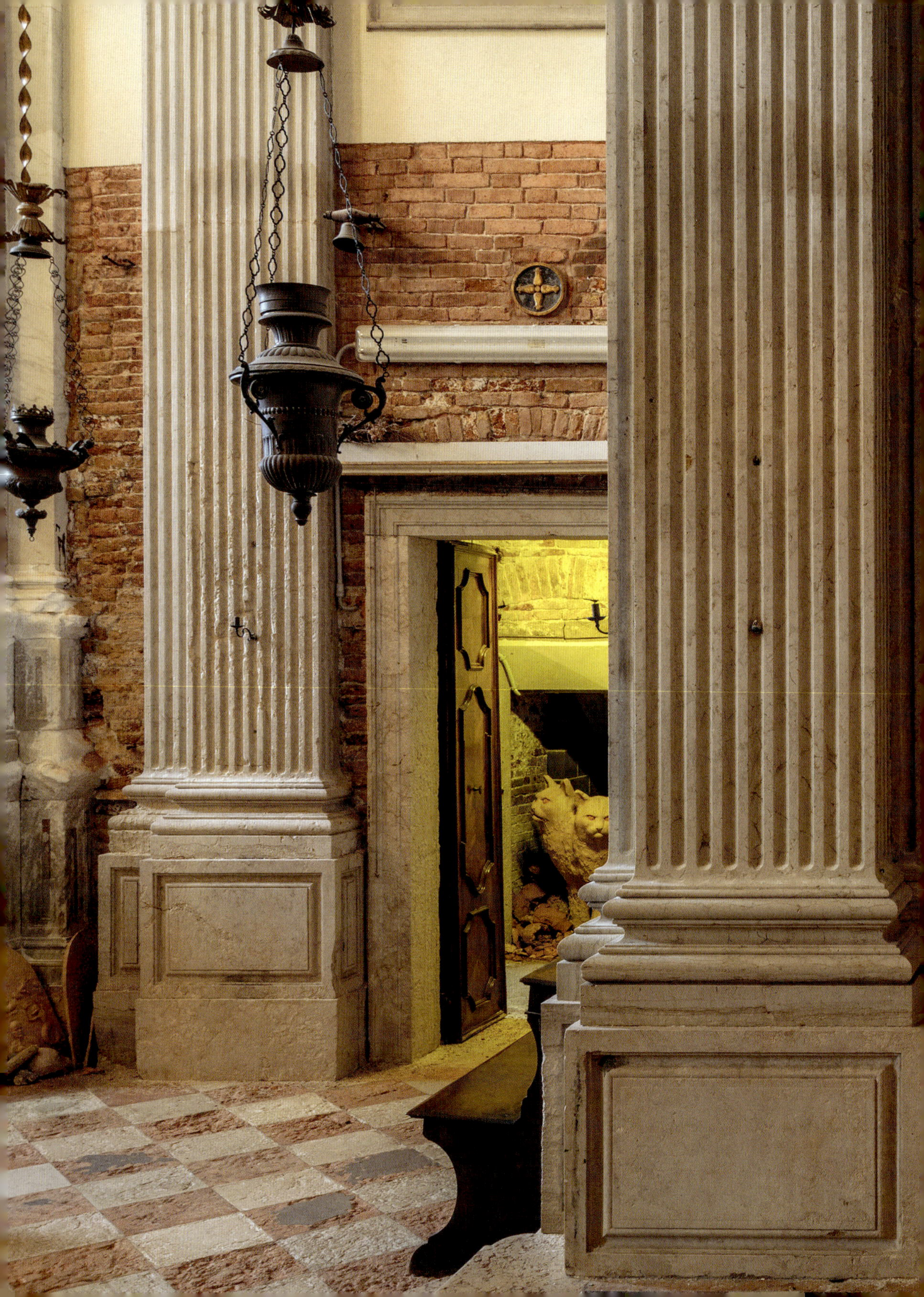

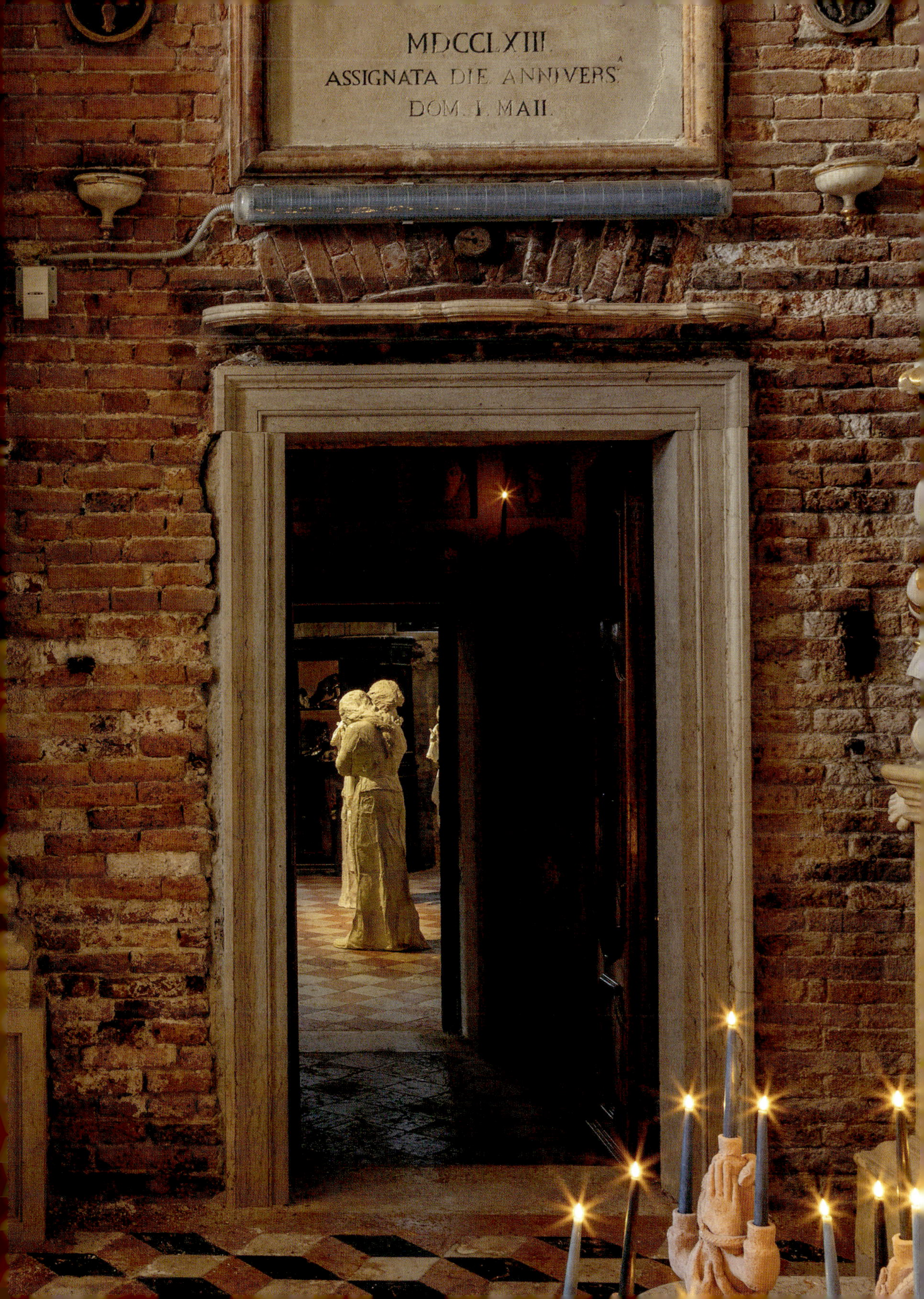
MDCCLXIII
ASSIGNATA DIE ANNIVERS
DOM. I. MAII

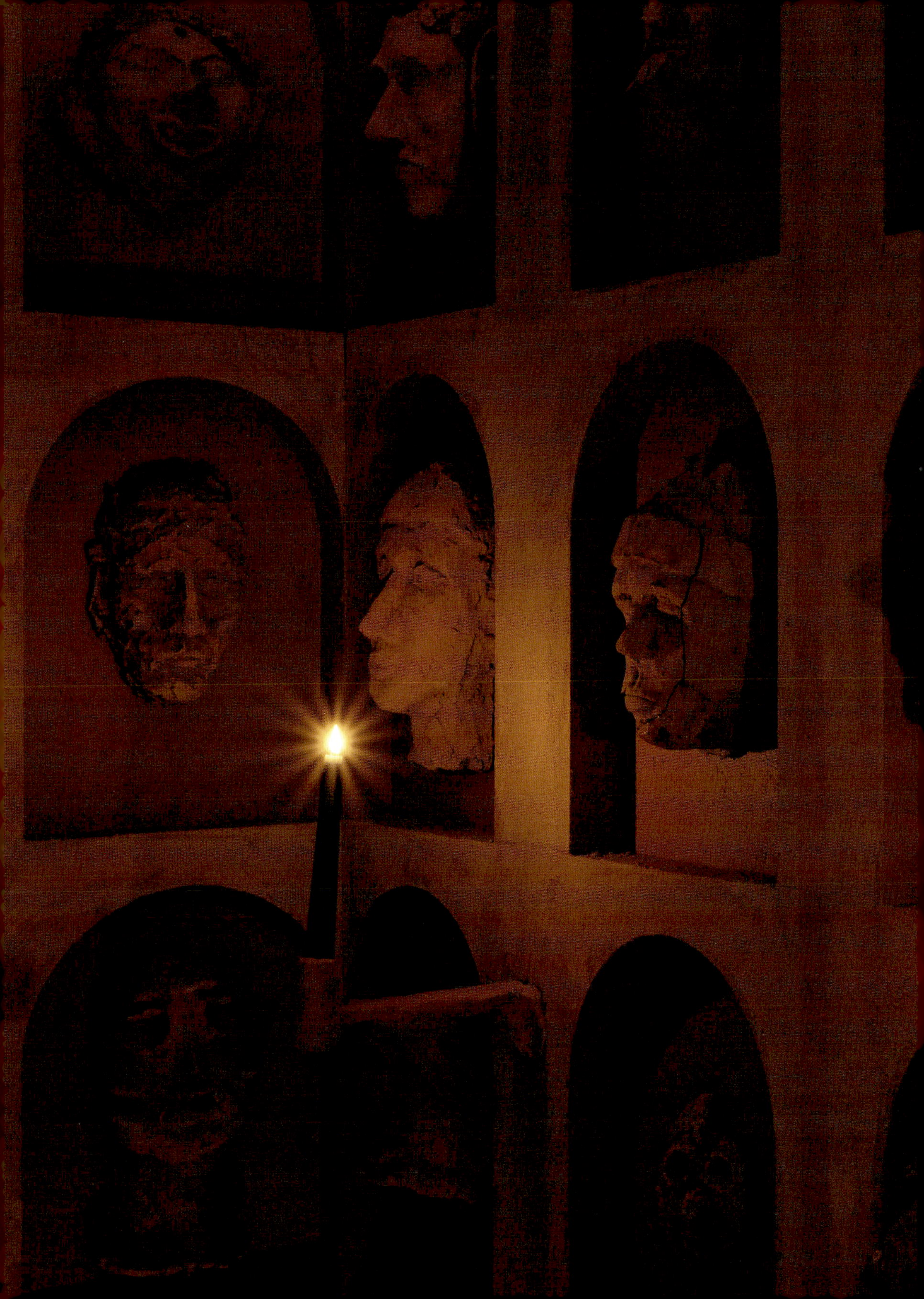

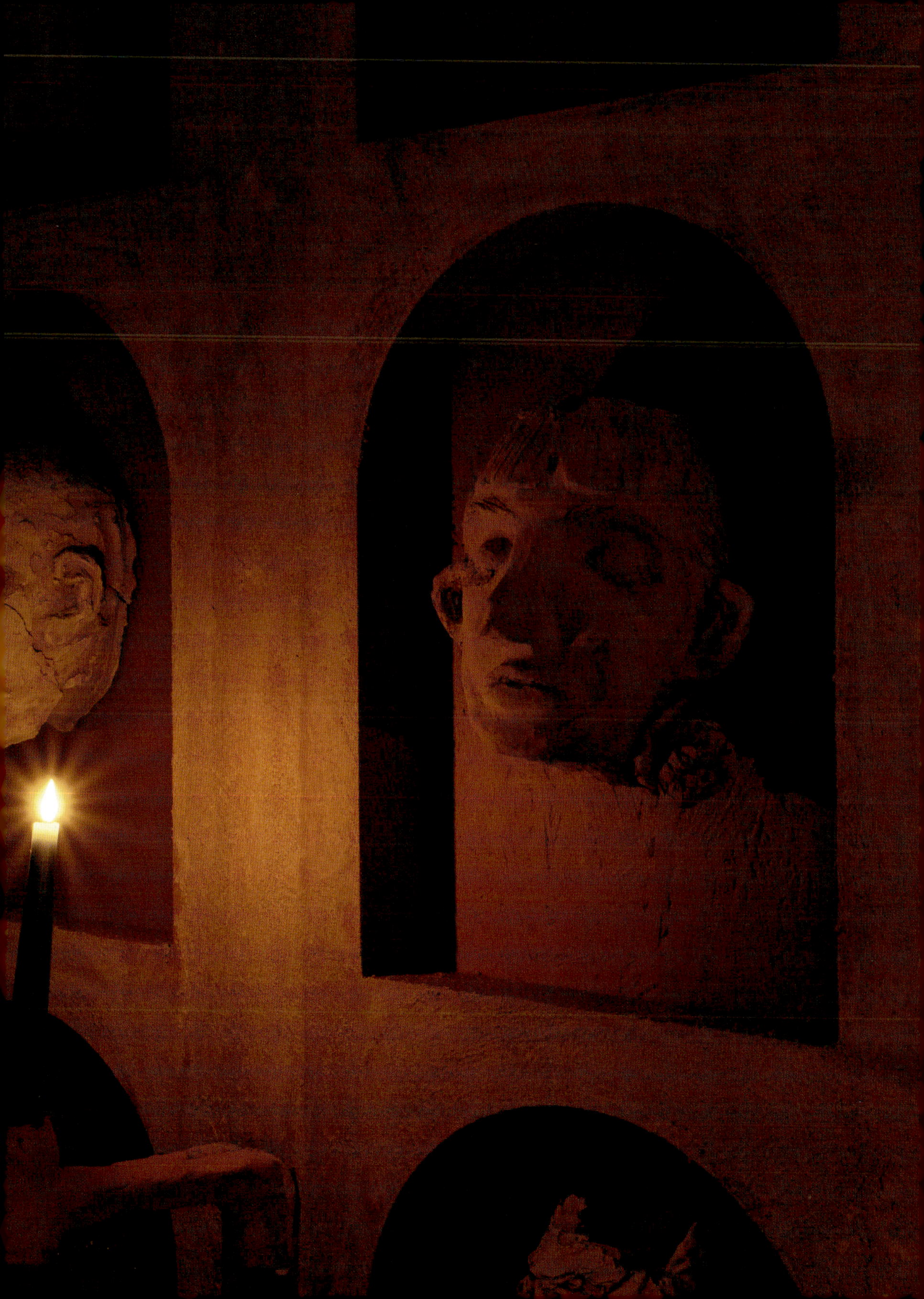

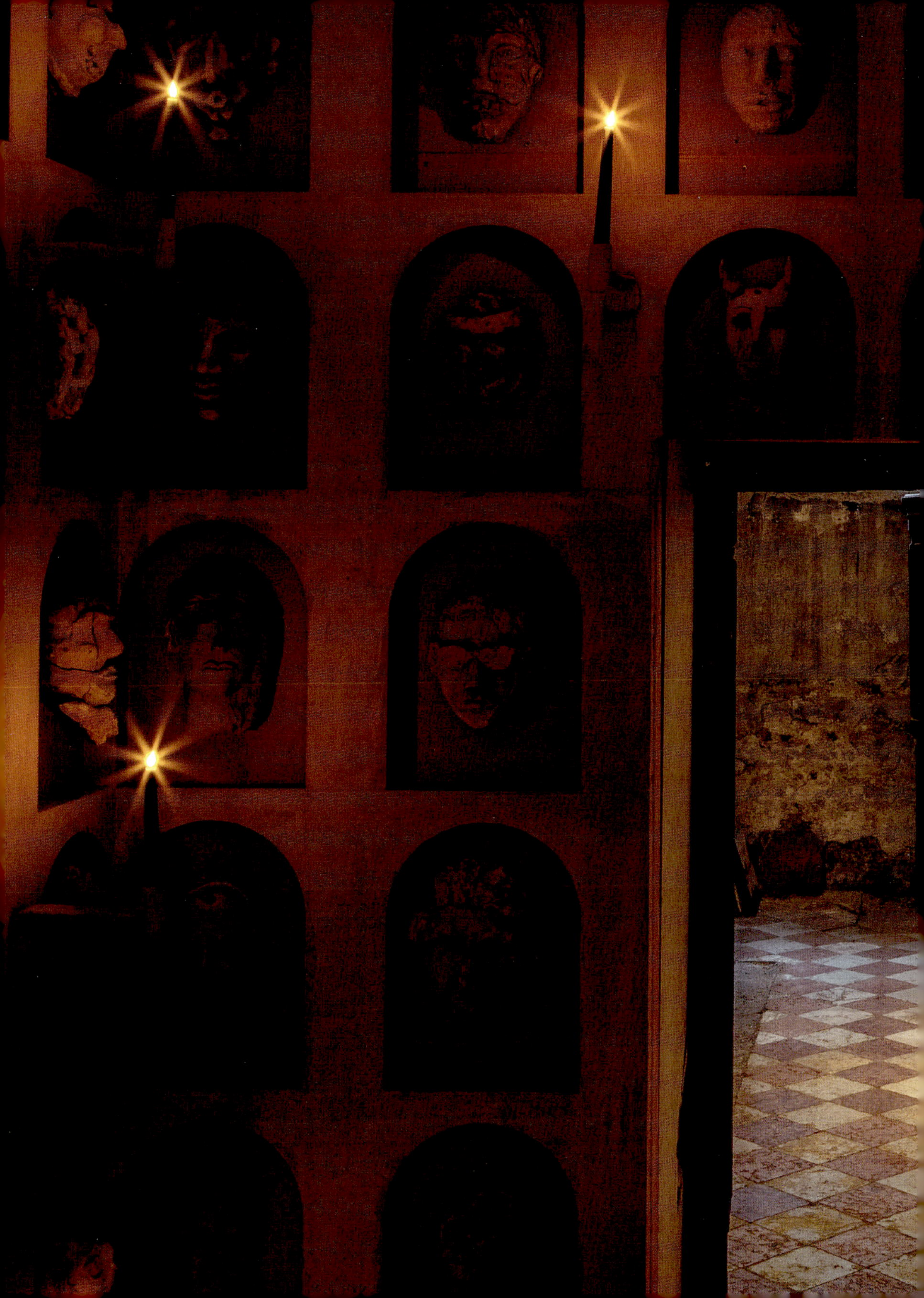

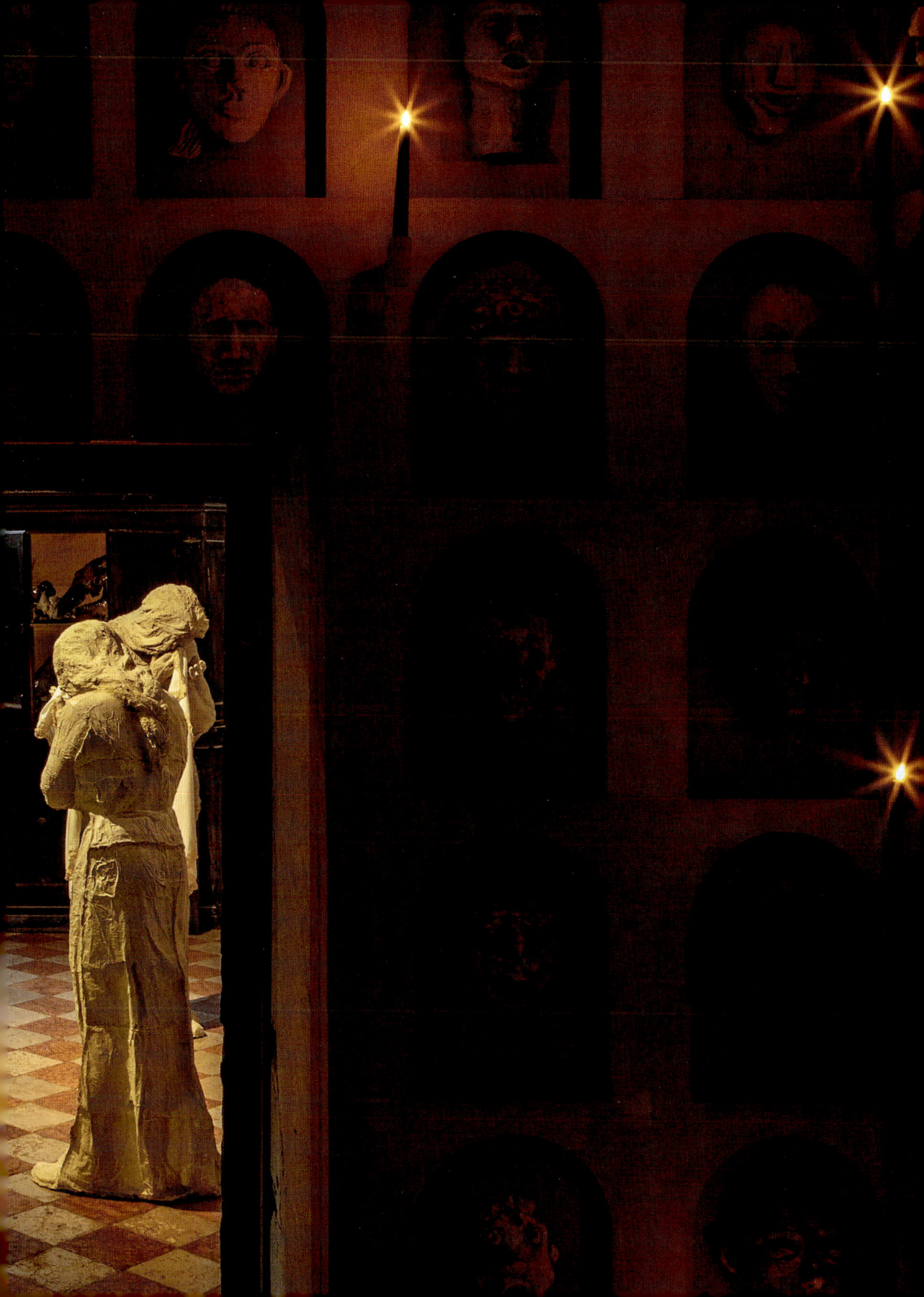

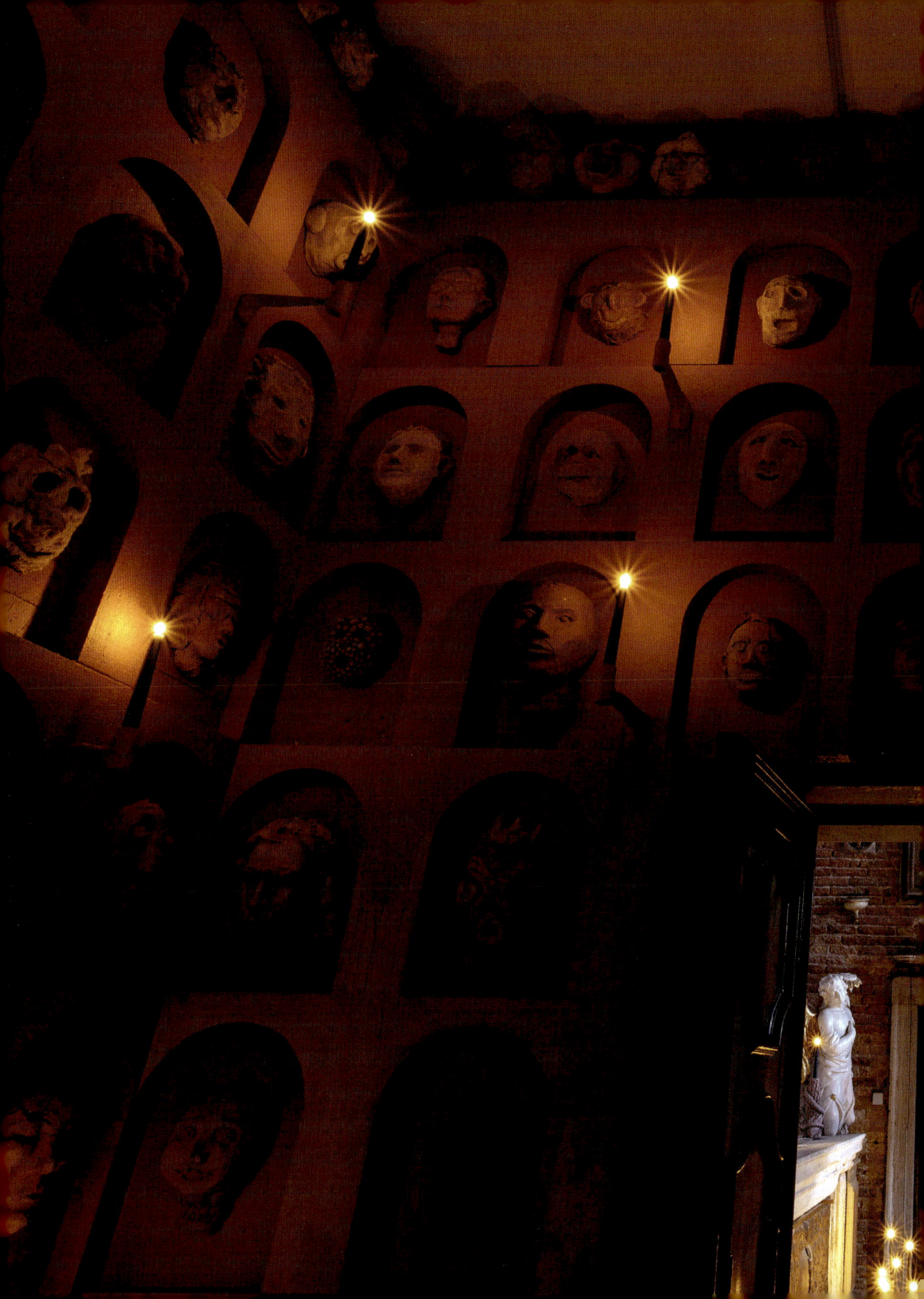

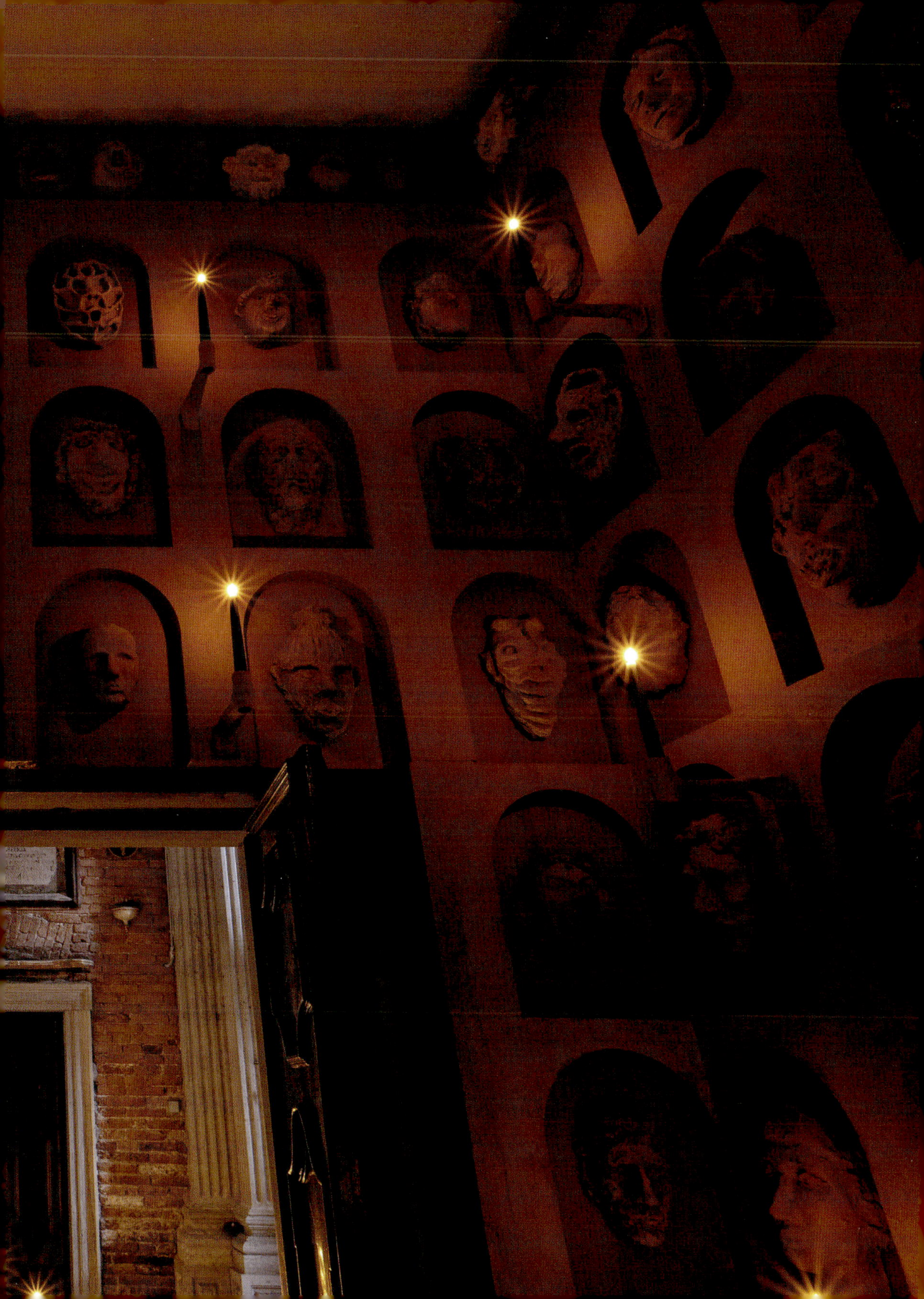

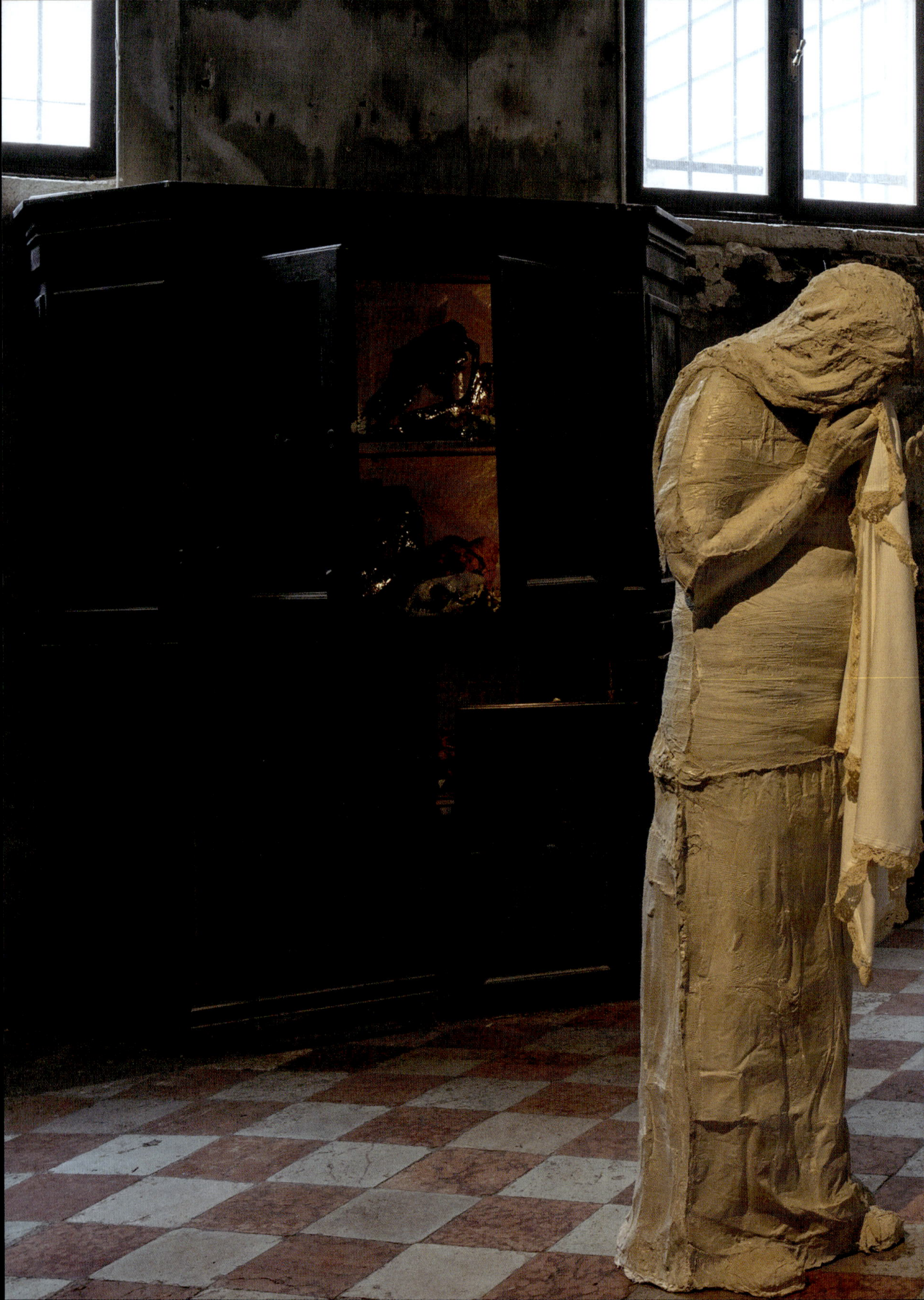

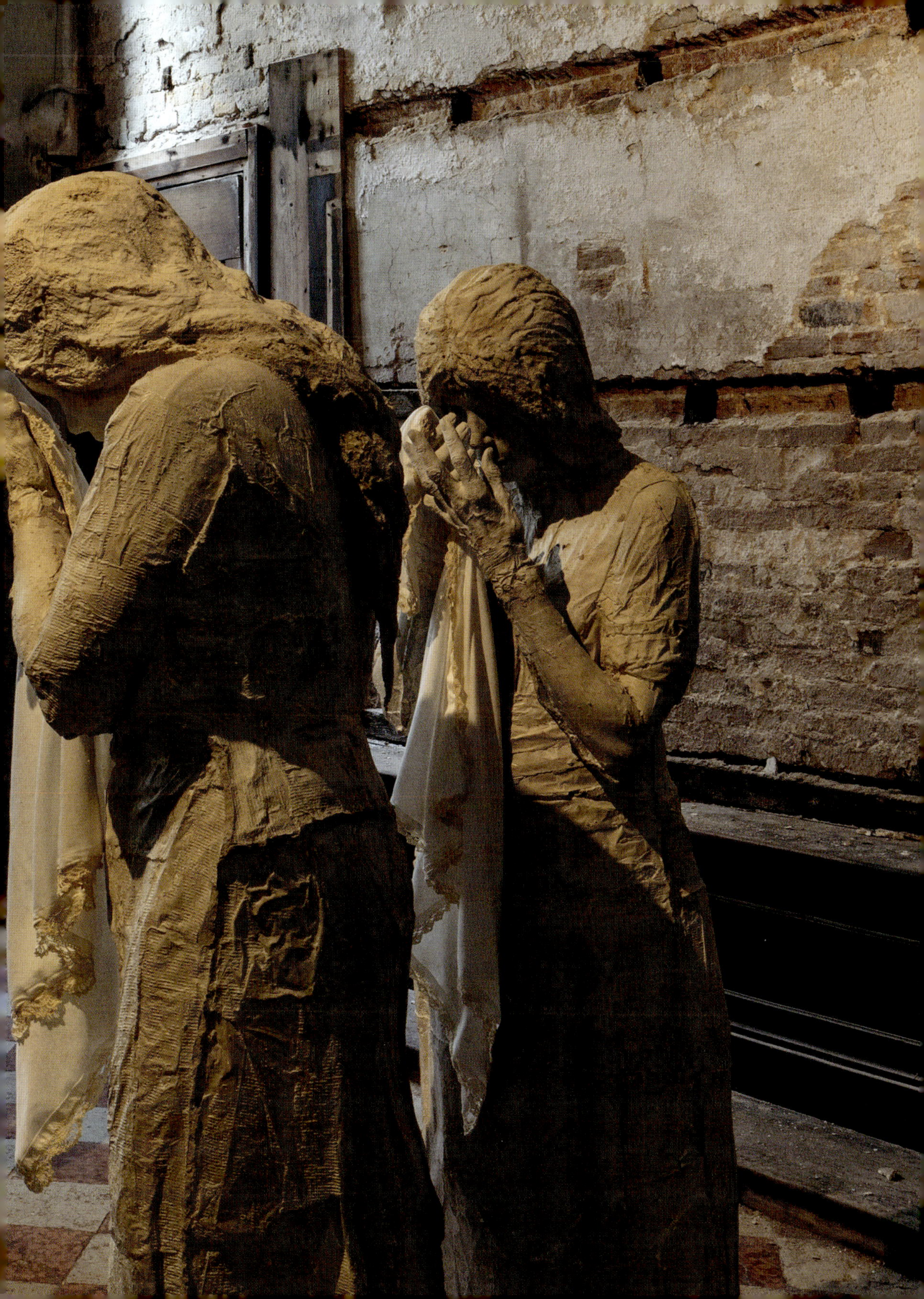

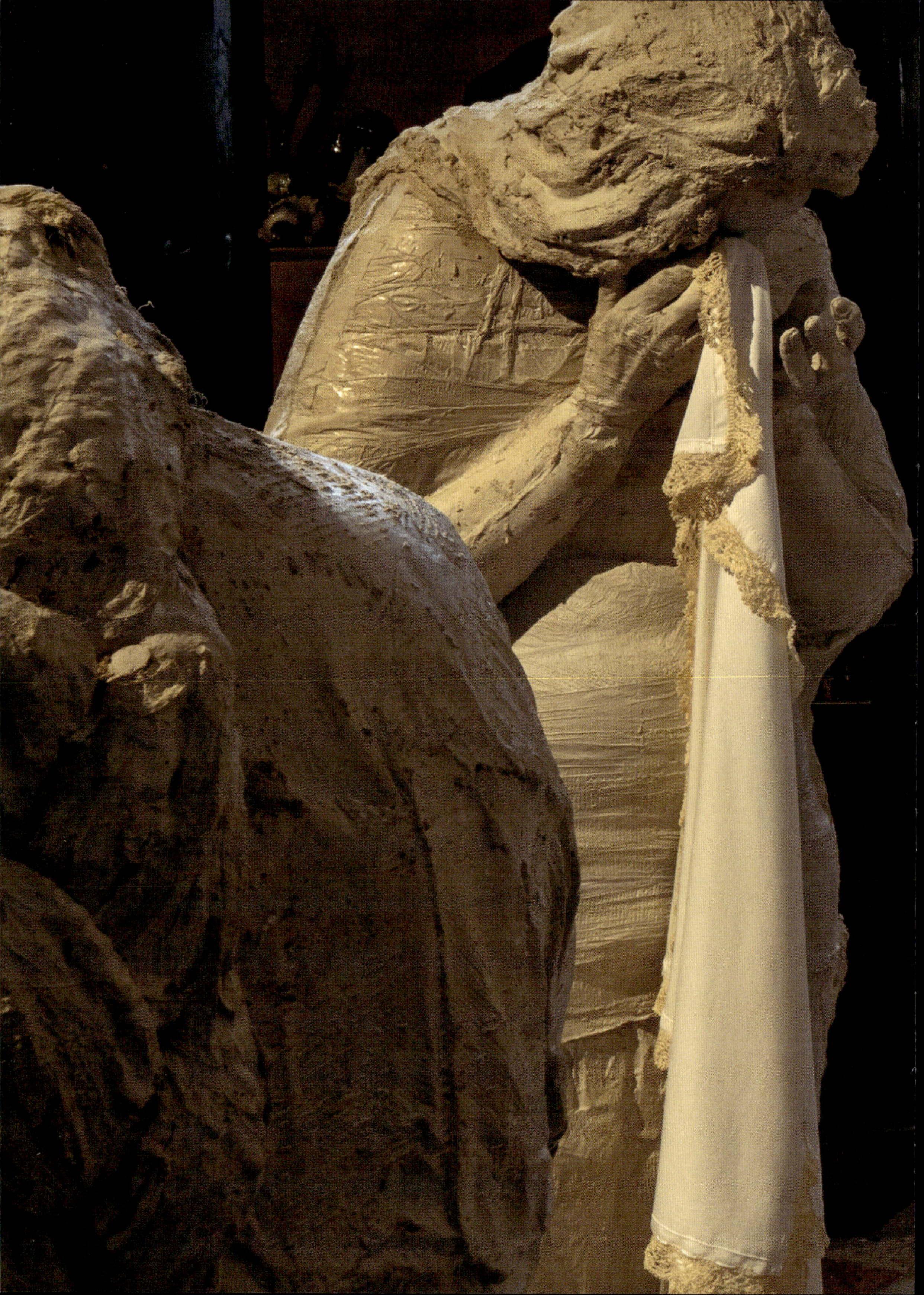

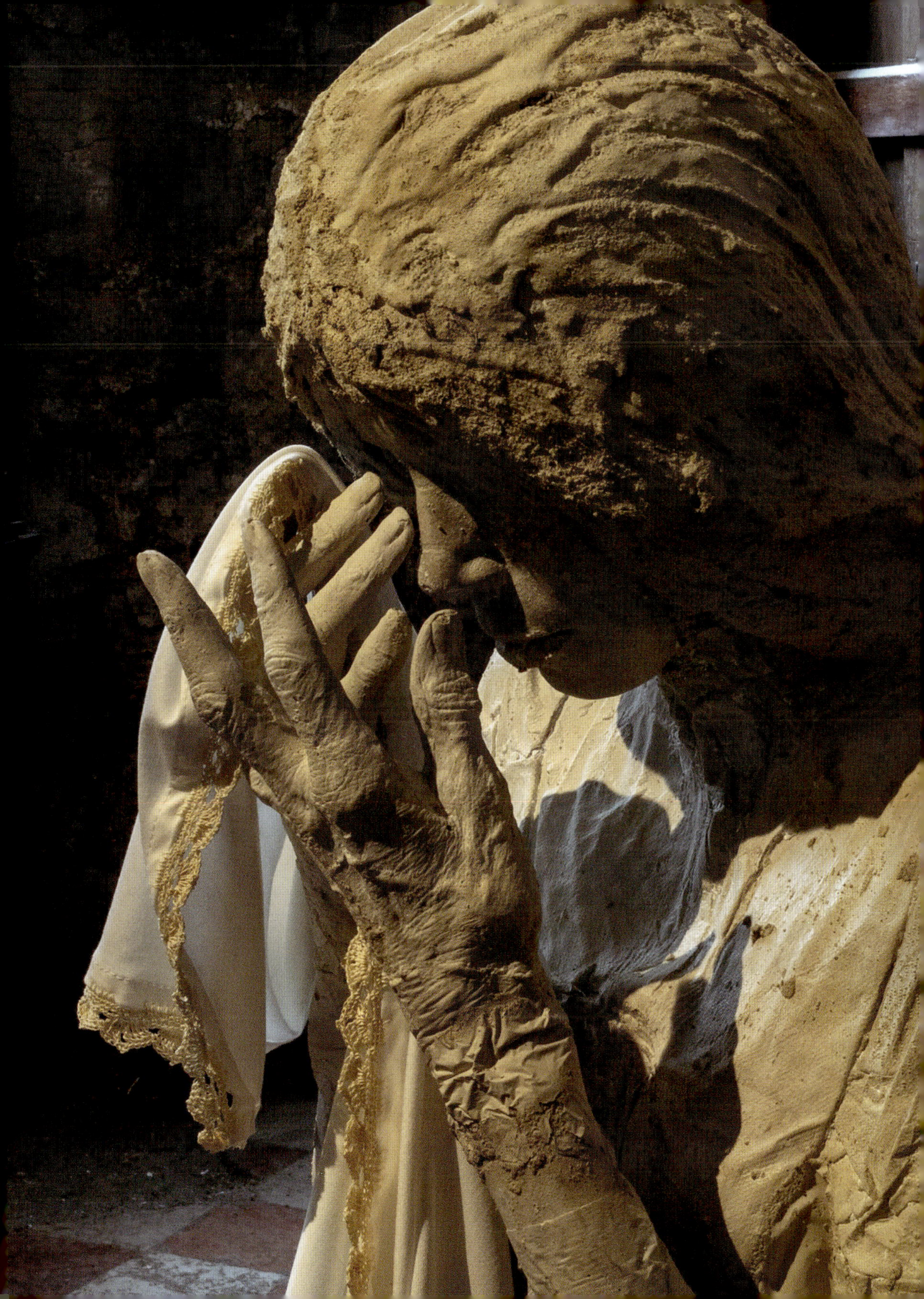

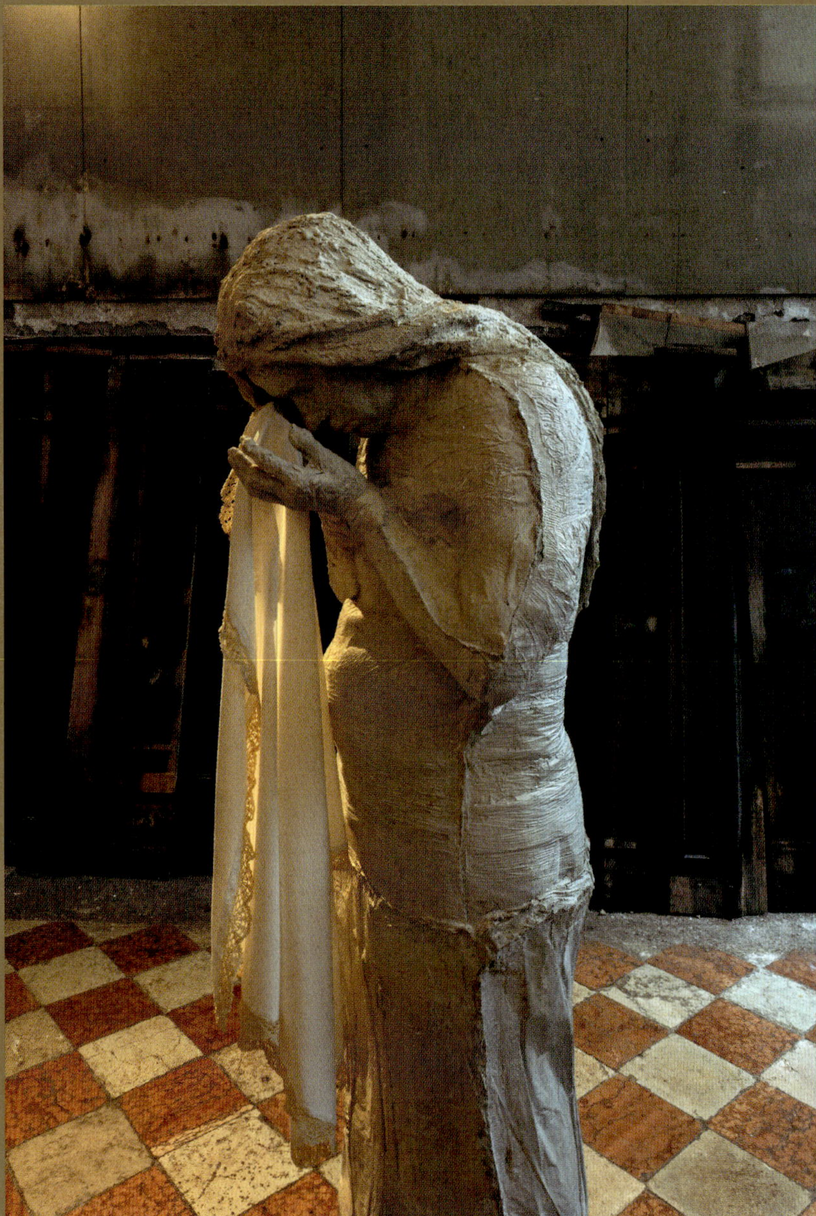

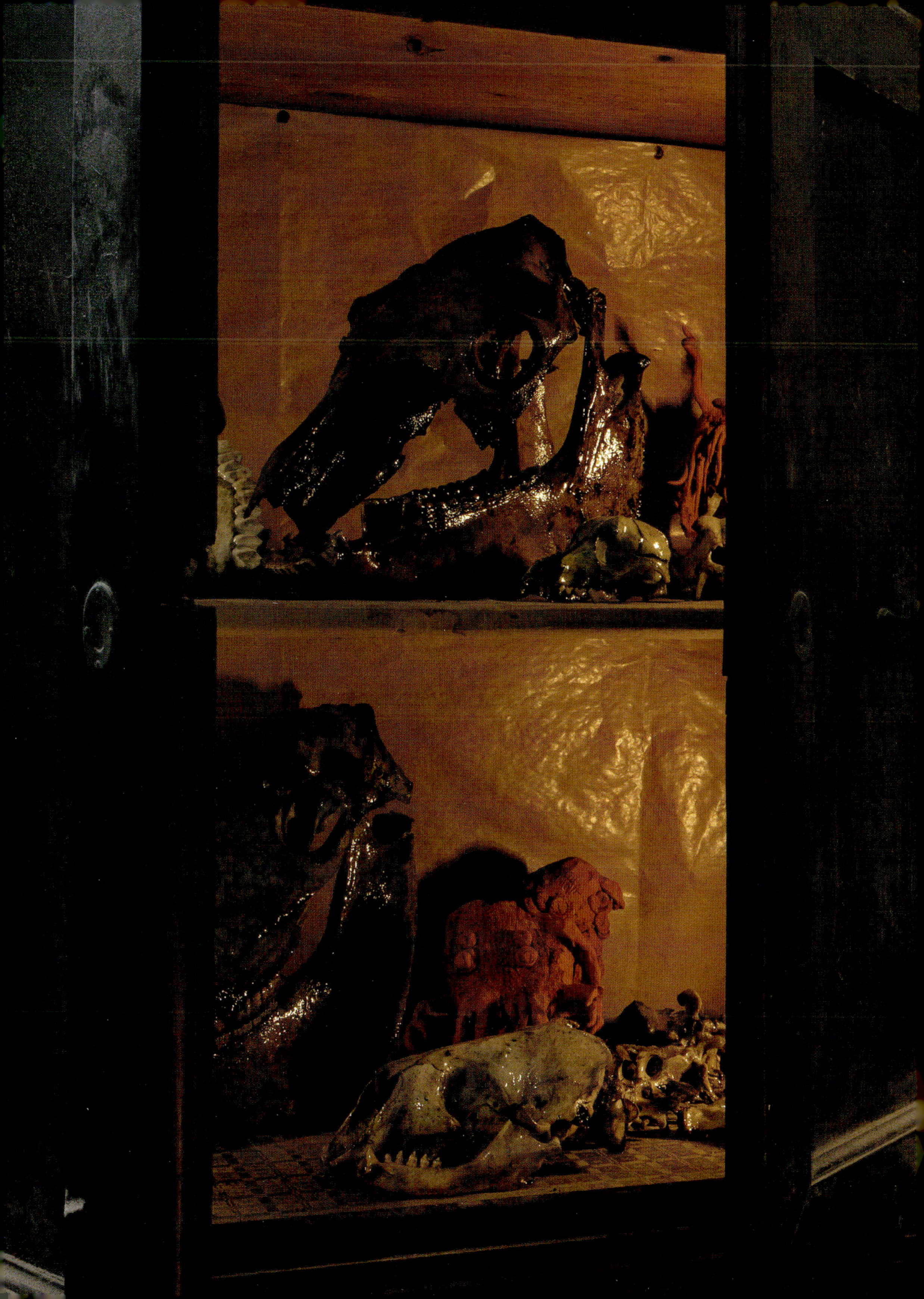

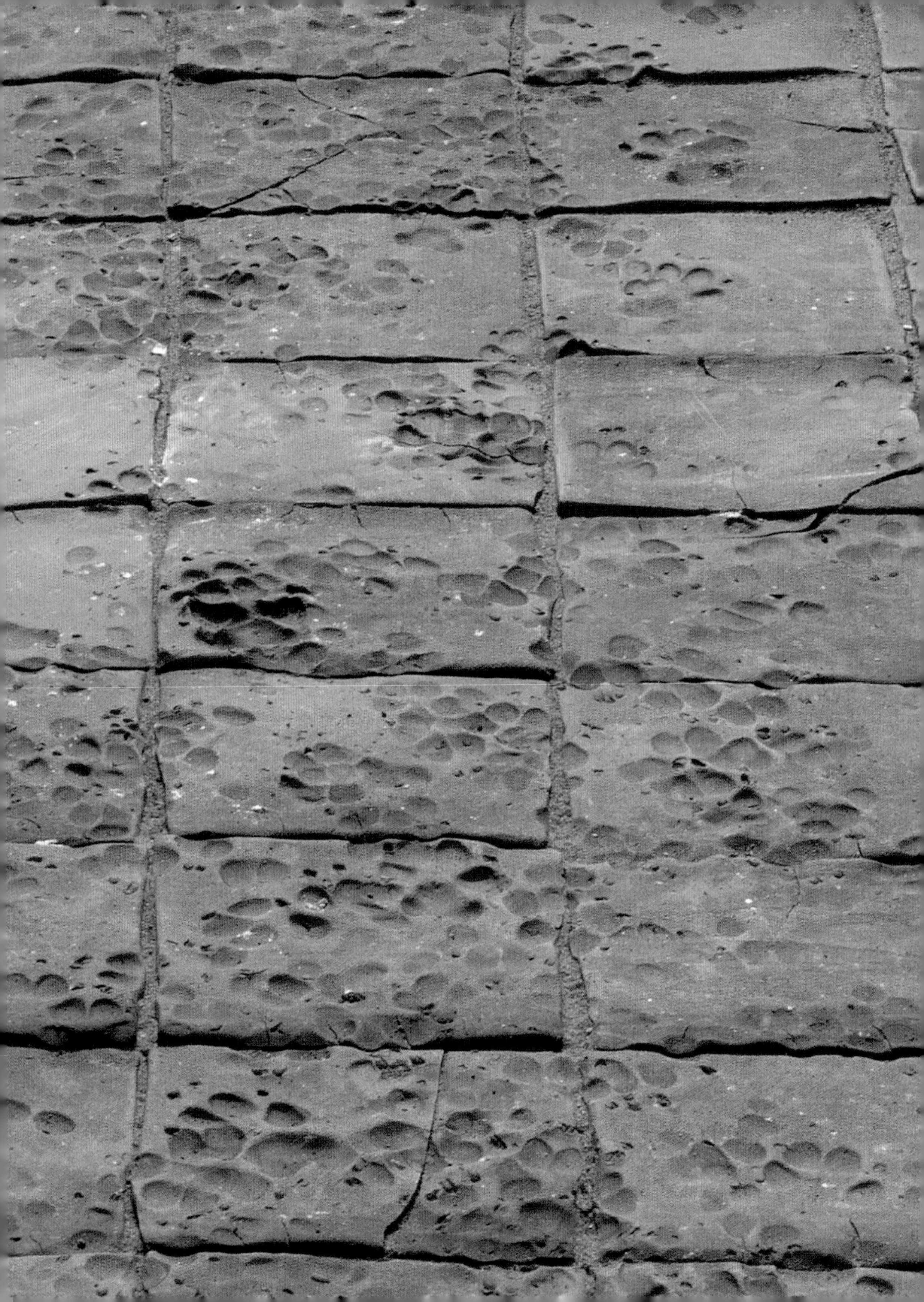

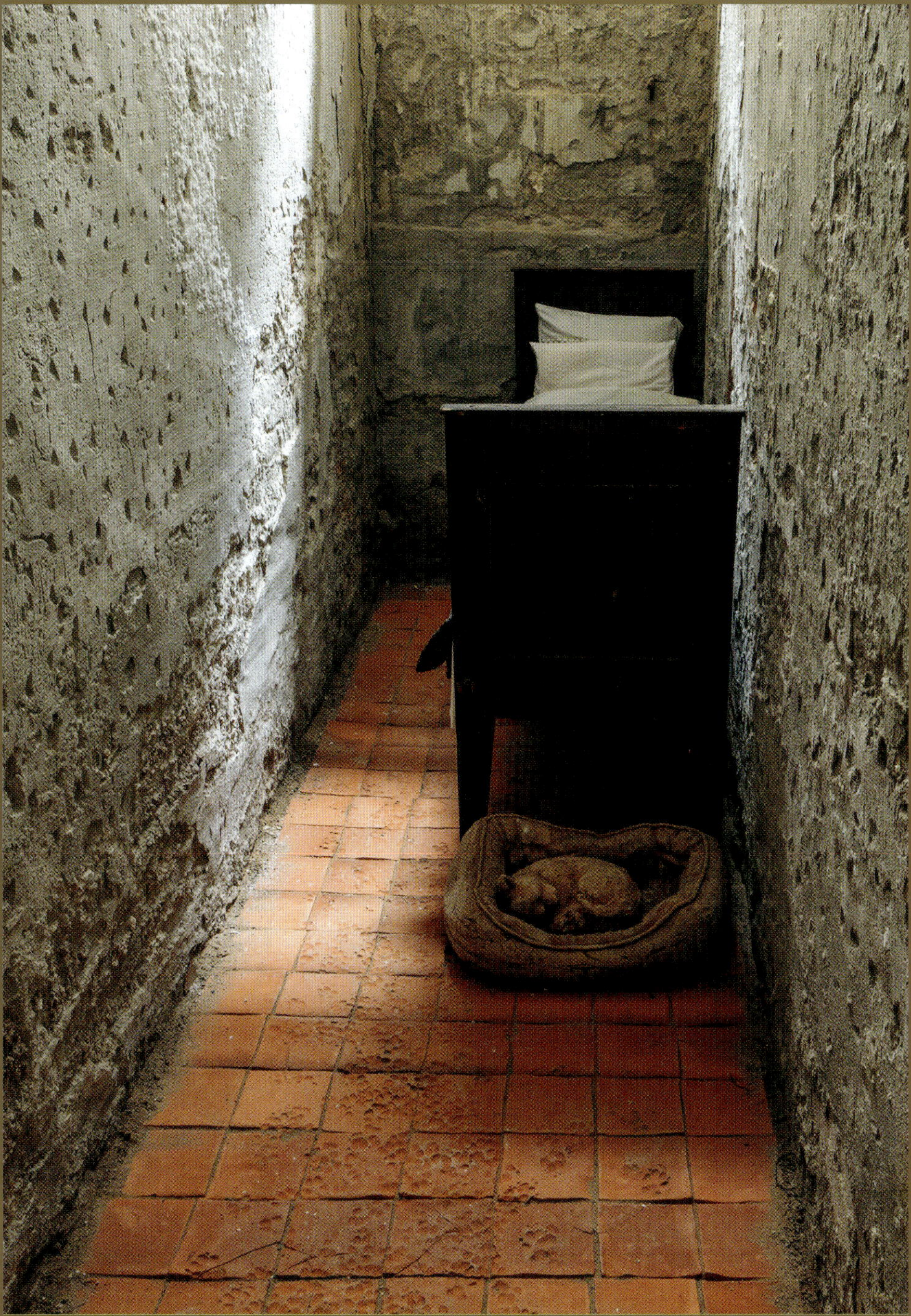

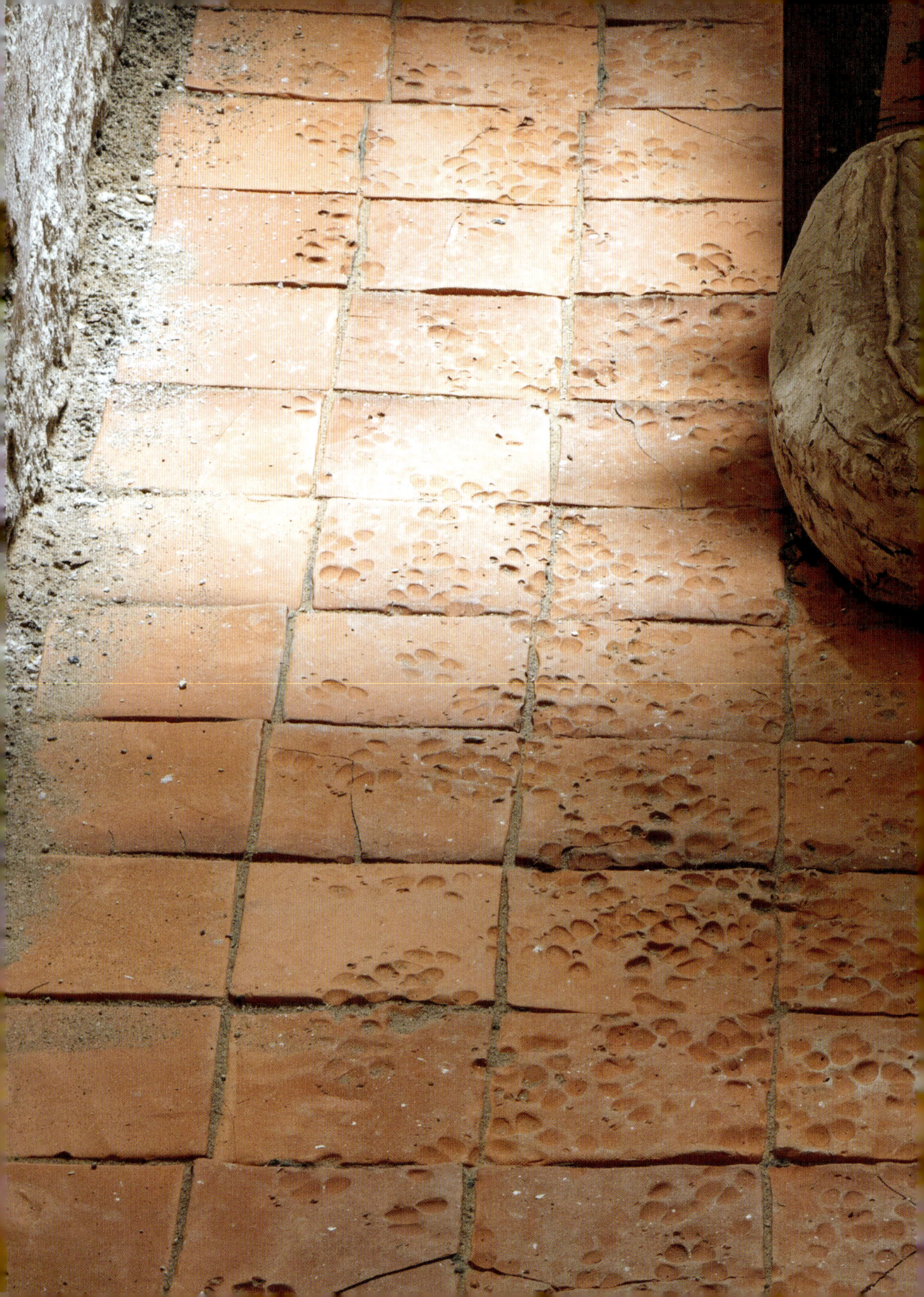

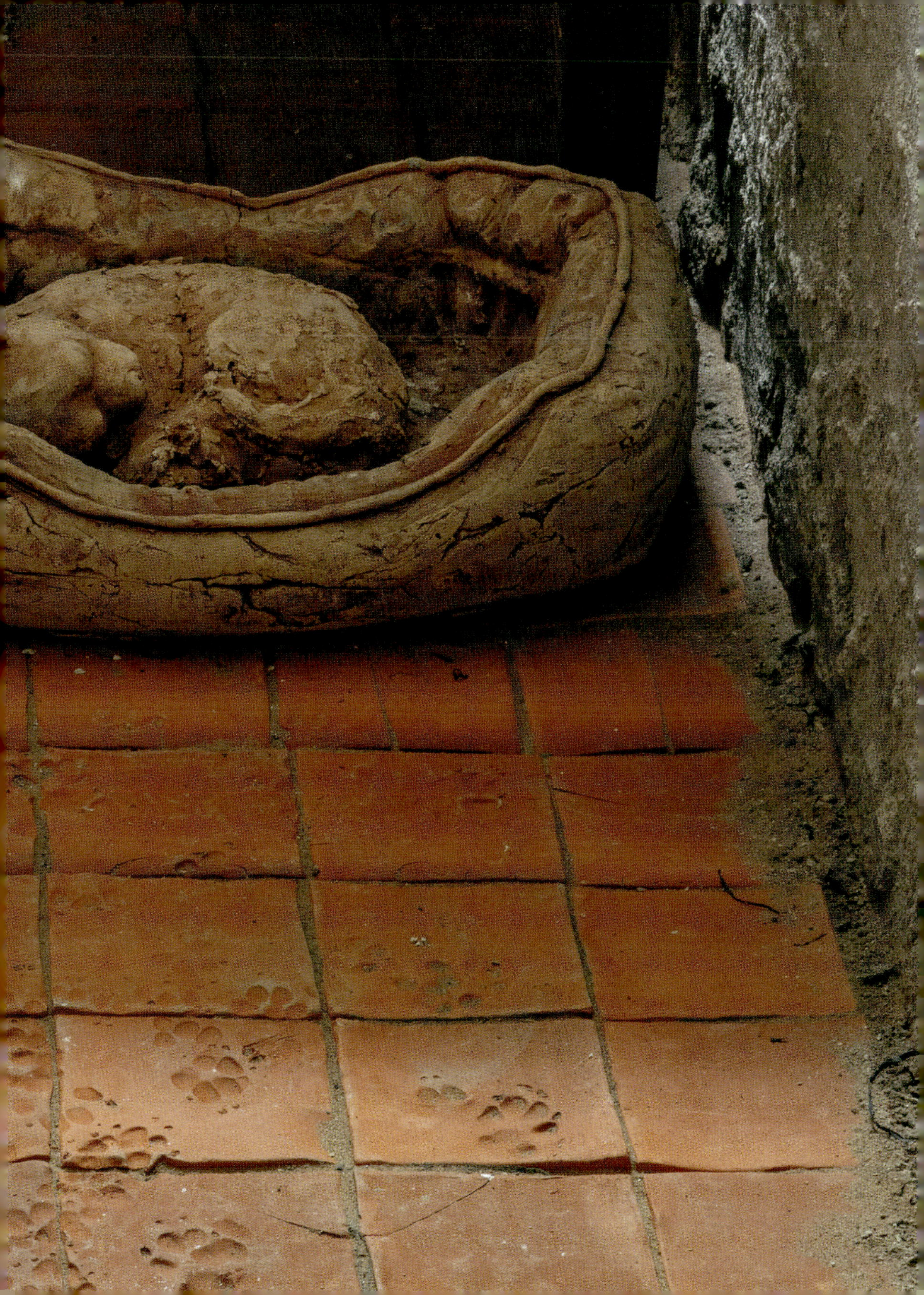

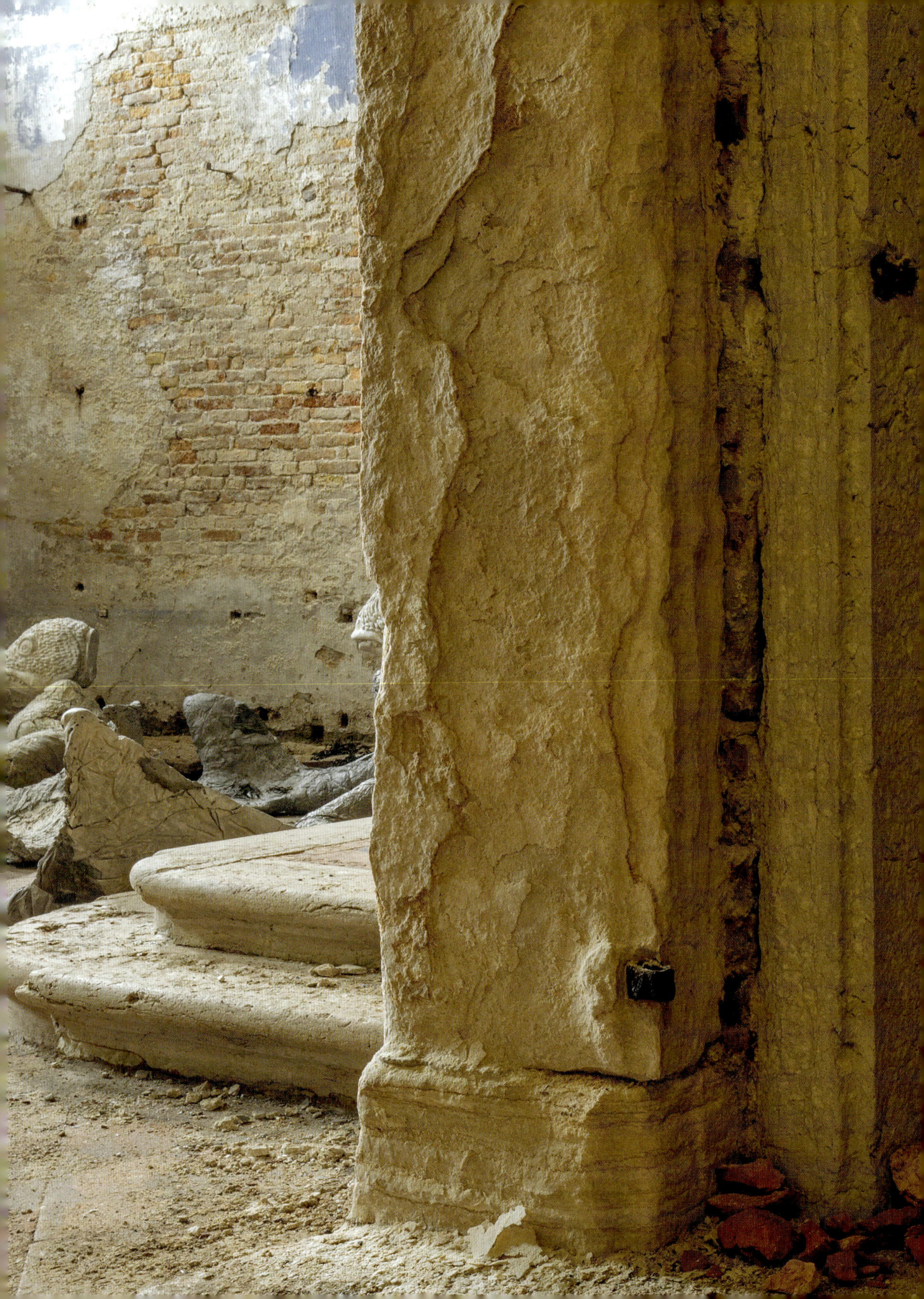

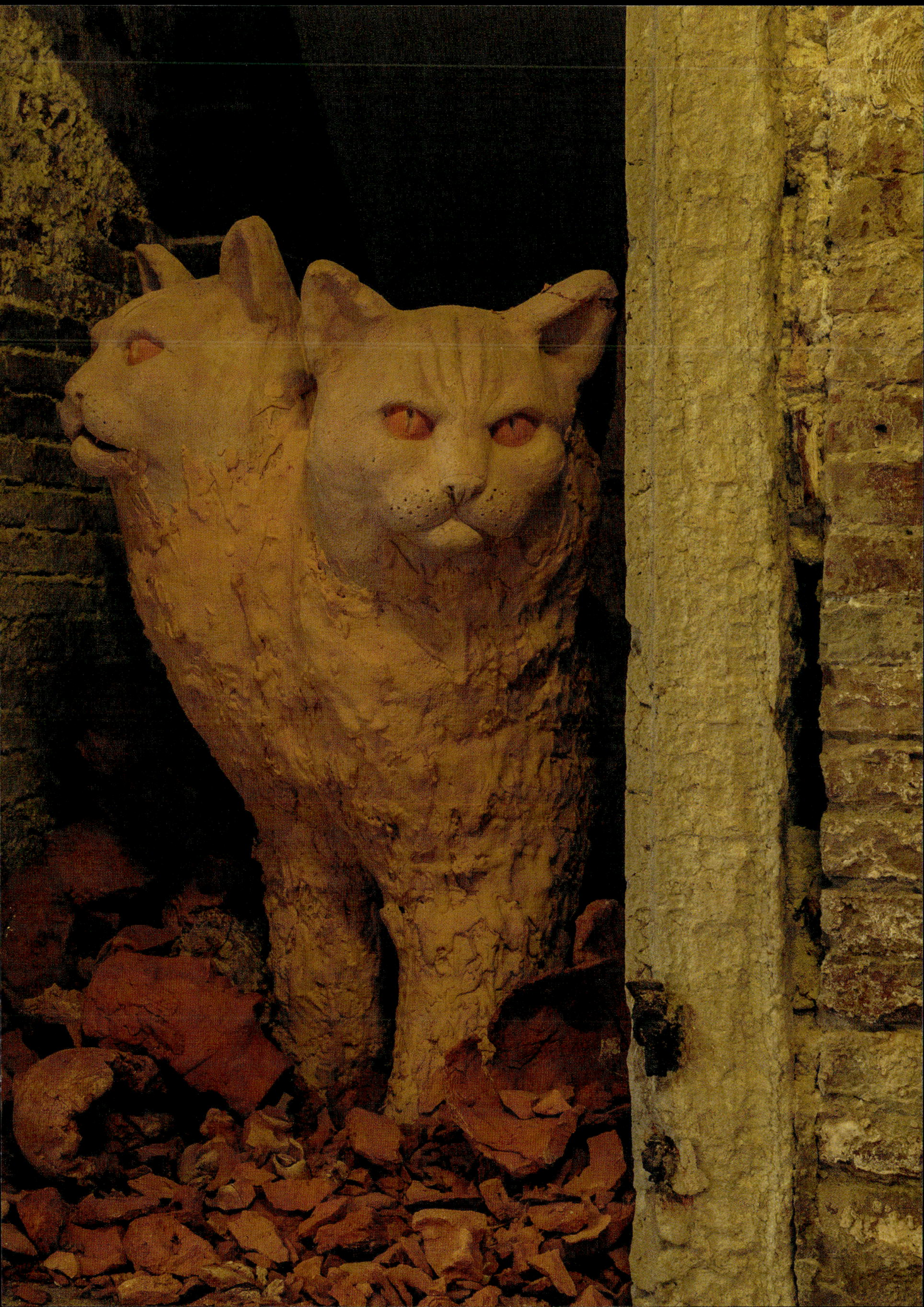

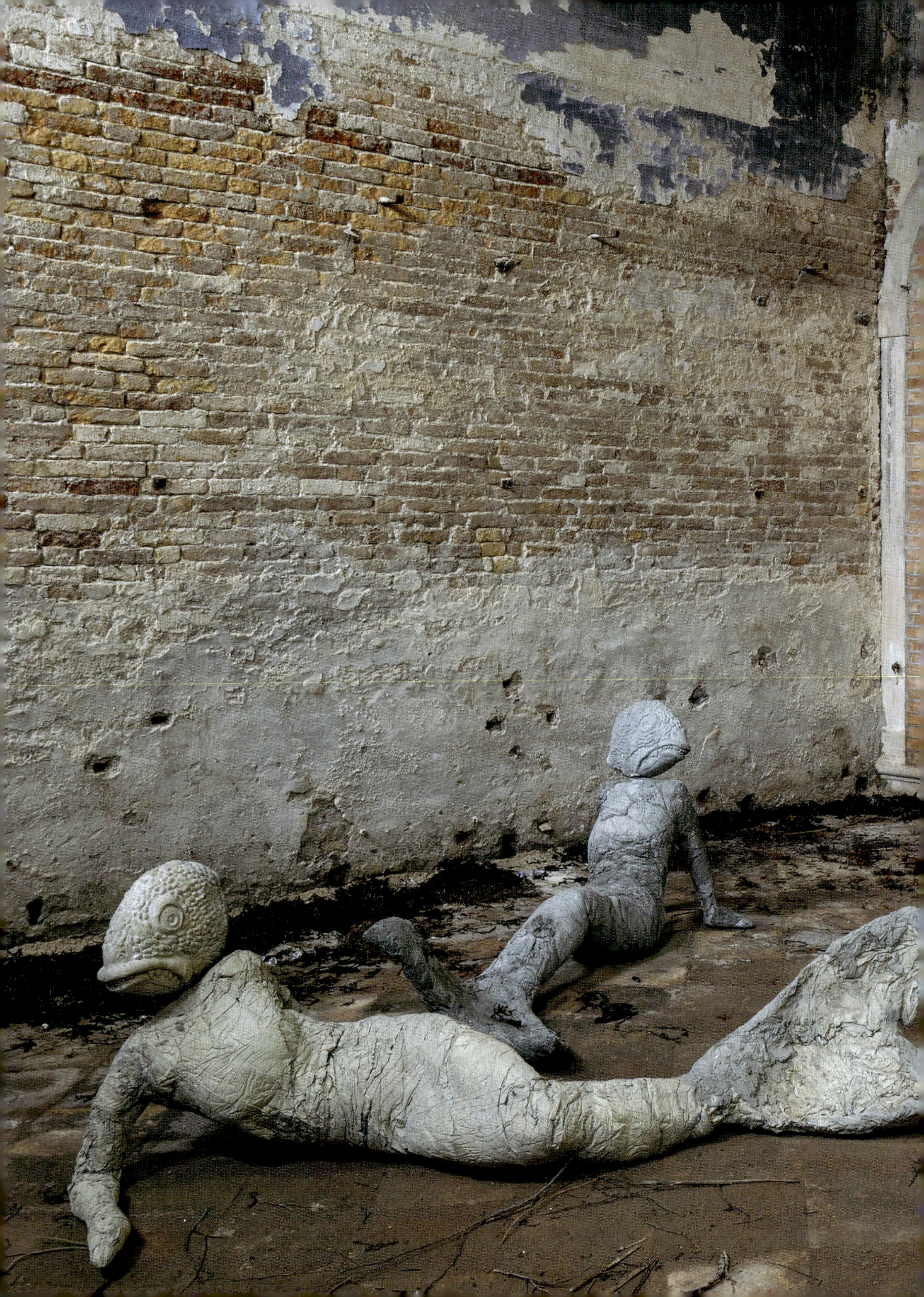

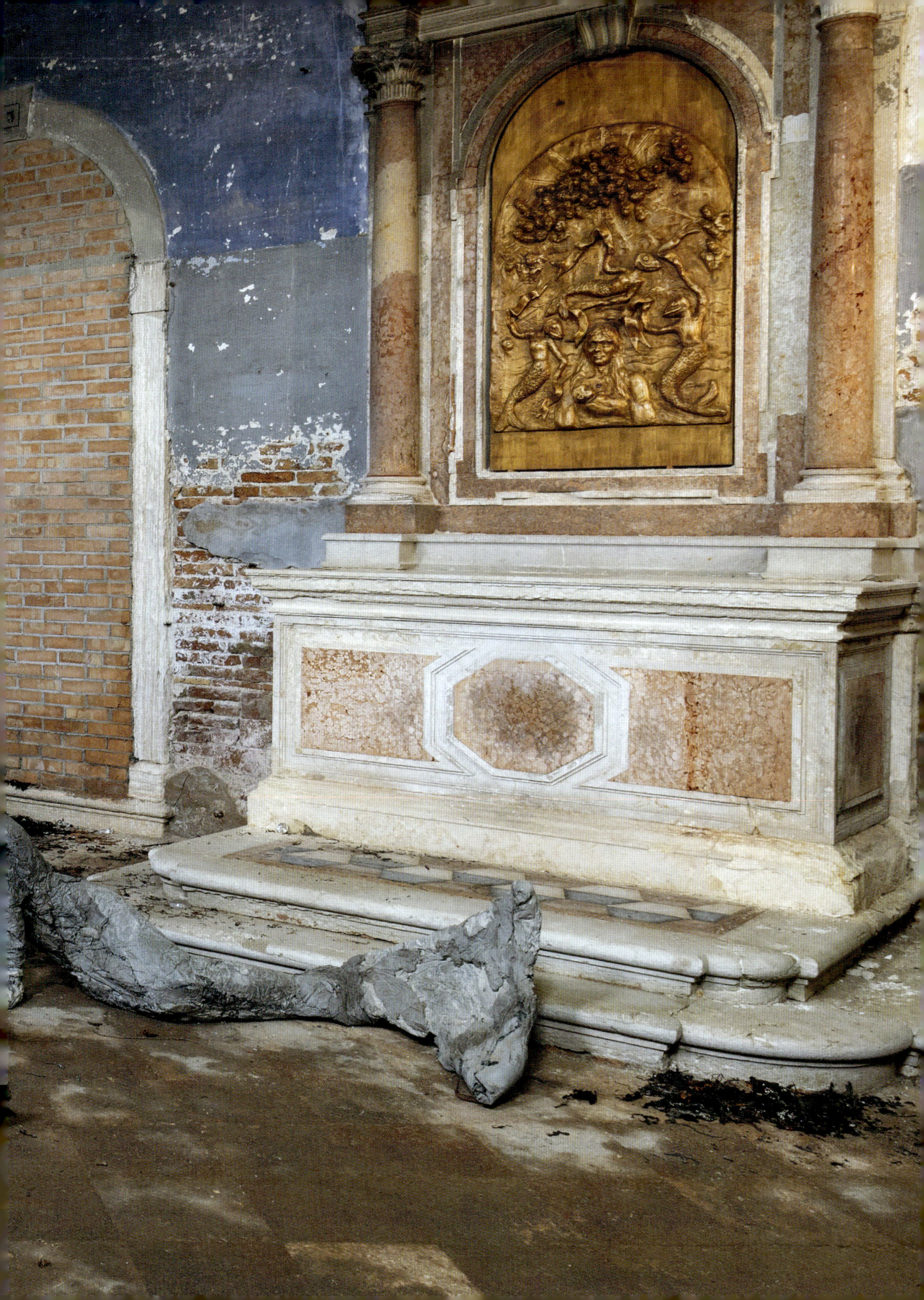

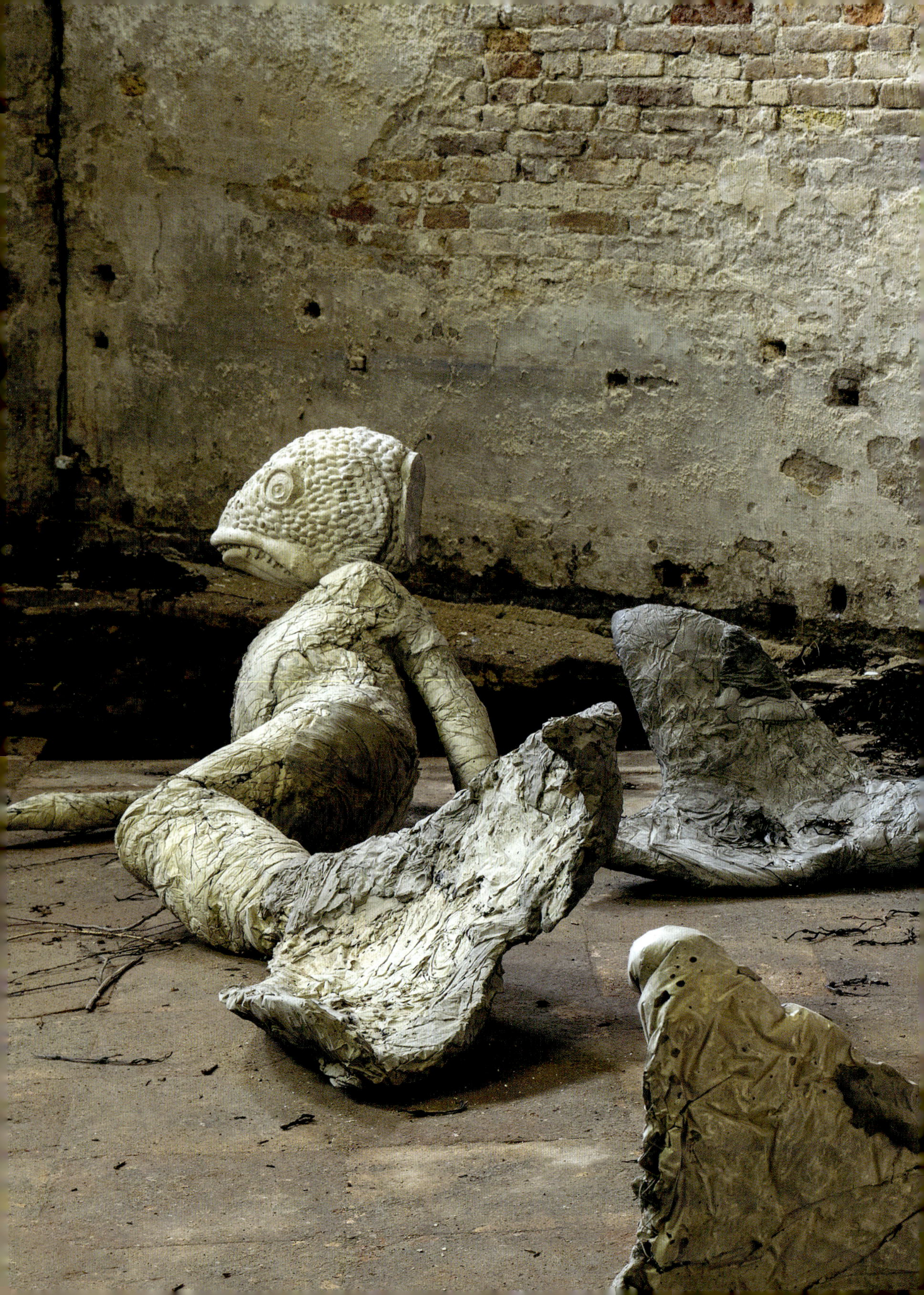

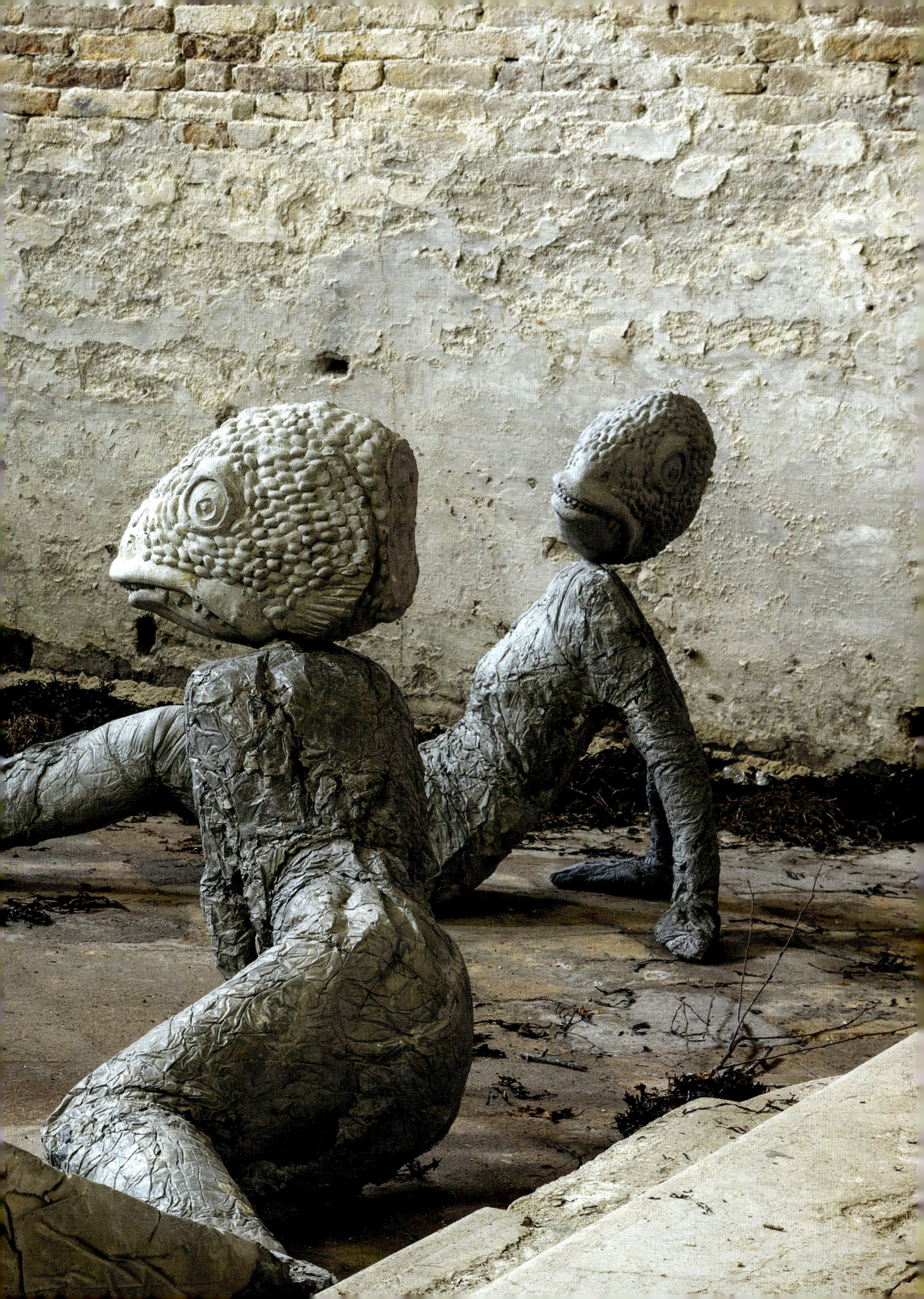

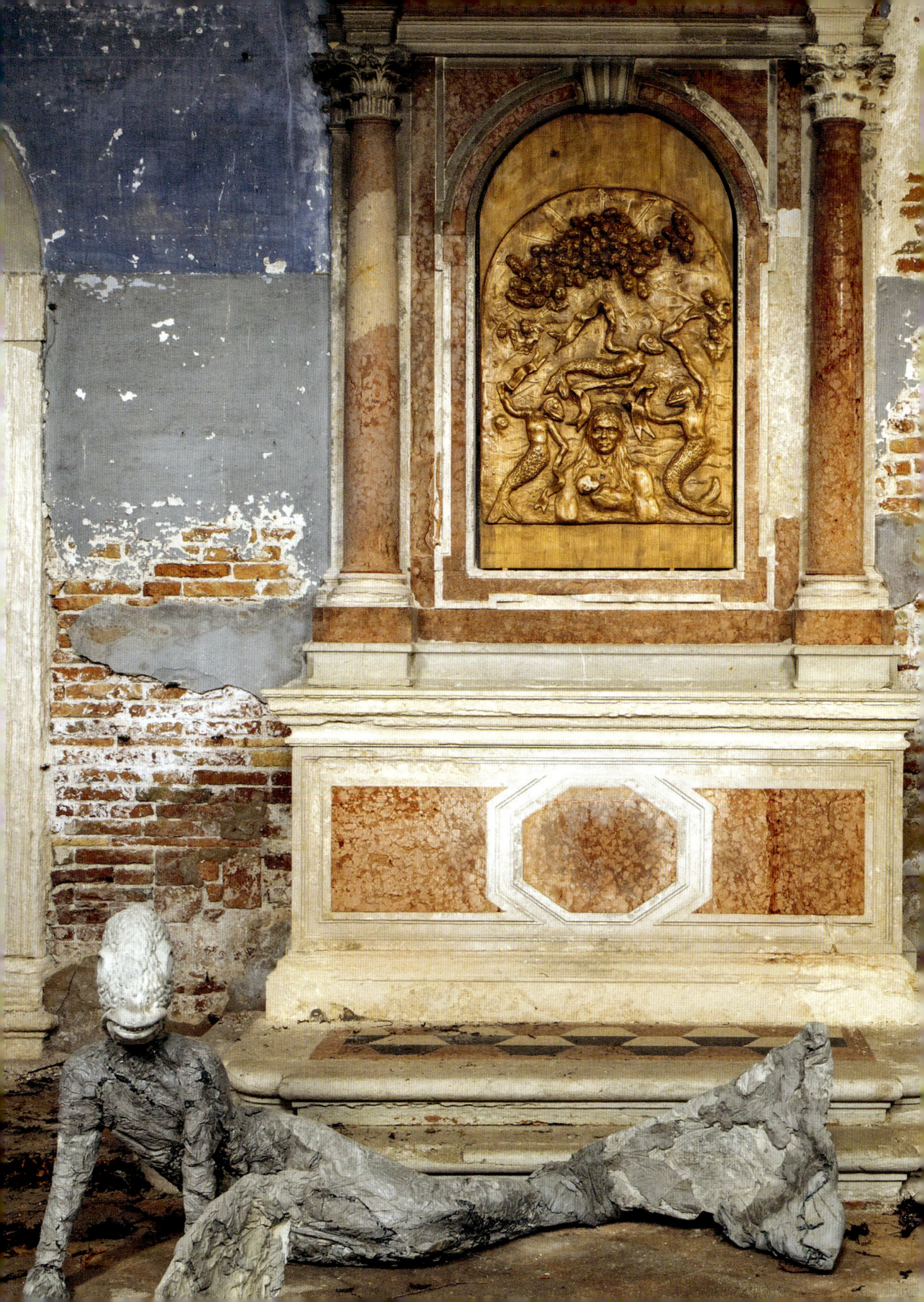

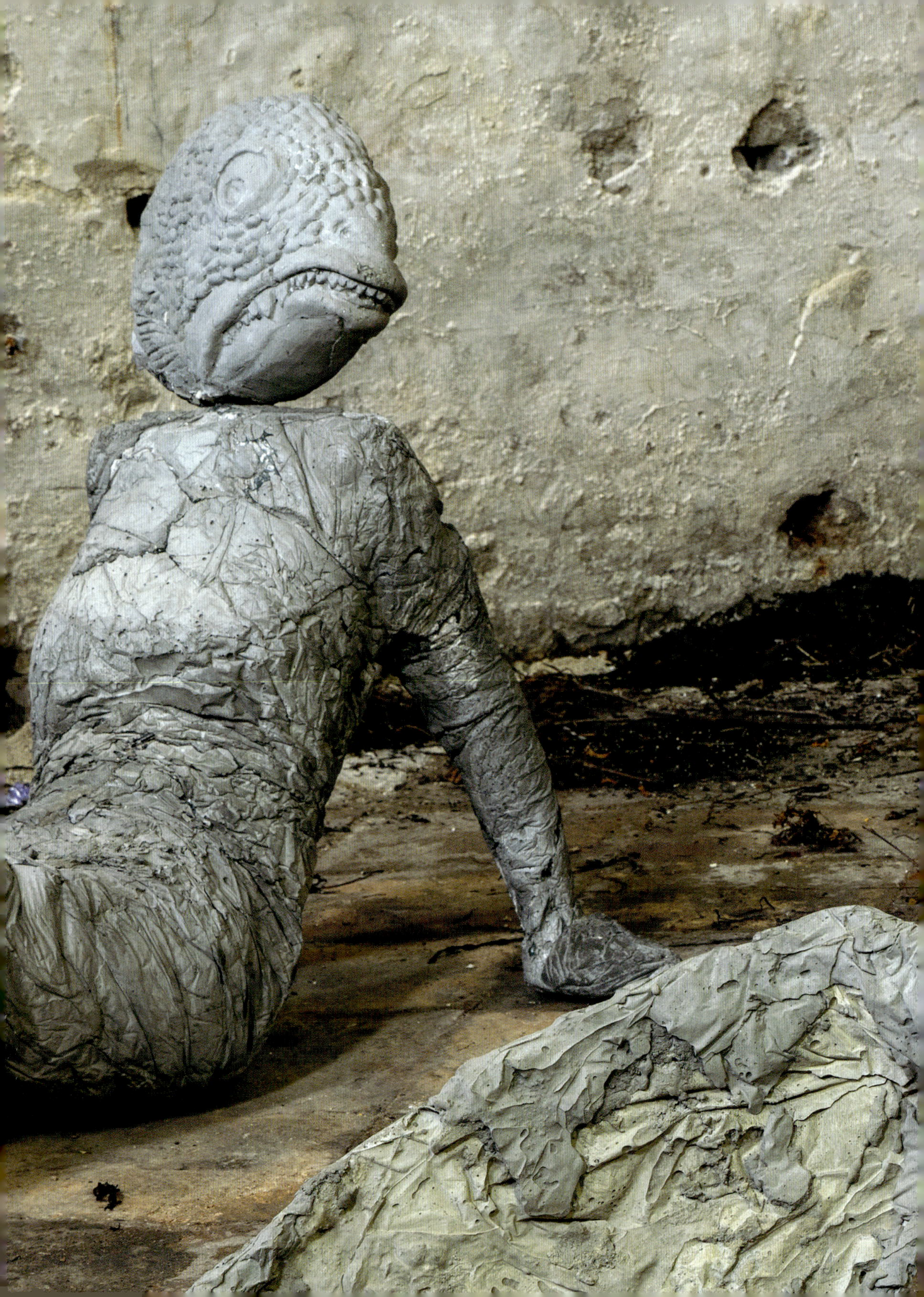

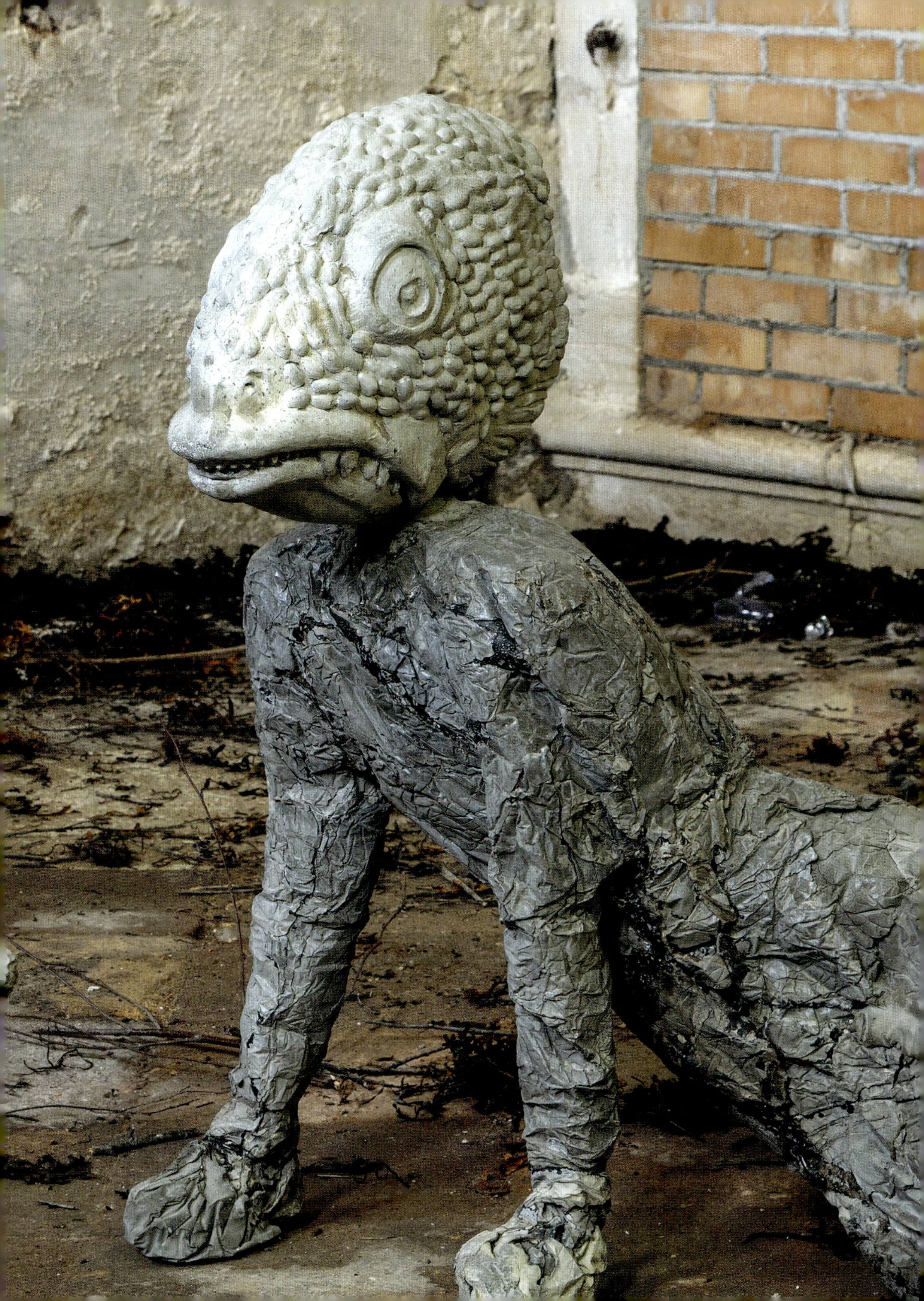

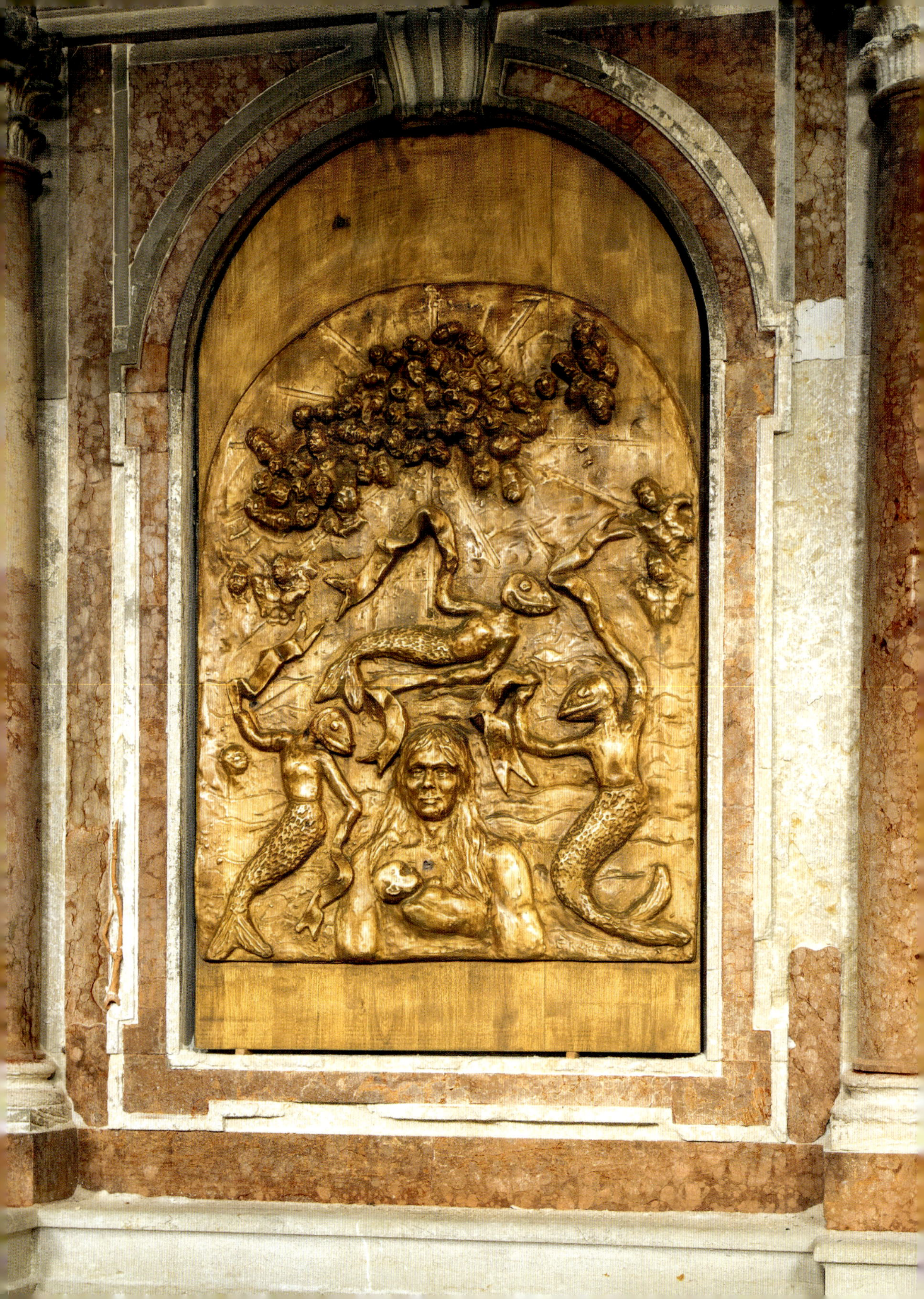

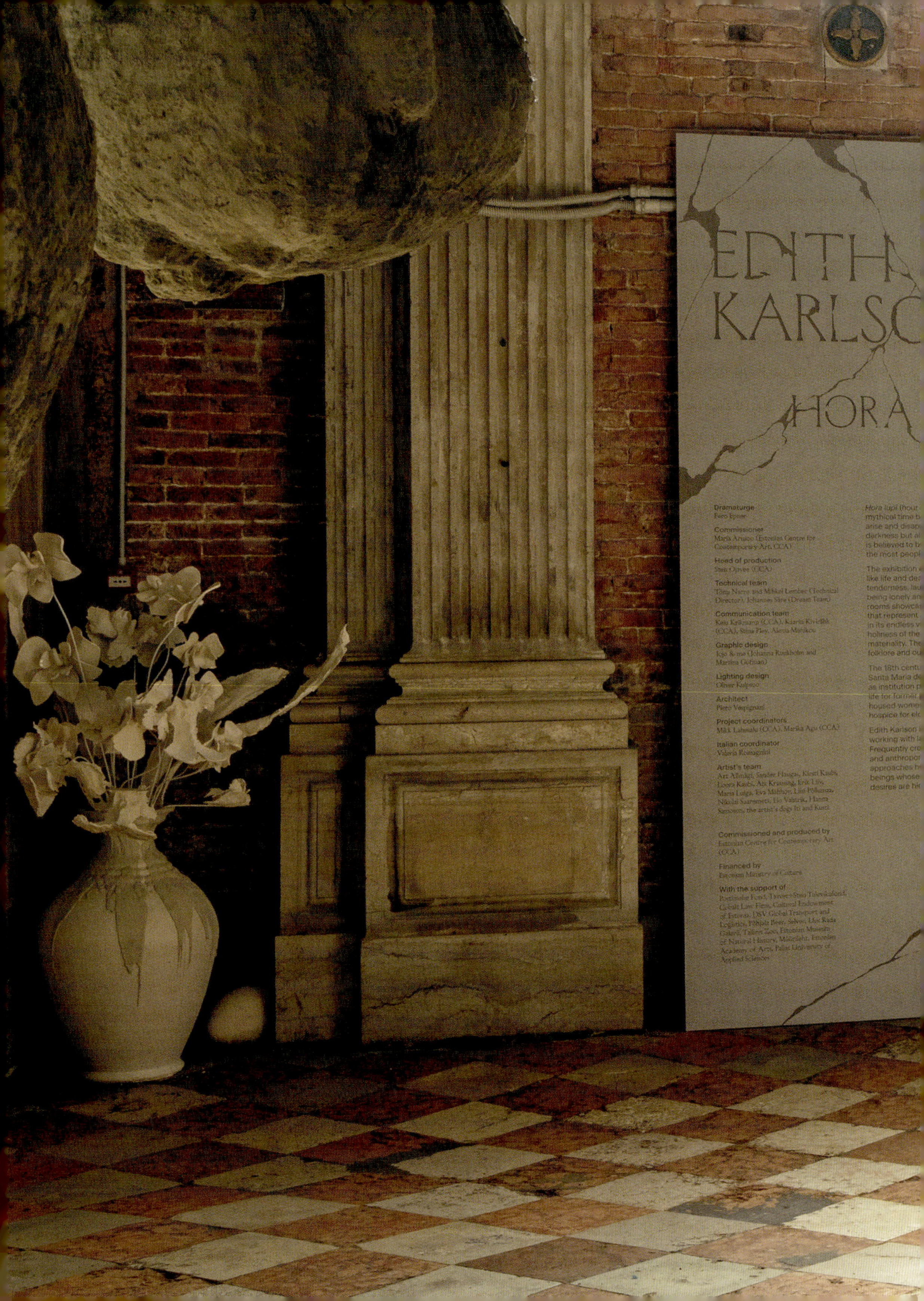
EDITH
HORA
Dramaturge
Commissioner
Head of production
Technical team
Communication team
Graphic design
Lighting design
Architect
Project coordinators
Italian coordinator
Artist's team
Commissioned and produced by
Financed by
With the support of

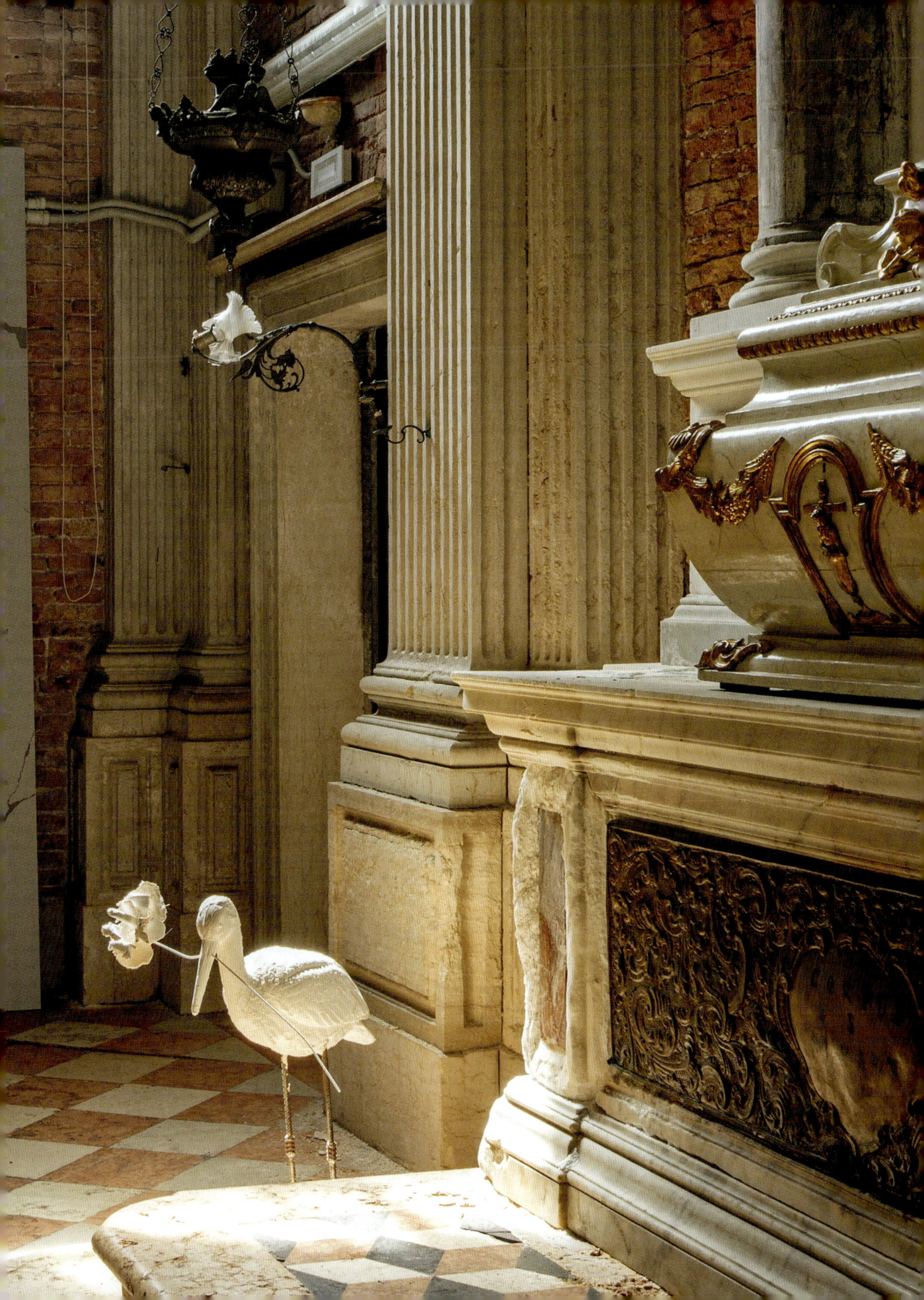

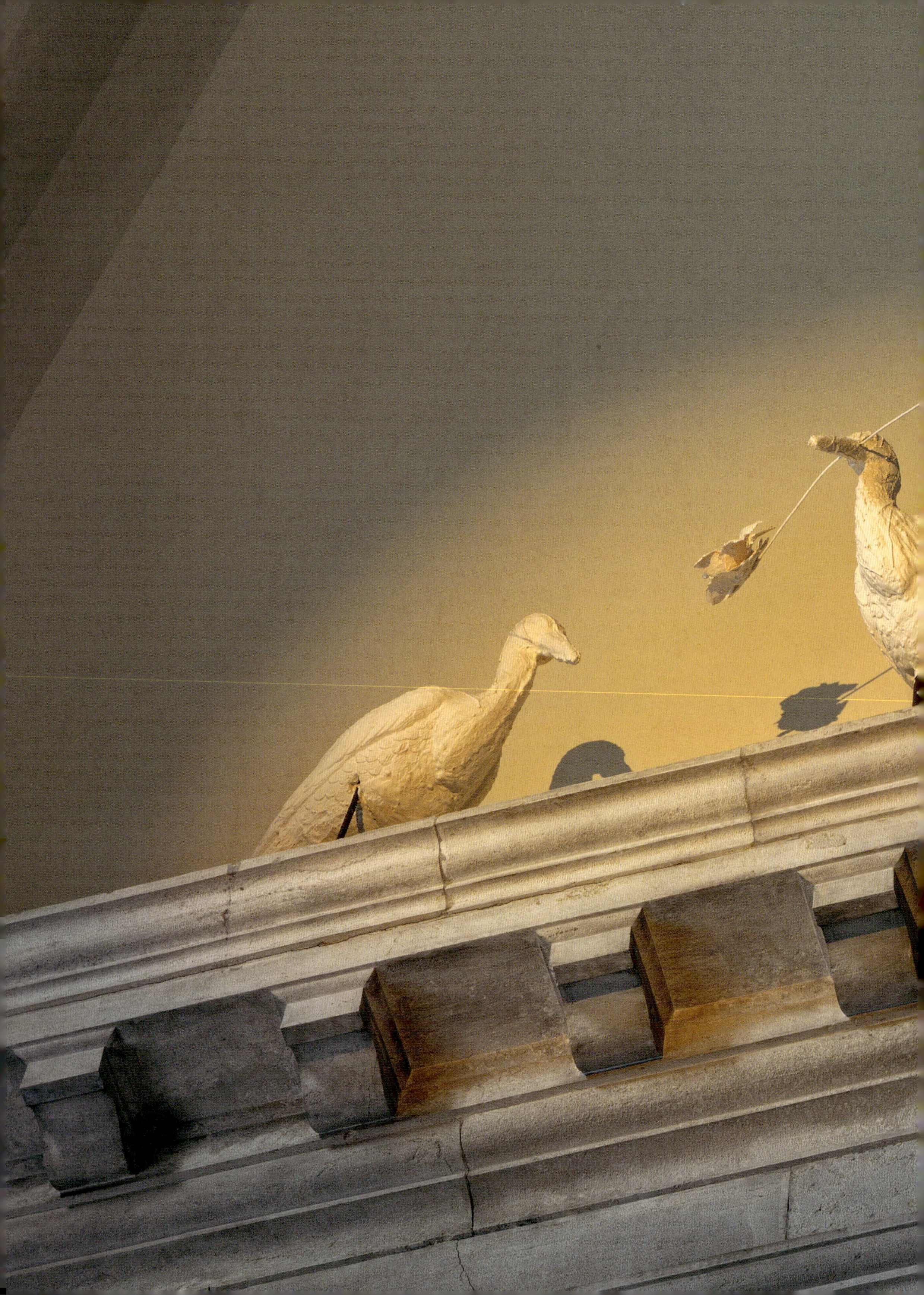

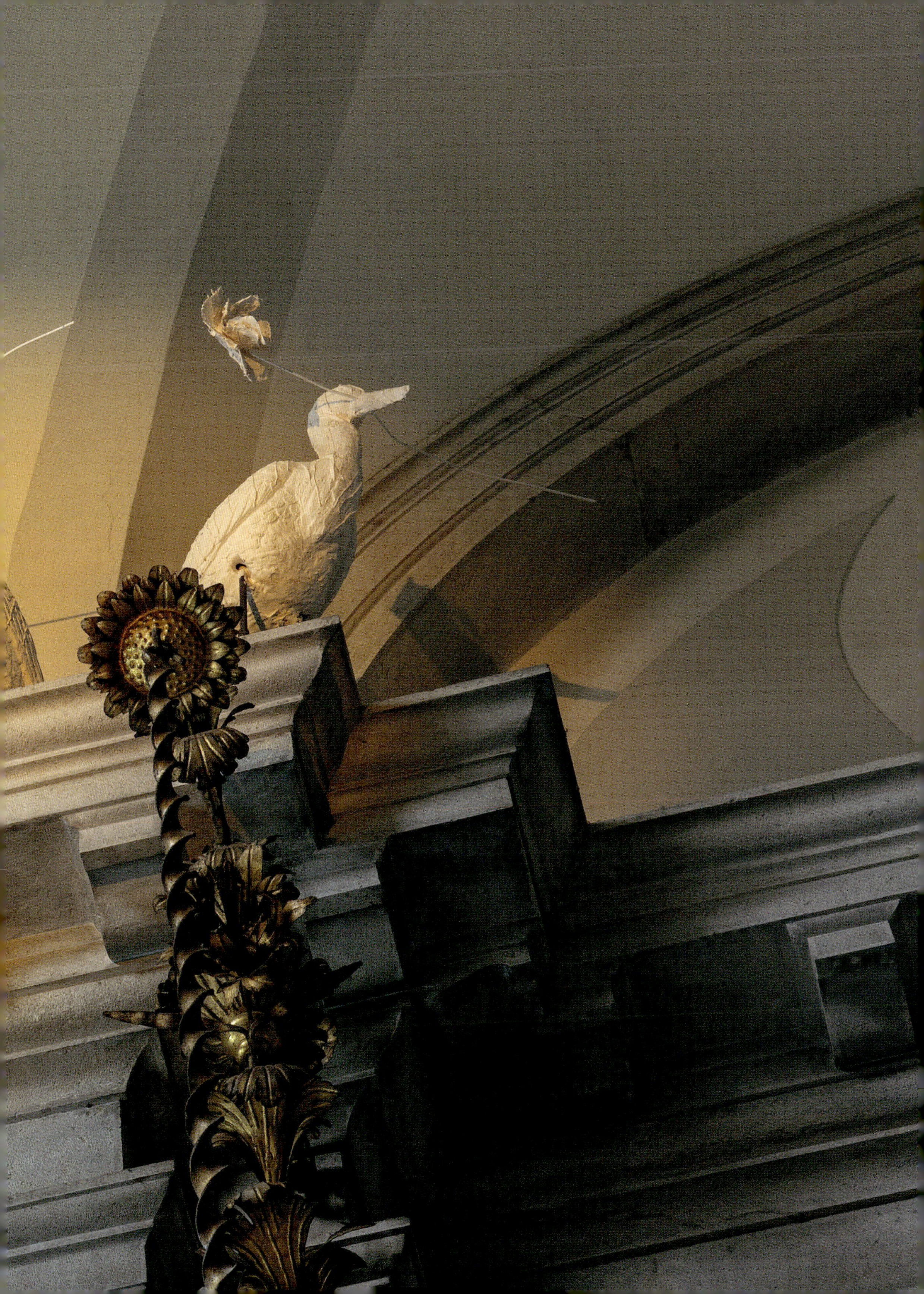

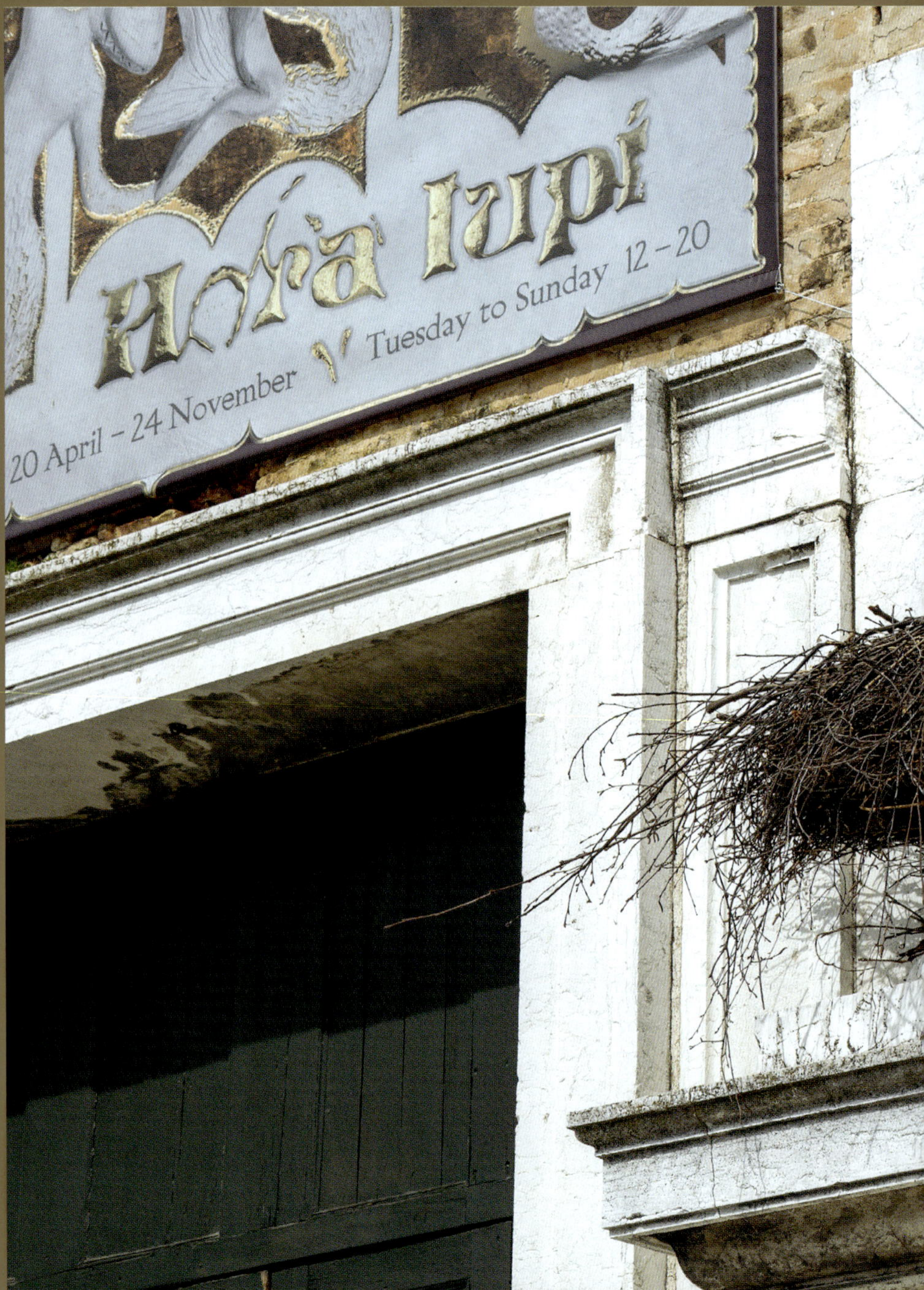
20 April – 24 November
Tuesday to Sunday 12 – 20

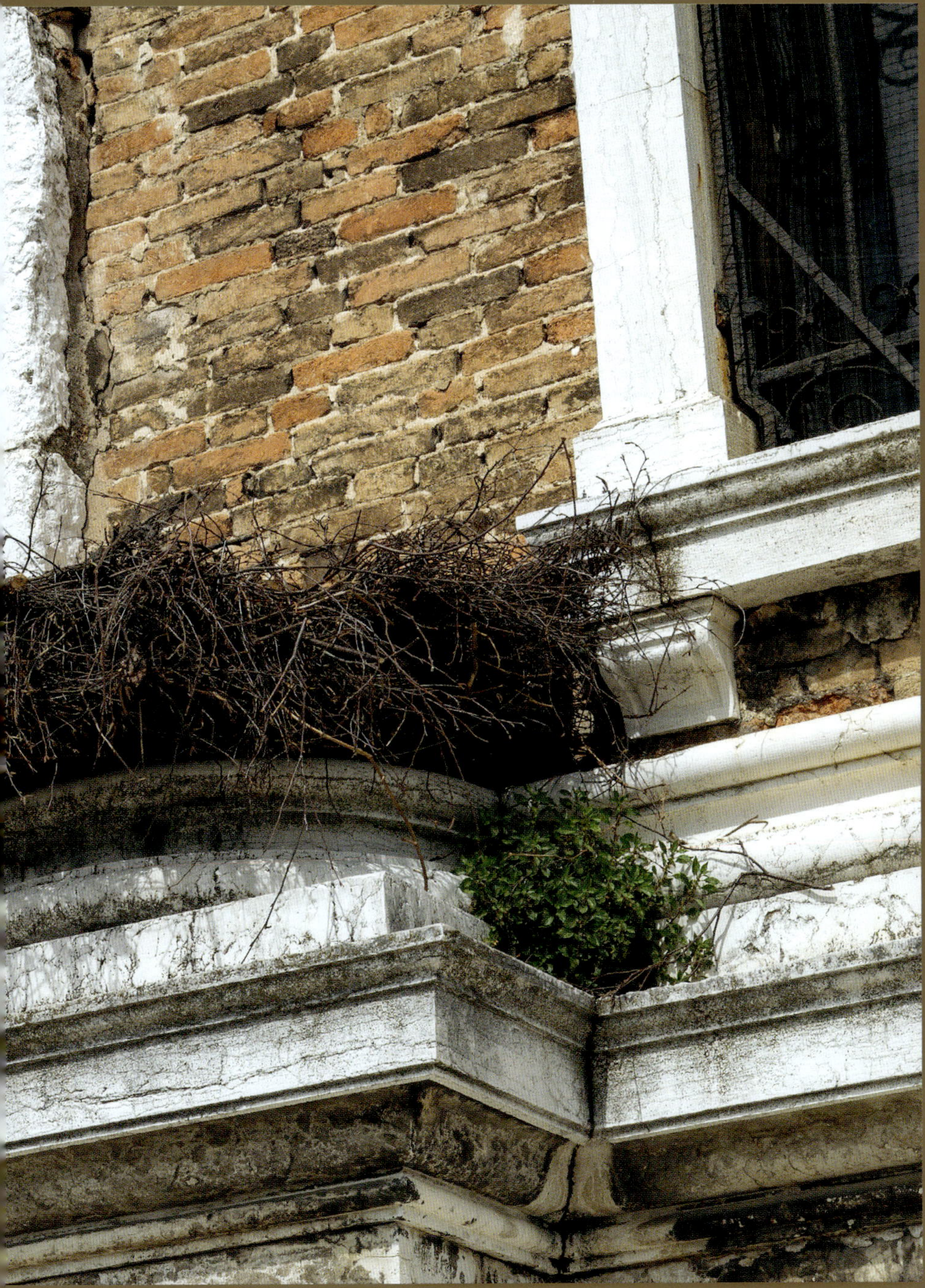

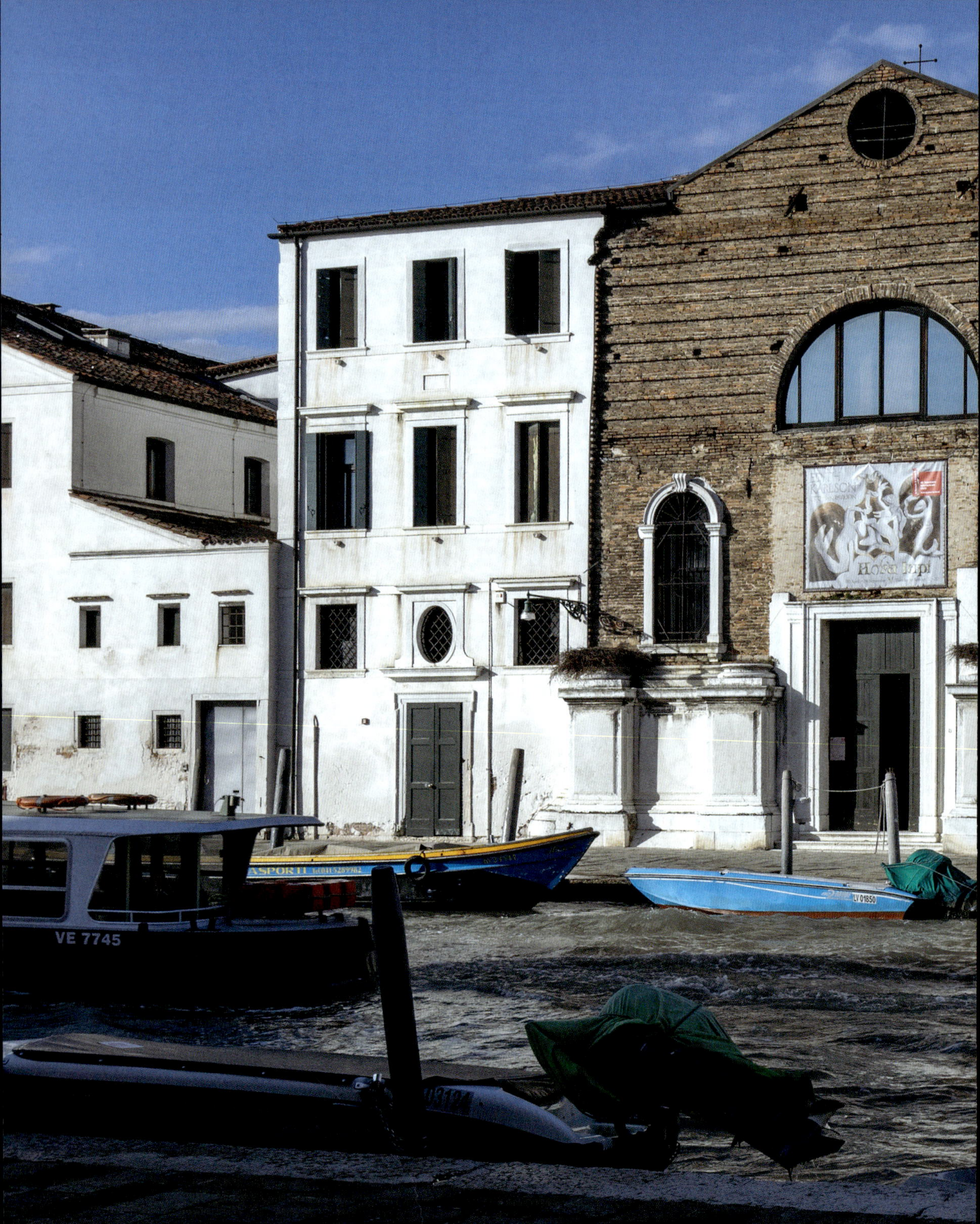
VE 7745
LV 01850

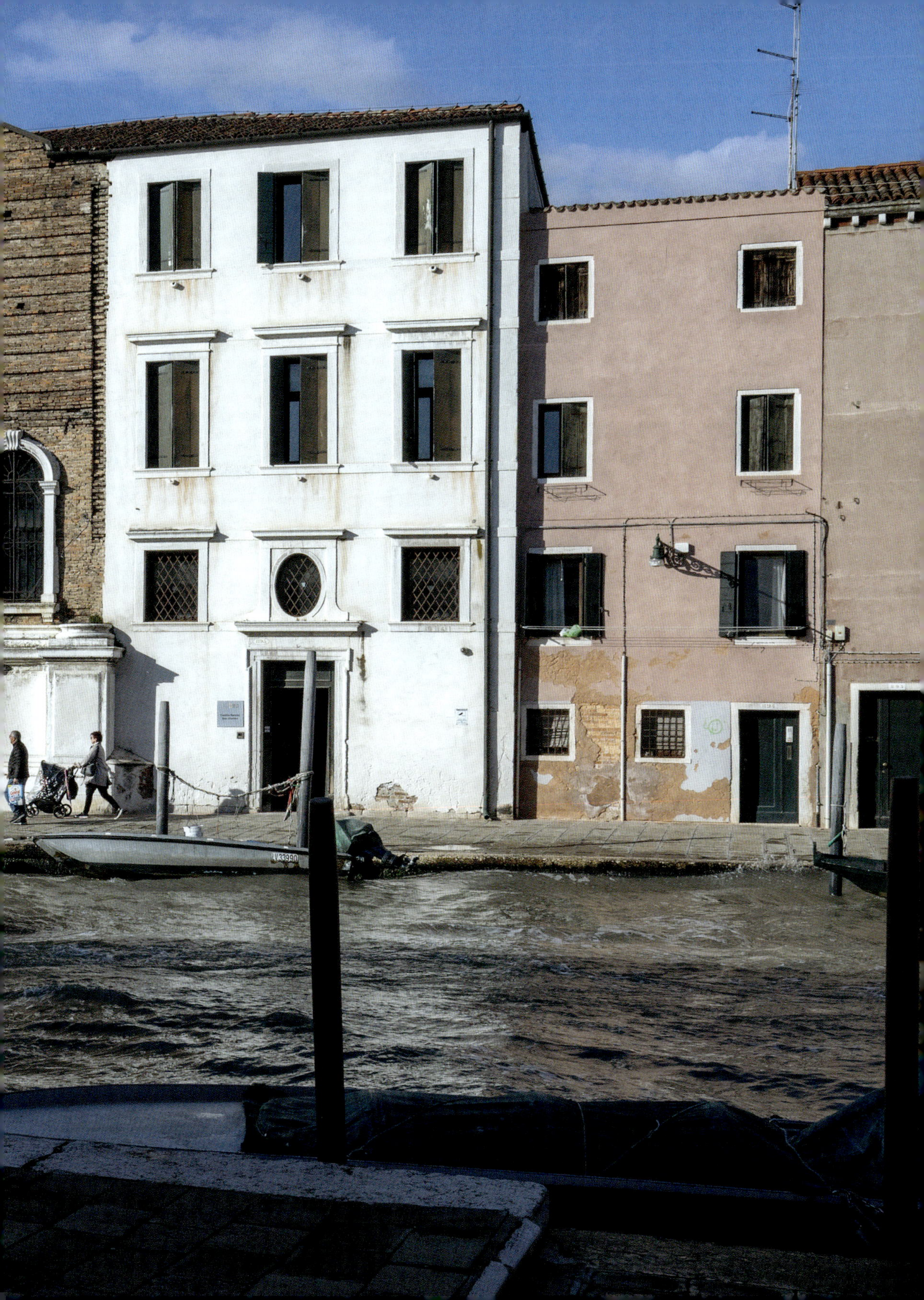

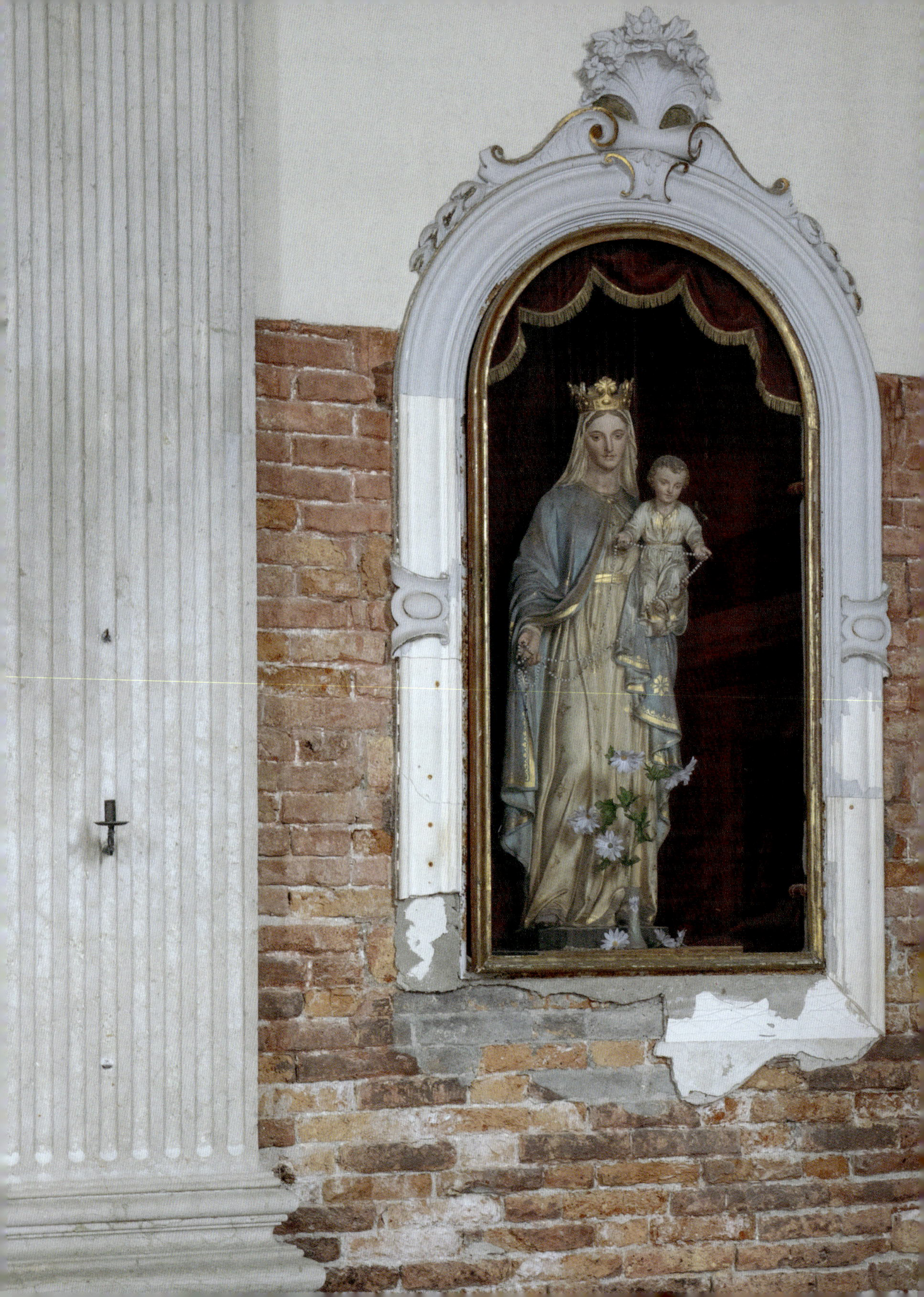

Piero Vespignani

CHIESA DI SANTA MARIA DELLE PENITENTI

HISTORICAL NOTES

Chiesa di Santa Marie delle Penitenti overlooks the Canareggio canal, in the homonymous sestiere located to the north-west of the historic centre of Venice. The complex is part of a network of charitable welfare structures established by the Republic of Venice. From its very origins, the republic, also known as *La Serenissima* was forced to deal with complex sanitary management, both because of its exposure to continuous trade flows (of people and things) and due to a high concentration of inhabitants in the city. Suffice it to say that Venice had 133,000 inhabitants in 1338 and 190,000 in 1440, and throughout the Renaissance it was one of the five most populous cities in Europe.

A high number of inhabitants inevitably also meant a high number of people living in poverty, which is why in the history of Venice, welfare institutions have always played an important role. Historically, the four most important institutions for the health and social care of the city were the Derelitti, the Incurabili, the Mendicanti and the Pietà complex. These institutions included the "pious place of the Penitents" founded in 1700 near Santa Marina and from 1705 based in San Giobbe. The function of this institution was to redeem former prostitutes who voluntarily agreed to submit to the rules of monastic seclusion. Penitents had to be no less than twelve years old and no more than thirty, be Venetian or have lived in the city for at least a year, be healthy in mind and body, not be pregnant and have abstained from a previous sinful life for at least three months.

These were institutions that gave shelter to people, on the condition that they learn a trade (e.g. lacemakers) and enhance their talents. It is curious how for the society at the time, one of the tools of social emancipation for these girls was a knowledge of music, with the ability to play an instrument or education in singing, leading to the formation of the so-called "chorus girls". In the eighteenth century, these institutions organised concerts by the girls and their performances were known throughout Europe. The Ospedaletto dei Derelitti concerts were the most famous as these were conducted by music master Antonio Vivaldi.

Work on the current seat of the Penitents began in 1725 thanks to the collection of substantial funds from the Venetian nobility, in particular the Da Lezze family. The project was created by Giorgio Massari, a notable architect active in the city (his works include the Palazzo Grassi, the Gesuati church, and the Pietà church), in whose work references to Palladio and Sansovino resonate clearly.

The Church of the Penitents was realised by the architect almost simultaneously with another work, the church of San Marcuola. The two churches clearly share a formal reference and the same compositional construction of the façade, despite their different dimensions. The base is built with the same proportions and the same mouldings, the same thermal window, and the same rose window. The stone portal has the same cornice but is made more humble by the absence of the two Ionic columns on either side. Curiously, both churches were not completed due to lack of funds.

The Penitents church is flanked and encompassed by two sym metrical buildings that extend in a continuous line along the canal and inside around the two cloisters, only one of which was finished. The architectural reference is the church of the Zittelle at the Giudecca, built by Palladio in 1588, who first proposed the church flanked and enclosed by two symmetrical buildings.

The entire complex was organised as an autonomous and self-sufficient citadel due to the need to keep the penitents away from the temptations of the city until redemption was complete. With the fall of the Republic of Venice, the Penitenti became a hospice for self-sufficient elderly ladies. During the twentieth century it also took in refugee women from Istria and the former African colonies. It was finally closed in 1995. In 2015 it was restored and is now a residence for the non-self-sufficient elderly and a centre for Alzheimer's patients.

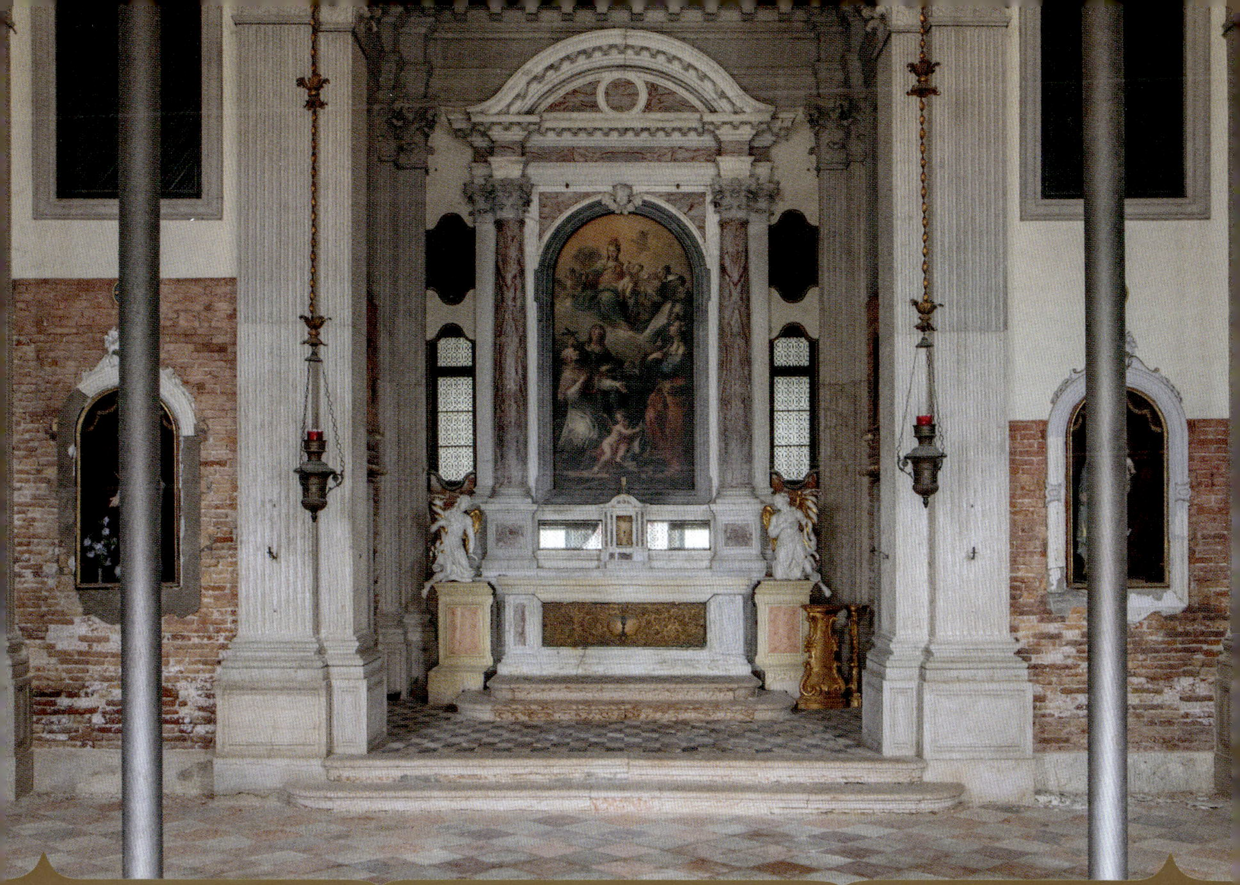
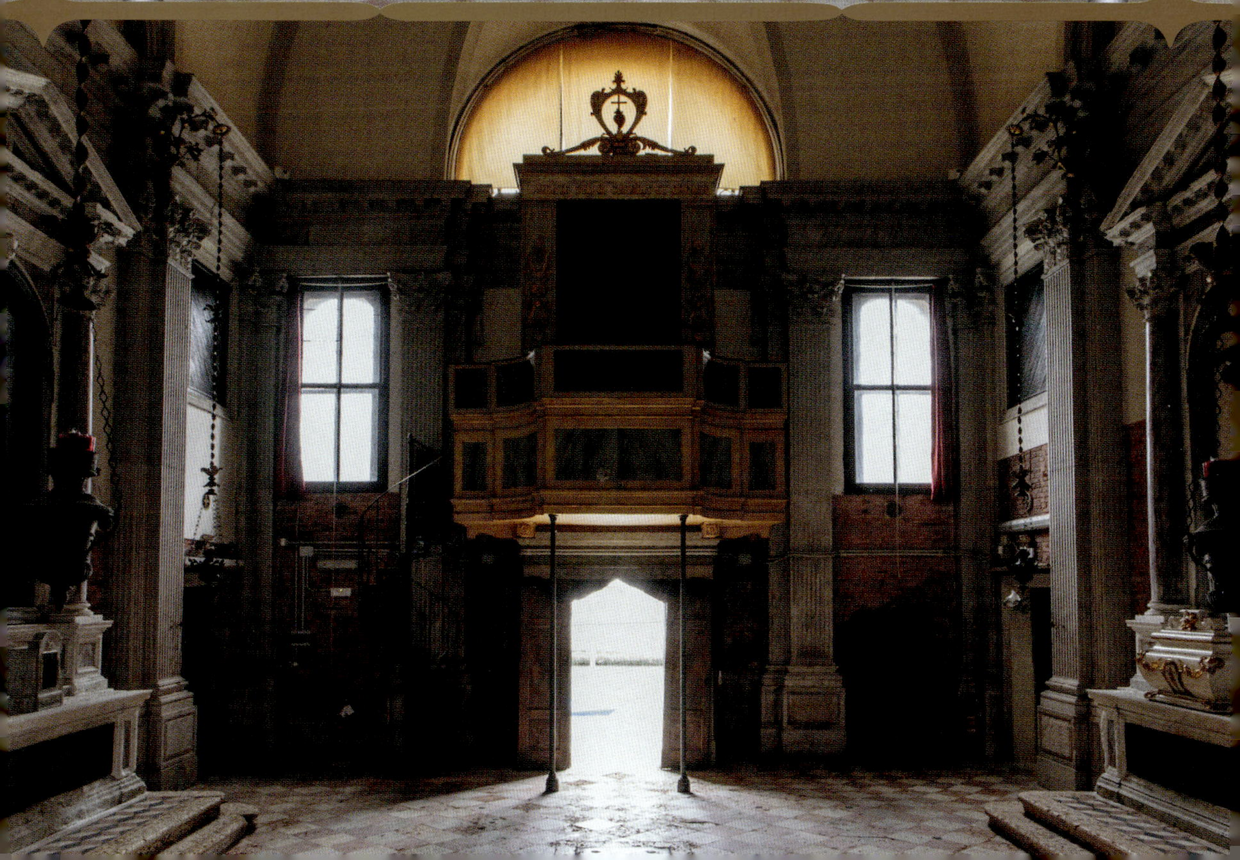

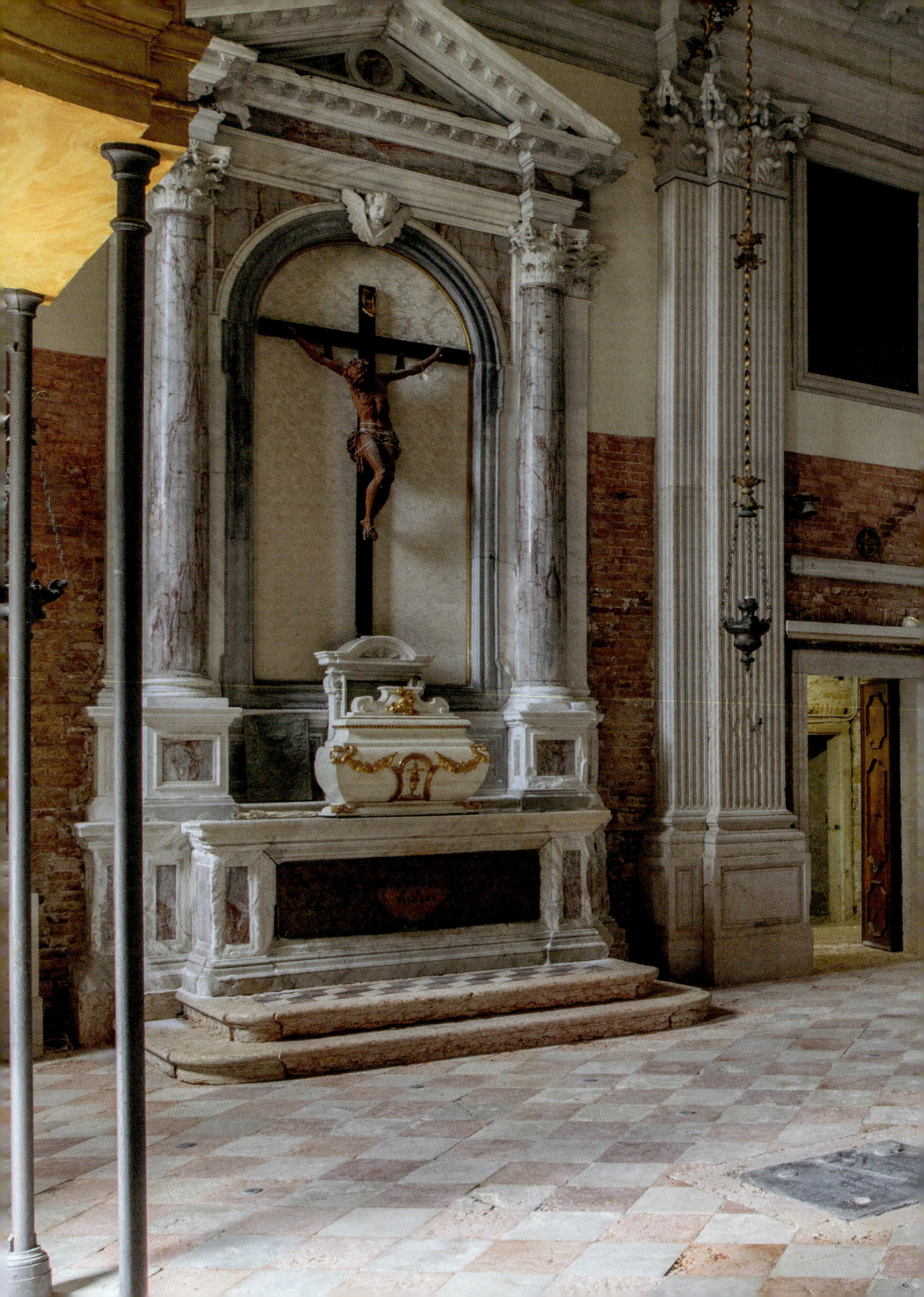

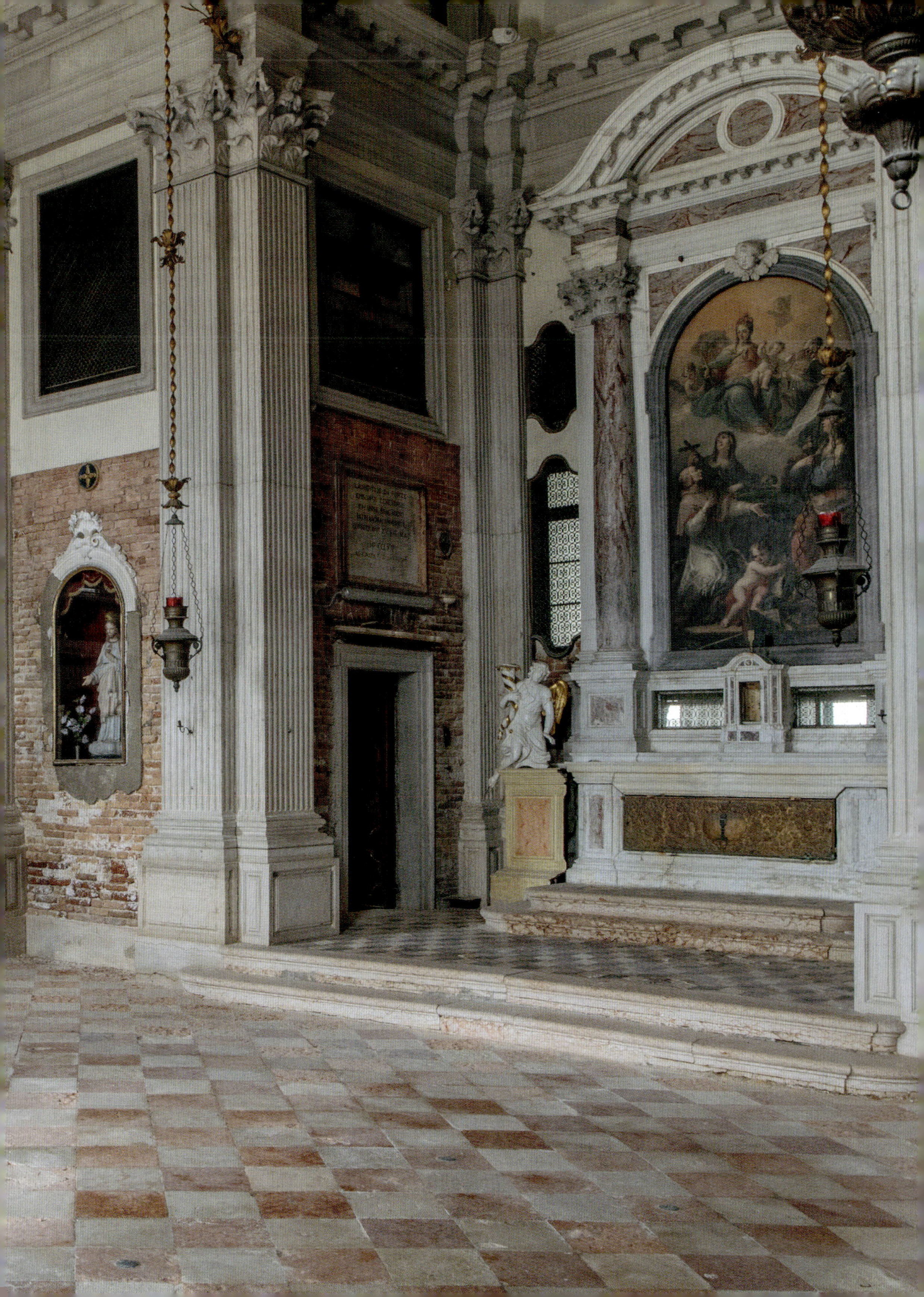

DESCRIPTION *of* THE EXHIBITION SPACES

The exhibition *Hora Lupi* occupies a portion of the Penitents' complex, specifically the church, the Chapel of St Anne, and the Sacristy.

The interior of the Penitenti church, with a single nave and short choir, retains its eighteenth-century architectural character and is spatially defined by the presence of three marble altars. The ceiling is decorated with a tondo replete with cherubs by Jacopo Marieschi, also the author of the painting *Glory of San Lorenzo Giustinian'*, once on the high altar and now preserved in Palazzo Contarini del Bovolo. On the two side altars, three nineteenth-century altarpieces by Alessio Revera replaced the seventeenth-century paintings. In the chapel to the left of the altar, we see a depiction of the Holy Family by an anonymous eighteenth-century artist.

The chapel of St Anne is located to the left of the church with di rect access from the canal. The space is a single room with a marble altar on the back wall symmetrically flanked by two round-headed portals, one of which is walled up. The floor is in terracotta and portions of the elegant boiserie that cov ered the side walls are still visible, while the ceiling has been completely lost.

The entrance wall also has fragments of wood panelling, but of lesser value, suggesting that the original chapel must have been a wooden casket.

The chapel leads to a narrow room leading to the sacristy. Portions of wooden panelling are also visible in this room, but the architec tural appearance of the room is less refined given its function. How ever, two ancient pieces of furniture are visible: a long bench with the backs removed and a wooden cupboard. Behind the long bench, grooves are visible in the masonry to fit the backrests. All surfaces show lacerations of plaster and wooden panelling.

The sequence of the rooms dedicated to the exhibition, although limited in number, allows for an interpretation of the complexity of the place as one quickly moves from the ornate and rich spaces of the church to the very simple, humble spaces of the sacristy.

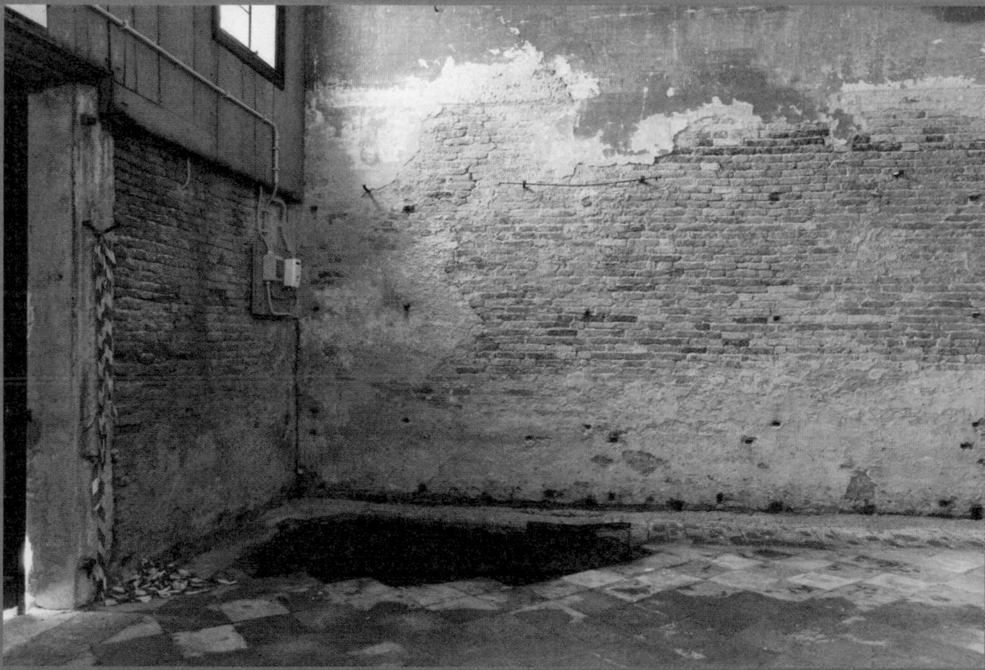

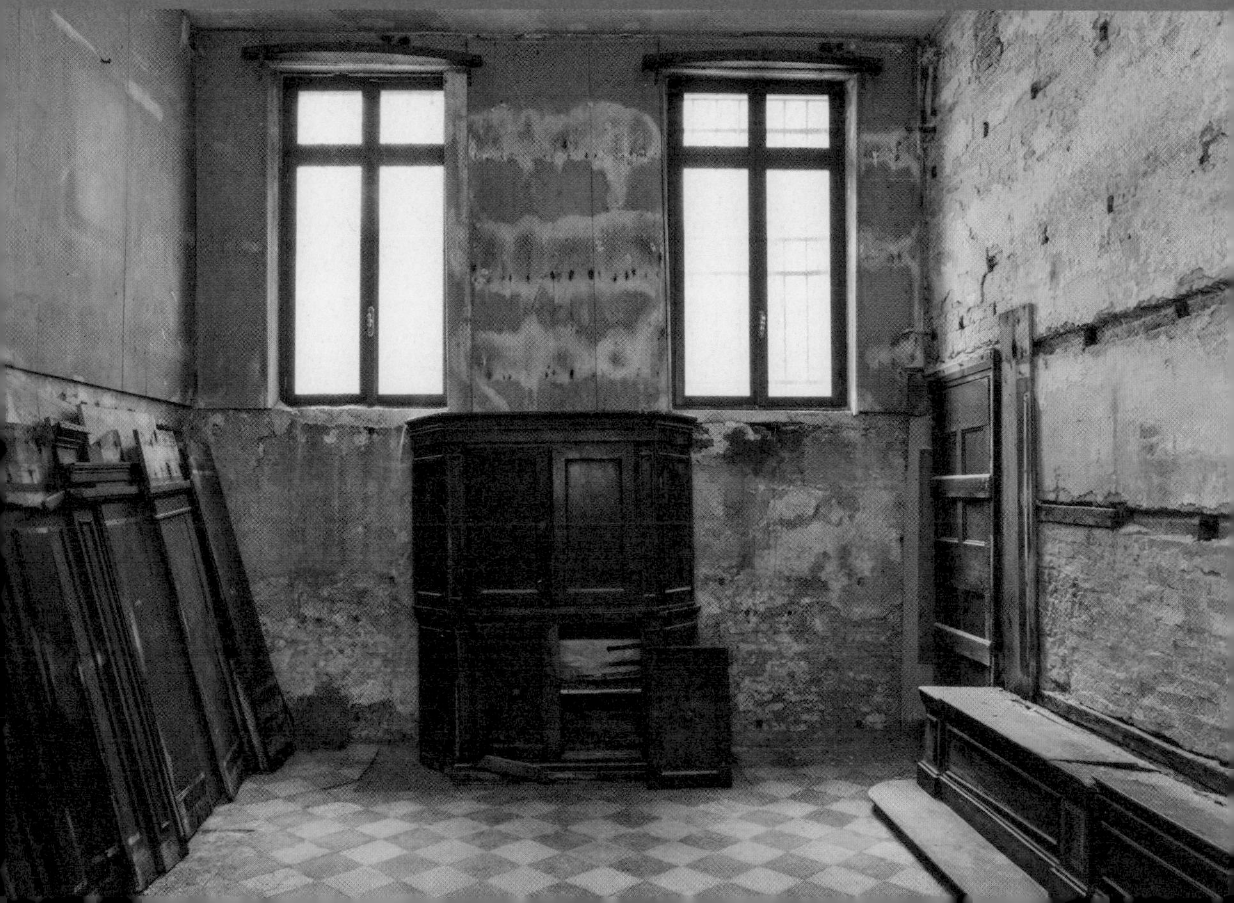

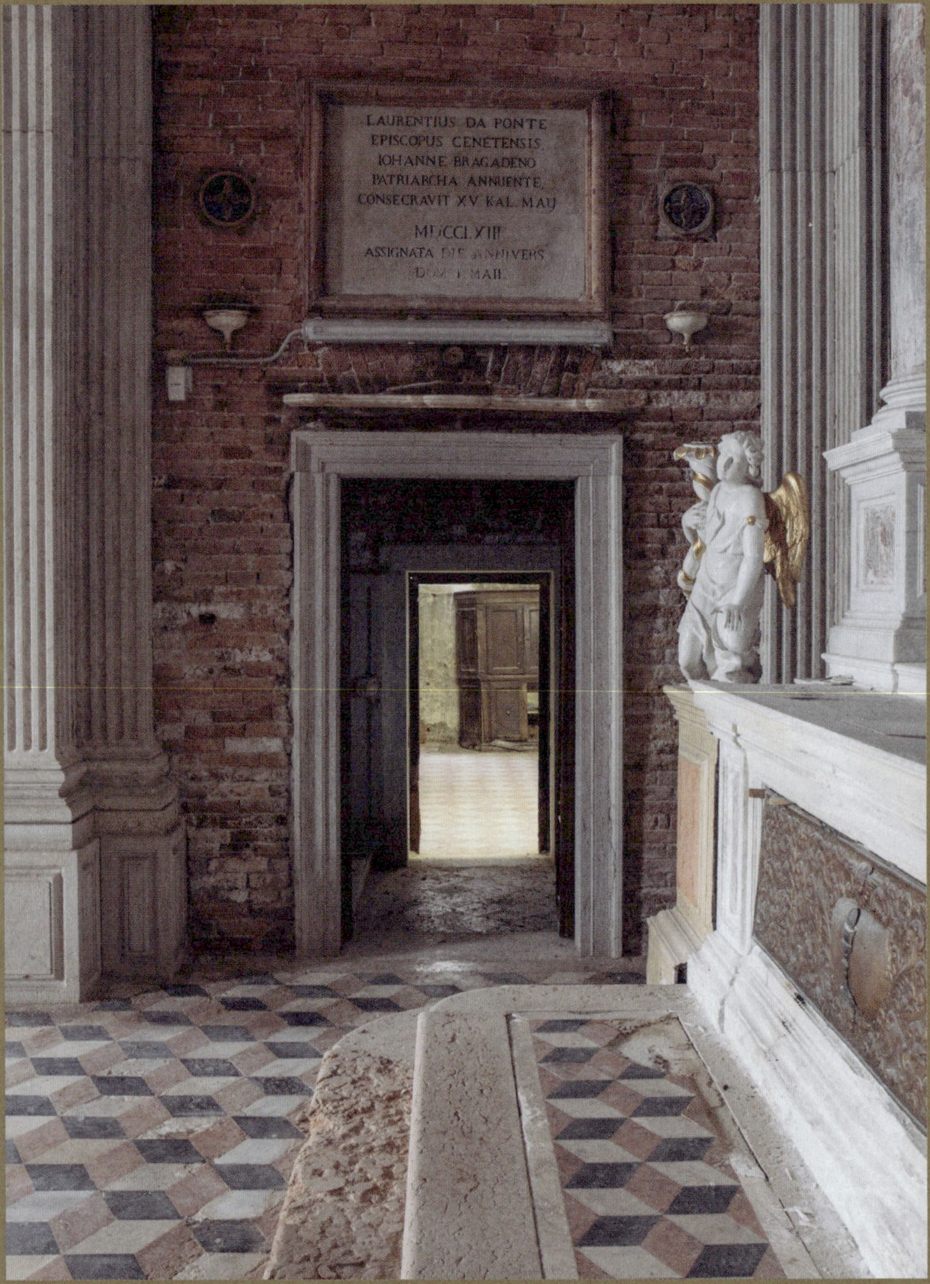
LAURENTIUS DA PONTE
EPISCOPUS CENETENSIS
IOHANNE BRAGADENO
PATRIARCHA ANNUENTE
CONSECRAVIT XV KAL. MAIJ
MDCCLXIII
ASSIGNATA DIE ANNIVERS
DOM I MAII

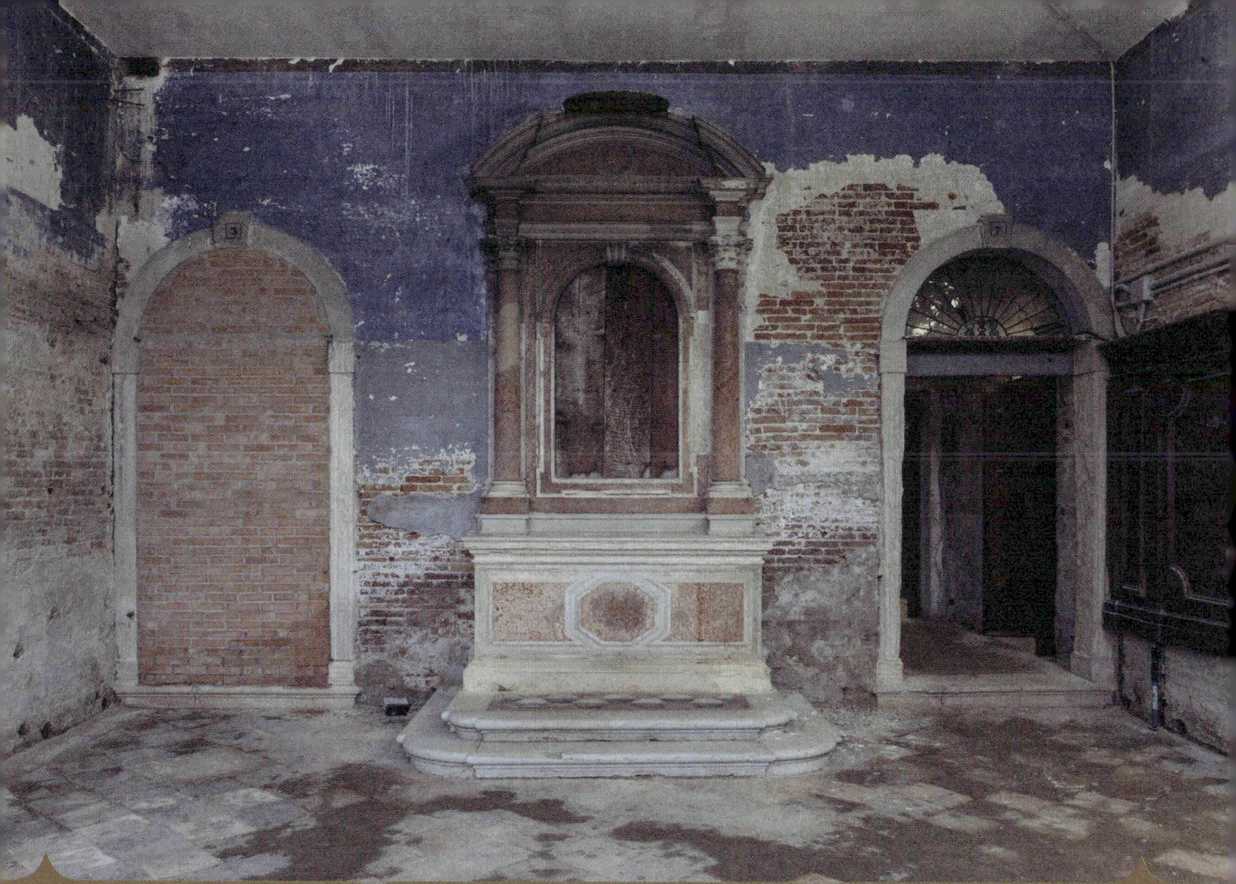

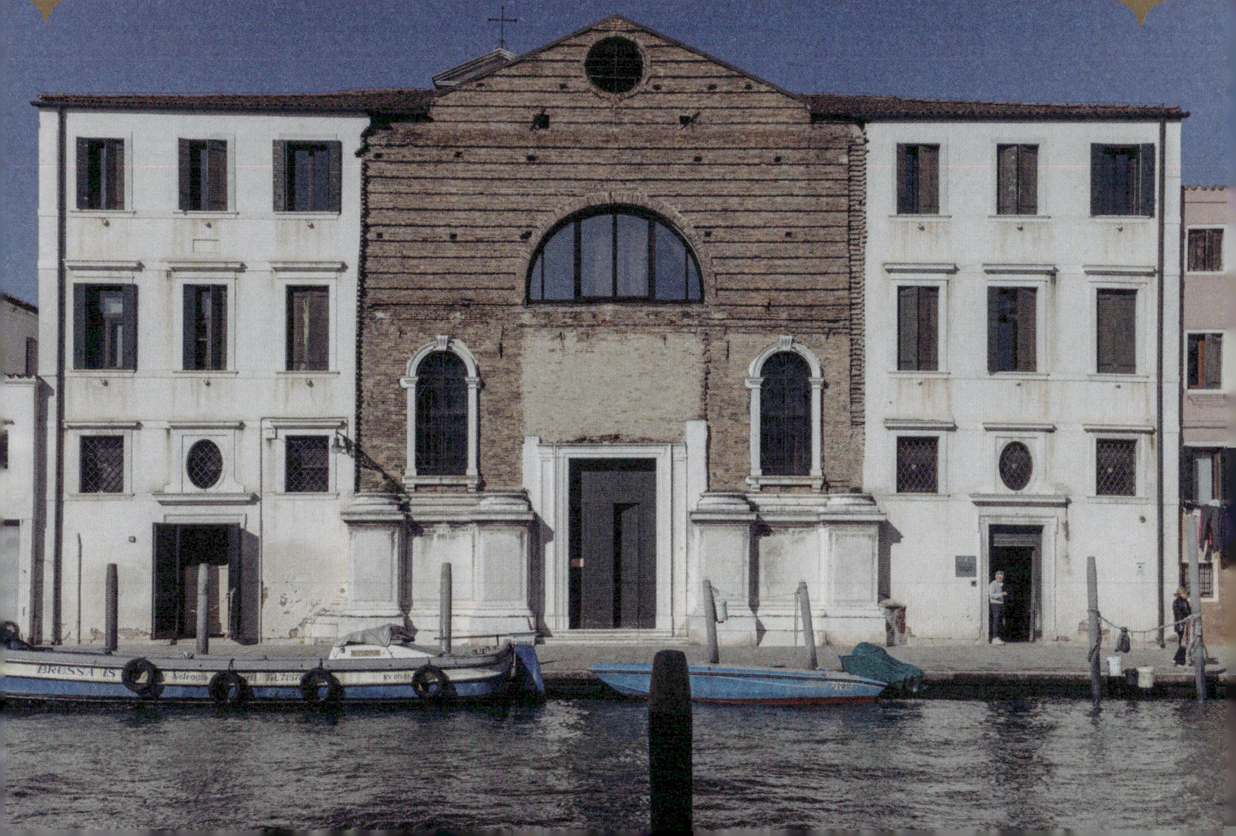
BRUSSA IS

Dieter Roelstraete

AMOR VACUI
EDITH KARLSON IN VENICE

Sometime in the fall of 2023, around the time when I was first invited to contribute to the present publication, a number of articles started circulating online that set out to find a name for our chaotic, "terrible twenties": a single word to describe that dizzying feeling that, for some time now — but *when* exactly did this start? — things only ever seem to get worse. ("Gaza, Trump, Ukraine.") The best contender so far has no doubt been the particularly witty notion of an "assholocene," which a certain Tadzio Mueller first introduced in an article titled "Beyond Ethics and Rationality" in reply to the following string of rhetorical questions:

> What should we call a society in which a prominent Conservative party politician — that is to say, not a fascist oddball or some random talking head — calls for "violence against irregular migration", i.e. for shooting migrants at the EU's borders; in which up to 30% believe that it is perfectly OK to vote for a party that is "in parts certified right-wing extremist", for which, read: fascist; in which "climate protection" means protection against climate activists, and "climate adaptation" does not mean building higher dikes, but building higher walls against migrants; in which migrants who, for completely incomprehensible reasons, want to migrate to the parts of the world that are still inhabitable (whereby of course the vast majority migrate to their home or neigh

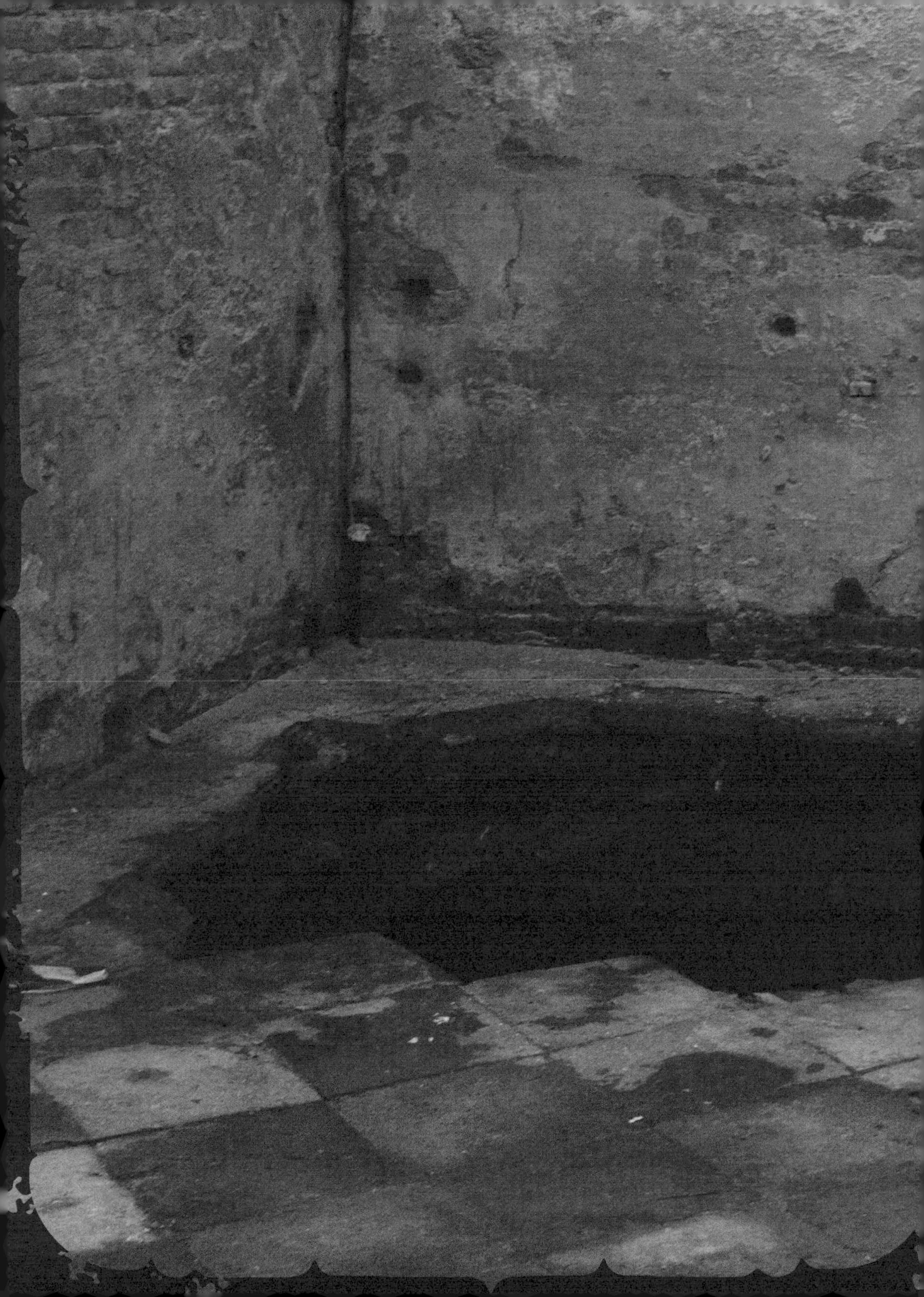

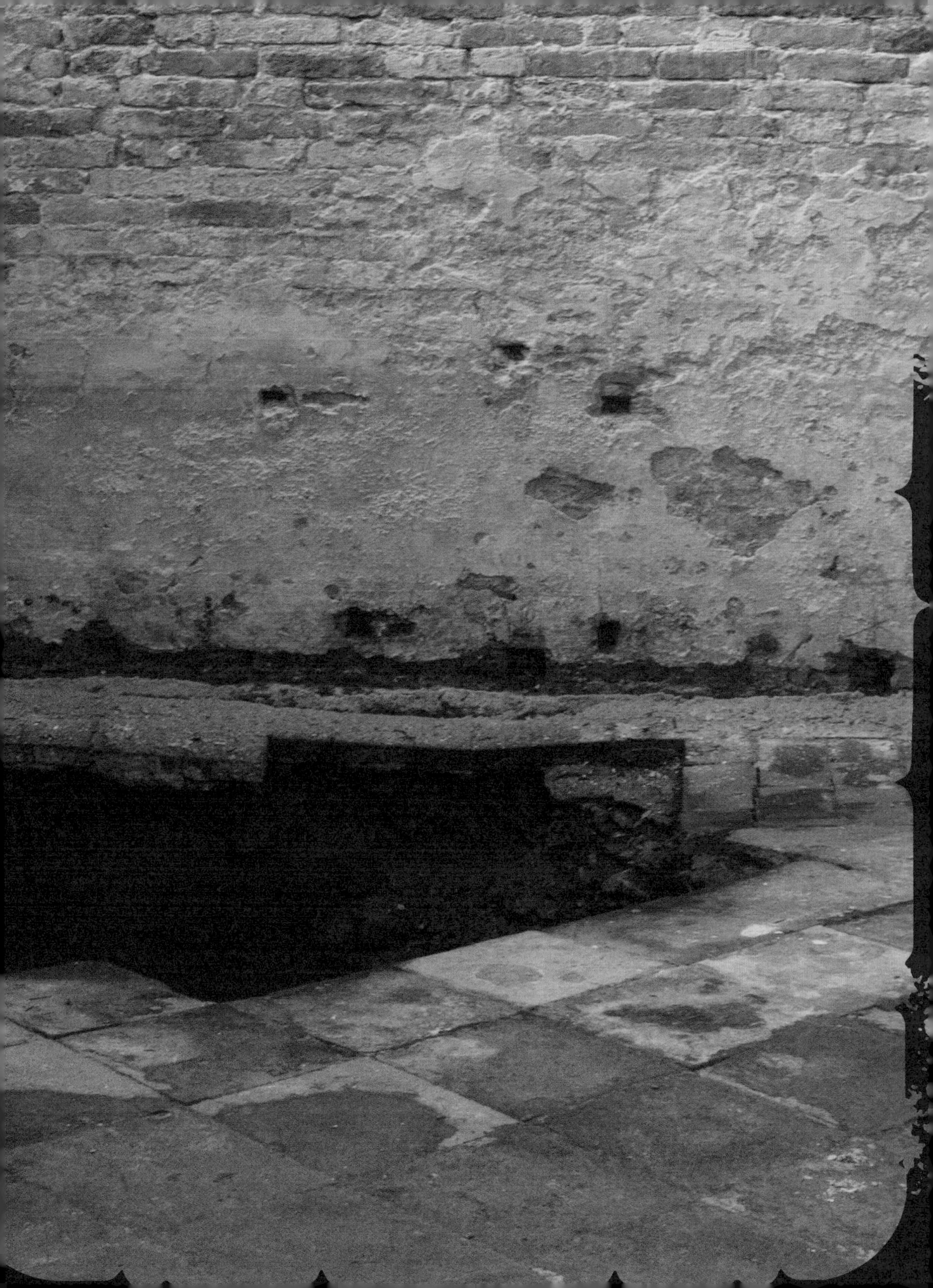

boring countries), are demonized as "criminal gangs of human traffickers", in order to legitimize a "war on mi gration/migrants"? (…) The epoch in human history in which assholization, i.e. the normalization of group-spe cific misanthropy, is a dominant political dynamic, and the nationalist, patriarchal asshole replaces the neoliberal sociopath as the dominant subject: this is what I call the *assholocene* — the age of assholes.[1]

For as long as art has existed, it has been haunted by the singularly vexing question "what to do about it": *Chto Delat,* in the face of this emerging "age of assholes" — which is ultimately not terribly different, of course, from all the preceding ages of assholes? (Being an asshole may well be the most dependably successful way in which one can assure the fact that "history" happens *at all* — that the wheels of history grind on.[2]) Indeed, one could call this haunting one reason for art's very being — or rather, for art's being *modern.* (I will return to this qualification shortly.) Here we are, despairing inhabitants of the assholocene: what, *if anything* — for this, of course, is truly the million-dollar question — can or *should* art do about it? Provided that art, in the peculiar guise of the art *world,* isn't just a contributing factor to the actual genesis and emergence of the assholocene — this is surely a distinct possibility — how should art *relate* to this moment of unprecedented awfulness? Should it merely register and "report" — and thereby, inevitably, also *replicate* — said awfulness, or should it actively fight it by continuing to remind us, in a variety of ways, that another world is possible — that things can and *should* be different? One self-evident manner in which it can do the latter thing is by providing *succor* — by becoming a refuge *from* the world or a "little island off the coast of society," as I have called it in an altogether different context.[3] (By looking *away.*) This is the path conventionally associated with aesthetic pleasure and, more troublingly still, *beauty,* which we are of course used to seeing castigated for its presumed role in fostering a so-named "escapist" agenda at a time — the assholocene — when *confrontation* rather than *escape* seems called for. ("Refusal" is just a slightly more activist, militant synonym for the same basic posture of *denial, evasion, flight, or retreat.*) In choosing "beauty" — or its various analogues comfort, contentment, joy, peace, quiet, etc. — this particular tradition in art sides squarely with a broader conception of culture that believes art's reason for being is to soothe and distract, to *please* rather than to *displease* — to make us feel *good* rather than *bad.* A high-flying theoretical corollary

1 https://steadyhq.com/de/friedlichesabotage/posts/a1c14c1a-feb9-42ec-9678-358be77f8d99. In a conversation with the author in December 2023, Karlson at one point suggested that the single most pressing question underlying her sculptural work — creatures all, from men to women and humans to animals and every "thing" in between — is quite simply: "why can't we all just get along?"

2 E.g., Adolf Hitler, Josef Stalin — or: Benjamin Netanyahu, Vladimir Putin, Donald Trump.

3 I have called the realm of art "a little island off the coast of society" in a publication by my current place of employment, the Neubauer Collegium for Culture and Society at the University of Chicago, in which I asked what the precise nature of the relationship of culture *to* society (or, mutatis mutandis, of art to the world) should be — suggesting that answering this question "may be a mere matter of hitting upon the right conjunction or preposition. Should we really think art *and* culture, or art *and* society? Should we look at art *as* culture, and find art *in* society? How about opting for art *instead of* culture, or art *contra* society? For a long and venerable tradition exists, naturally, of opposing art to culture — and a much longer one still pitting art against society. In this view, "true" art is inimical

of this stance is that the very existence of art as a paradigmatic instantiation of *das ganz Andere* may serve as a symbolic *indictment* of the world as everything that is the case — a resounding denunciation, pure and simple, of all that exists. (A dramatic variation of this apocalyptic claim can be found in Nietzsche's assertion, made in *The Birth in Tragedy,* that "it is only as *an aesthetic phenomenon* that existence and the world are eternally *justified.*") This is one of the basic tenets of the ideology of avant-garde art as a secular version of *negative theology* — the site of quasi-religious redemption in a world that, because of its presumed modernity, can no longer indulge in the cultivation of outright religious fantasies.

To please, or nor to please, then: the work of Edith Karlson has no intention, of course — much less the ambition — to answer any of the questions about art's presumed essence or end goal listed above; so many of art's problems in the past have stemmed, in part, from an immoderate aspiration to do so. (That being said: there is no denying that Karlson's work is rooted in a grounding sense of *displeasure* — in a founding feeling of, and for, *irritation.*) Nor is Edith Karlson a religious person (as far as I know[4]), much less a religious artist. But here we are, looking at art — looking at *her* art — in a *church.* And not just any old church, of course: not only is the desecrated eighteenth-century church of Santa Maria delle Penitenti in which Karlson has installed her work notable for its peripheral siting so far away from the hustle and bustle of both "overtourist" Venice and the art world's Venice (located in the northwestern corner of Cannaregio, Santa Maria delle Penitenti has its facade defiantly turned towards the proletarian ignominy that is Mestre), it also happens to have been founded as a local Venetian variant on the primarily Protestant phenomenon of the Magdalena Asylum — a charitable institution devoted to sheltering and improving the lot of so-called "fallen women," i.e. penitent prostitutes anxious to turn their back on the world of their day, which we may legitimately assume to have been something of an assholocene as well, back then. The habit of looking at art inside a church is obviously an ancient one — in the first instance because western art as we know it could be said, quite simply, to have originated from the Latin (Roman, Catholic) church, and art and religious feeling may therefore be doomed to forever coexist even in the most thoroughly agnostic or atheist recesses of our mind. But the habit of looking at *contemporary* art inside a church, whether desecrated or not, is just as well established, and in it, archaic echoes of the aforementioned genealogical entanglement of art and religious feeling obviously persist — in a way, perhaps, that may lead one to immodestly assume that art

to the very idea of culture as we know it today — of culture as diminished to a mere jumble of cogs in the entertainment industry machine. This is a tradition weighed down by a certain degree of nostalgia and romantic naïveté, perhaps, but one that we nonetheless continue to hold dear. Our vision of art is one that seeks to secure a measure of refuge for the utopian impulses of negation, of contradiction — not so much art as merely opposed to culture and society, but rather art as *actively opposing what passes for culture and society in our fractured here and now.* Art as "something else" — a dependable island of otherness in our culture's all-encompassing ocean of sameness from which it so often seems no escaping is possible. Such is our idea of art, in 'culture and society'." Venice during summer is exactly that, of course: a veritable island off the coast of society whose insularity is guaranteed in part by its wholesale dedication to the whims of art.

4 In the conversation alluded to earlier on, Karlson shared only this shred of religious recollection from a childhood marred by recurrent migraines: an indissoluble association of Christian images of suffering — much of which was habitually inflicted on female bodies in particular — with headaches.

is in effect the primary site of religious feeling in today's secular world. (Which it evidently isn't, and — God help us! — shouldn't be either.) Long stretches of the history of the Roman-Catholic church (and indeed of most organised religions stemming from the Judeo-Christian tradition, which is just another term for western civilisation pure and simple) have been defined by and large by the architecture, quite literally, of retreat and seclusion, withdrawal and isolation, and art has found a welcome refuge — respite from the assholocene that has shadowed human history since its very inception — in its various voids. This void, so bliss fully free of "feeling," is Edith Karlson's home.

La Biennale di Venezia

60. Esposizione Internazionale d'Arte

Partecipazioni Nazionali

This book is published in conjunction with the exhibition *Hora lupi* at the Estonian Pavilion at the 60th International Art Exhibition – La Biennale di Venezia

Published and distributed by
Mousse Publishing – Contrappunto s.r.l.
Via Pier Candido Decembrio 28, 20137,
Milan–Italy in collaboration with
Estonian Centre for Contemporary Art
Suur-Karja 23, Tallinn, Estonia

Available through Mousse Publishing, Milan, and Estonian Centre for Contemporary Art
moussemagazine.it
cca.ee

First edition: 2024

Print run: 1000

Printed in Estonia by Printon
ISBN 978-88-6749-654-9

35€ / 40$

EDITORS
Maria Arusoo & Keiu Krikmann

GRAPHIC DESIGN
Jojo & me

LANGUAGE EDITING
Jaq Body

TRANSLATIONS
Keiu Krikmann

Jaan Tõnisson – Postimehe Fond
Taavet Sten
Eesti Kultuurkapital
EAS Enterprise Estonia
DSV
COBALT LAW FIRM
Tallinn city of music

EXHIBITION TEAM

ARTIST
Edtih Karlson

COMMISSIONER
Maria Arusoo (Estonian Centre for Contemporary Art, CCA)

DRAMATURGE
Eero Epner

HEAD OF PRODUCTION
Sten Ojavee (CCA)

TECHNICAL TEAM
Tõnu Narro and Mihkel Lember (Technical Director), Johannes Säre (Dream Team)

COMMUNICATION TEAM
Keiu Krikmann (CCA), Kaarin Kivirähk (CCA), Stina Pley, Alexia Menikou

DESIGNERS
Jojo & me (Johanna Ruukholm and Martina Gofman)

LIGHTING DESIGNER
Oliver Kulpsoo

SOUND DESIGNER
Raul Saaremets

ARCHITECT
Piero Vespignani

PROJECT COORDINATORS
Mikk Lahesalu (CCA), Marika Agu (CCA)

PROJECT COORDINATOR IN ITALY
Valeria Romagnini

ARTIST'S TEAM
Art Allmägi, Sander Haugas, Kirsti Kaubi, Loora Kaubi, Ats Kruusing, Erik Liiv, Maria Luiga, Eva Mahhov, Liisi Põllumaa, Nikolai Saaremets, Hanna Samoson, Elo Vahtrik, artist's dogs Iti and Kusti

COMMUNICATION
Kaarin Kivirähk, Keiu Krikmann(CCA), Stina Pley, Alexia Menikou

COMMISSIONED AND PRODUCED BY
Estonian Centre for Contemporary Art

FINANCED BY
Estonian Ministry of Culture

WITH THE SUPPORT OF
Postimehe Fond, Taavet+Sten Tulevikufond, Cobalt Law Firm, Cultural Endowment of Estonia, Enterprise Estonia, Tallinn City of Music, DSV Global Transport and Logistics, Põhjala Beer, Selver, Uus Rada Galerii, Tallinn Zoo, Estonian Museum of Natural History, Müürileht, Berengo, Estonian Academy of Arts, Pallas University of Applied Sciences

THE ARTIST WOULD LIKE TO THANK
Katrin Kissa, Ene-Liis Semper, Raul Saaremets

Image credits:

Chiesa di Santa Maria delle Penitenti, pages 154163, 166167 by Agne Raceviciute © 2023

Documentation of Hora lupi, pages 9, 13, 62, 65, 7677, 79153 by Anu Vahtra © 2023

Documentation of making of Hora lupi, pages 35, 3861, 7273 by Alana Proosa © 2023

Illustrations pages 2634 by Nikolai Saaremets © 2023